Lecture Notes in Computer Science 1950

Edited by G. Goos, J. Hartmanis and J. van Leeuwen

Springer
Berlin
Heidelberg
New York
Barcelona
Hong Kong
London
Milan
Paris
Singapore
Tokyo

Randomness and Completeness in Computational Complexity

 Springer

Series Editors

Gerhard Goos, Karlsruhe University, Germany
Juris Hartmanis, Cornell University, NY, USA
Jan van Leeuwen, Utrecht University, The Netherlands

Author

Dieter van Melkebeek
Institute for Advanced Studies
Einstein Drive, Princeton, NJ 08450, USA
E-mail: dieter@ias.edu

Cataloging-in-Publication Data applied for

Die Deutsche Bibliothek - CIP-Einheitsaufnahme

Melkebeek, Dieter van:
Randomness and completeness in computational complexity /
Dieter van Melkebeek. - Berlin ; Heidelberg ; New York ; Barcelona ;
Hong Kong ; London ; Milan ; Paris ; Singapore ; Tokyo : Springer, 2000
    (Lecture notes in computer science ; Vol. 1950)
    ISBN 3-540-41492-4

CR Subject Classification (1998): F.2, F.1, F.3

ISSN 0302-9743
ISBN 3-540-41492-4 Springer-Verlag Berlin Heidelberg New York

Springer-Verlag Berlin Heidelberg New York
a member of BertelsmannSpringer Science+Business Media GmbH
© Springer-Verlag Berlin Heidelberg 2000
Printed in Germany

Typesetting: Camera-ready by author, data conversion by PTP-Berlin, Stefan Sossna
Printed on acid-free paper   SPIN: 10780945   06/3142   5 4 3 2 1 0

Preface

This book contains a revised version of the dissertation the author wrote at the Department of Computer Science of the University of Chicago. The thesis was submitted to the Faculty of Physical Sciences in conformity with the requirements for the PhD degree in June 1999. It was honored with the 1999 ACM Doctoral Dissertation Award in May 2000.

Summary

Computational complexity is the study of the inherent difficulty of computational problems and the power of the tools we may use to solve them. It aims to describe how many resources we need to compute the solution as a function of the problem size. Typical resources include time on sequential and parallel architectures and memory space. As we want to abstract away from details of input representation and specifics of the computer model, we end up with classes of problems that we can solve within certain robust resource bounds such as polynomial time, parallel logarithmic time, and logarithmic space. Research in complexity theory boils down to determining the relationships between these classes – inclusions and separations.

In this dissertation, we focus on the role of randomness and look at various properties of hard problems in order to obtain separations. We also investigate the power of nondeterminism and alternation, as well as space versus time issues.

Randomness provides a resource that seems to help in various situations. We study its use in the area of proof checking. We show that every property that has a bounded-round interactive proof system has subexponential size classical proofs (for infinitely many input sizes) unless the polynomial-time hierarchy collapses. This provides the first strong evidence that graph nonisomorphism has subexponential size proofs. Under a stronger hypothesis we can scale the proof size down to polynomial size. We obtain our result by derandomizing Arthur-Merlin games. The same technique applies to various other randomized processes. We show how it works for the Valiant-Vazirani random hashing procedure which prunes the number of satisfying assignments of a propositional formula to one, the exact learning of Boolean circuits using equivalence queries and access to a satisfiability oracle, the construction of matrices with high rigidity, and generating polynomial-size universal traversal sequences.

Completeness arguably constitutes the single most pervasive concept of computational complexity. A problem π is hard for a complexity class if we can efficiently reduce every problem in the class to π, i.e., we can efficiently solve any problem in the class when given access to an oracle providing solutions to instances of π. If π itself also belongs to the class, we call π complete for the class. Several complexity classes have complete problems under various reducibility notions. One often focuses on decision problems, or equivalently, on the corresponding language of yes instances. In this thesis, we develop techniques for separating complexity classes by isolating a structural difference between their complete languages. We look at various properties from this perspective:

> Sparseness — the *density* of complete languages.
> Autoreducibility — the *redundancy* of complete languages.
> Resource-bounded measure — the *frequency* of complete languages.

Sparseness forms a candidate differentiating property that interests complexity theorists because of its connections to nonuniform complexity and to isomorphism questions. A language is sparse if it contains no more than polynomially many instances of each size. Showing that polynomial time has no sparse hard language under logarithmic space reductions would separate polynomial time from logarithmic space. We establish the logical completeness of this approach for reductions that can ask a bounded number of queries: If polynomial time differs from logarithmic space then there exists no sparse hard language for polynomial time under logarithmic space reductions with a bounded number of queries. The proof works for various other classes as well, e.g., for nondeterministic logarithmic space versus logarithmic space, and for logarithmic space versus parallel logarithmic time. Another instantiation states that no sparse hard language for nondeterministic polynomial time exists under polynomial-time randomized reductions with a bounded number of queries unless we can solve nondeterministic polynomial time in randomized polynomial time.

Autoreducibility defines the most general type of efficient reduction of a problem to itself. A problem is autoreducible if we can solve a given instance in polynomial time when allowed to ask an oracle the solution to any other instance. We establish that large complexity classes like doubly exponential space have complete languages that are not autoreducible, whereas the complete languages of smaller classes like exponential time all share the property of autoreducibility. The specific results we get yield alternate proofs of known separations. We also show that settling the question for doubly exponential time either way, would imply major new separations: It would either separate polynomial time from polynomial space, and nondeterministic logarithmic space from nondeterministic polynomial time, or else the polynomial-time hierarchy from exponential time.

Resource-bounded measure formalizes the notions of scarceness and abundance within complexity classes such as exponential time. From the separation point of view, the theory seems particularly suited for separating randomized polynomial time from exponential time. Within the formalism of resource-bounded measure, most languages turn out to be hard for randomized polynomial time under relatively powerful reductions. On the other hand, by establishing a small span theorem and using other approaches, we prove that exponential time and several subclasses only have a few complete or hard languages under weaker reducibilities. A very narrow gap between the power of the reductions remains, and bridging it would separate randomized polynomial time from exponential time.

Another approach for settling this problem, similar in spirit to the probabilistic method of combinatorics, tries to show that randomized polynomial time is a small subclass of exponential time. We prove the logical completeness of this strategy, i.e., if randomized polynomial time differs from exponential time then it is a small subclass of exponential time. As a byproduct, we obtain the first nontrivial example of a class for which the equivalent of Kolmogorov's 0-1 Law in resource-bounded measure holds.

One can view resource-bounded measure as a restriction of classical Lebesgue measure preserving properties like additivity and monotonicity. Whether invariance under permutations also carries over, remains open. If it does, then the class of autoreducible languages is small. We show that a resource-bounded version of permutation invariance holds if efficient pseudo-random generators of exponential security exist, and that if it holds, then randomized polynomial time differs from exponential time. We develop betting games as the basis for an alternate to resource-bounded measure for quantifying the frequency of properties within complexity classes, with permutation invariance built in.

Acknowledgments

To many people I owe a lot for their support during my graduate studies. It is my pleasure to thank them here.

First there are the people directly related to this dissertation. Above all is my advisor, Lance Fortnow. While still in Belgium, I had a hard time tracking down some of the references of the paper "MIP = NEXP" [17] which I had started reading. I finally emailed Lance, one of the authors of the paper. I gave him a list of three references which I couldn't get a hold of, and asked him whether he could send me copies. I wasn't expecting much of a reply. To my happy surprise, one week later, I found an envelope with the three papers in my mailbox! I contacted Lance again when I was considering a visit to the Department of Computer Science at the University of Chicago. Lance was very enthusiastic about it. He became my host during the visit and later my advisor. I am thankful to Lance for bringing me to Chicago, for his inviting attitude towards research, and for his advice and support over the years.

I am also grateful to the other members of my committee, Laci Babai and Janos Simon. In particular, I would like to thank Laci for his inspiring lectures as well as for his support. I'll be happy if I'll be able to carry over even a fraction of Laci's inspiration to others. I thank Janos for his broad enlightening perspective on almost anything.

I am indebted to all members of the theory faculty, including Stuart Kurtz, Ketan Mulmuley, and Robert Soare, for the things I learned from them, and to the Department of Computer Science in general for the research and teaching opportunities I received. Thanks also go to Barbara Castro, Margaret Jaffey, Karin Lustre, Rory Millard, and Shirley Proby for the administrative help.

Much of the work reported in this thesis was a joint effort. For their collaboration and for their permission to include our results in my dissertation, I am grateful to my coauthors: Harry Buhrman, Lance Fortnow, Adam Klivans, Ken Regan, D. Sivakumar, Martin Strauss, and Leen Torenvliet. I would also like to thank Jack Lutz, Mitsu Ogihara, and Shiyu Zhou for the work we did together.

I would like to express my sincere gratitude towards Ashish Naik for his encouragement when I made my first steps in the world of computational complexity, as well as to Jin-Yi Cai, Mitsu Ogihara, and D. Sivakumar. I would like to thank Jin-Yi especially for having served as a reference on several occasions.

I have been very fortunate to get the chance to visit various institutes during my graduate studies. I am grateful to Eric Allender and the NSF for the summer of '96 which I spent at DIMACS. Eric was an excellent host and I have been very lucky to receive his advice and support ever since.

Harry Buhrman played a major role in my visit to CWI during the academic year '96–'97. I am thankful to him and to the European Union for the opportunities I got. Leen Torenvliet provided me with office space at the University of Amsterdam during that period.

I owe thanks to Allan Borodin, Steve Cook, Faith Fich, Charlie Rackoff, and to the Fields Institute in Toronto for inviting me to the Special Year on Computational Complexity from January till June '98. I am particularly grateful to Steve for the class he taught and for his interest and support.

I acknowledge Dirk Janssens and Jan Van den Bussche for the Belgian connection they offered.

On the more personal level, I would like to thank the following people for having been around: Amber S., Anna G., Barb M., Bernd B., Brian S., Dave K., Duke W., Dustin M., Fran G.-H., Gerry B., John R., John T., Juliana E., Kass S., Kati F., Kousha E., Louis S., Mark F., Micah A., Patrick P., Peter G., Peter K., Pradyut S., Robert S., Ronald d.W., Ruth M., Sandy K., Satya L., Shiyu Z., Silvia G., Sophie L., Steve M., Thomas W., Tom H., Tom M., and Vassilis A. Special thanks go to my office mate at the University of

Amsterdam, Bas Terwijn, to Valentine Kabanets in Toronto, and to my office and room mate in Chicago, Marcus Schäfer. Most of all, I would like to thank my room mate and best friend Behfar Bastani for all the discussions we had and the things we did together.

I also want to thank my long-time friends in Belgium: Bart, Jeroen, Patrick, and Peter. For their hospitality and interest, I am very grateful to Marijke, Bruno, Sigrid, and Shanti, my relatives on this side of the ocean. Similarly but on the other side of the ocean, I want to thank my grandma, sister, brother-in-law, and my nephews Jonas, Saul, and Tibo. Just seeing their smiles made every trip over the ocean more than worthwhile.

Finally, there are my parents. Words to describe my deep gratitude towards them done. Their continuous support – even when I made decisions which they would have preferred to see fail me differently – was invaluable.

Aan jullie, moeke en vake, draag ik dit werk met veel genoegen op!

Chicago, May 1999   *Dieter van Melkebeek*

Contents

1. Introduction

How can we solve a problem using computers in a reasonable amount of time? Computational complexity studies the inherent difficulty of problems and the power of the tools we may engage to solve them.

1.1 Issues in Computational Complexity

1.1.1 The Power of Randomness

Randomness provides a tool that we can often use to our advantage. King Arthur, on his quest for the Holy Grail, already knew that. One day, Merlin claimed to have found the sword Excalibur and showed it to the king. Arthur, however, could not tell the difference between that sword and his own. "But can't you see that this one is more tinted than yours?" Merlin replied. Arthur knew that Excalibur looked pretty much like his own sword but had a darker color. Arthur himself was color blind, though, so he would not be able to distinguish the swords based on their colors. There was a lengthy and tedious test which would determine whether Merlin's sword really was Excalibur. But in the past several people had claimed to have found Excalibur. Each time the determination test had been applied, and had refuted the claim. And each time Arthur had realized later on that there really had been no need to run the test because the sword could not be Excalibur for an obvious reason. Of course, this time is wasn't just anyone making the claim: It was his own adviser Merlin. Nevertheless, Arthur was reluctant to start the test procedure. "Maybe Merlin's sword is just a copy of mine," he thought. He decided he first wanted to be convinced that the swords were really different before embarking on any serious testing. He came up with the following simple procedure.

He would take his and Merlin's swords, and turn around so that Merlin could not see what he was doing. He would flip a coin. If the outcome was heads – or whatever was one that side of the coins in these days – he would take his sword; otherwise he would take Merlin's. Then he would show the sword he picked to Merlin and ask him whether that was Excalibur. Arthur figured that if the swords were identical, then, no matter how smart Merlin was, he would only have a 50/50 chance of coming up with the right answer.

D. van Mehlkebeek: Randomness and Completeness in Computational Complexity, LNCS 1950, pp. 1–11, 2000.
© Springer-Verlag Berlin Heidelberg 2000

Repeating the test a couple of times and Merlin passing each one of them would convince Arthur beyond reasonable doubt that Merlin could tell the two swords apart.

The outcome of the process is well-known: Arthur's coin came up heads and Merlin answered "yes." Arthur felt strongly about this. He sentenced Merlin to the dungeons and ordered him to design new molecule structures for the twentieth century carbon chemists. Merlin had to develop a new one every day and show it to the king.

One day, Merlin was lazy. Instead of thinking of a new molecule, he just took his layout of the previous day and redrew it in a different way. The molecule he came up with the previous day had the structure of Figure 1.1. The little circles represent carbon atoms, and the lines the chemical bonds

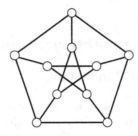

Fig. 1.1. A molecule design

between them. He interchanged the inner and outer atoms to obtain a structure as in Figure 1.2, and showed it to Arthur. Merlin was unlucky: Arthur

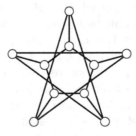

Fig. 1.2. Another molecule design?

discovered that the molecule was the same as the one he showed him the day before, and sent him back to the dungeons to redo his work for that day. Merlin came back, and showed his king Figure 1.3. But now Arthur had become suspicious again. Although he could not see a way to transform Figure 1.1 into Figure 1.3, he suspected there may be a less obvious way to do it than in case of Figures 1.1 and 1.2. Merlin understood Arthur's doubts and presented him with a proof that Figures 1.1 and 1.3 were really different. He

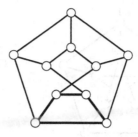

Fig. 1.3. A really new molecule design?

showed Arthur the heavy cycle of 4 atoms in Figure 1.3 and claimed that
any cycle in Figure 1.1 contained at least 5 atoms. But Arthur did not want
to spend the time verifying that no 4 or fewer atoms in Figure 1.1 formed a
cycle. Instead, he thought about the randomized test he had used before to
check that two swords were different, and came up with a similar trick.

Now, he would not just take one of the two molecules at random, show
it to Merlin and ask him which one of the two it was. That would be too
easy to figure out. Instead, after picking one of the molecules at random,
Arthur would randomly permute the atoms, i.e., randomly interchange their
positions. For instance, starting from the molecule in Figure 1.1, he could end
up with the one in Figure 1.4. He would then show this molecule to Merlin

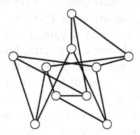

Fig. 1.4. A random permutation of Figure 1.1

and ask Merlin which of the two original molecules he started out with. In
case of different molecules, like Figures 1.1 and 1.3, Merlin would be able to
answer that question correctly with certainty. He could find a correspondence
between the atoms of the molecule in Figure 1.4 and the one in Figure 1.1,
like in Figure 1.5 for example. Merlin's correspondence may well differ from
the permutation Arthur effectively used to obtain Figure 1.4 from Figure
1.1. But Merlin knows Arthur could not have started from Figure 1.3: There
is no correspondence between the atoms of that molecule and the ones of
Figure 1.4, as Figures 1.3 and 1.4 represent different molecules. On the other
hand, if the two original molecules were identical, as in case of Figures 1.1
and 1.2, showing Merlin Figure 1.4 gives him no clue as to which of the two

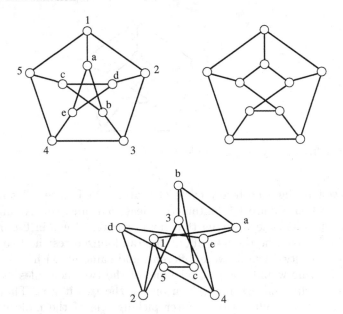

Fig. 1.5. Merlin's problem in case of different molecules

original molecules Arthur picked at the beginning. As is illustrated in Figure 1.6, Merlin could find a correspondence between the atoms of Figures 1.4 and 1.1, but also between the atoms of Figures 1.4 and 1.2. Given Figure 1.4, the odds that Arthur started from Figure 1.1 or from Figure 1.2 are the same.

As before, a 50% chance of catching identical designs did not suffice, so Arthur repeated the procedure a few times until he felt confident. In the historical case, Merlin passed all the tests and could relax for the rest of the day – albeit in the dungeons.

We sketched two situations where randomness seemed to help. Many more exist, and we will describe some of them in Chapters 2 and 3. In both of the above cases, Arthur could perform the task he wanted without the use of randomness but it would take him much longer. In the sword example, he could use some involved physical test. In the molecule example, he could verify Merlin's claim about the absence of 4-cycles in Figure 1.1, or more generally, he could try all possible ways of associating the atoms in one molecule to the atoms in the other molecule, and check that at least one chemical bond did not match under that association. In the historical examples, there would be 3,628,800 possible associations to rule out, though. How much more efficient solutions can become through the use of randomness, forms a major issue in computational complexity.

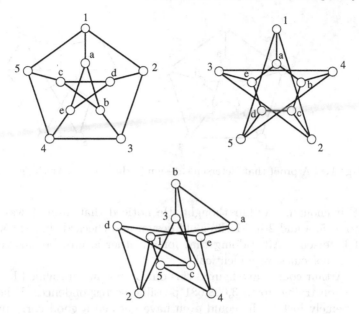

Fig. 1.6. Merlin's problem in case of identical molecules

1.1.2 The Power of Guessing

We are a couple of years later in time now. People had heard about Arthur's project and started sending him proposals for new molecules. Almost all of them had been discovered by Merlin before but one day Petersen came up to the king's castle and presented him the layout of Figure 1.7. Arthur liked the elegant design and he was embarrassed that his own adviser had not come up with it yet. He sent a note to Merlin in the dungeons together with a copy of Figure 1.7. Merlin – having spent years on this problem – recognized right away that this was the same molecule as the one he had engineered a long time ago, namely Figure 1.1. Merlin was sure the king had not forgotten about that design. The next day, he sent the king Figure 1.8. The correspondence showed that Merlin did come up with Petersen's molecule before. It would not take much of his majesties precious time to verify that, Merlin claimed.

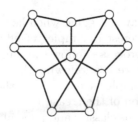

Fig. 1.7. Petersen's design

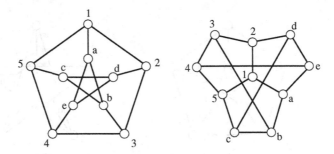

Fig. 1.8. A proof that Petersen's design is the same as Merlin's

"Fair enough," Arthur thought. He noticed that atom 1 was connected to atoms 5, a and 2 in Merlin's old design and checked that the same was true of Petersen's. After doing that for all other atoms, he was convinced that both molecules were identical.

Arthur could have figured this out on his own, provided he spent enough time on trying up to 3,628,681 possible correspondences. If he was lucky – extremely lucky – he could even have guessed a good correspondence from the first time and then performed the same check to verify that it worked. The same pattern occurs very frequently with decision problems of current interest. Often, figuring out the right decision requires, to the best of our knowledge, a lot of work. But if the answer is "yes" then there is an easily verifiable proof that the answer should be "yes."

The most prominent problem in computational complexity is the question whether coming up with such proofs is harder than verifying them. In other words, does the ability to guess proofs help us. It seems obvious that it makes a difference but so far no-one has been able to establish that intuition mathematically.

1.1.3 The Power of Memory

After a number of years, Arthur judged Merlin had produced enough molecule blue-prints to keep the twentieth century carbon chemists busy. Arthur released Merlin from the dungeons and assigned him a more frivolous task. He had to help the king with good strategies for finding a treasure hidden in a maze.

Arthur used to play this game when he visited friends. Over the years, he had developed an interest in simple yet efficient strategies. He had realized that the right-hand process – follow the wall on your right hand until you hit the treasure and then return following the wall with your left hand – did not always work. For example, it did not for the maze in Figure 1.9, where the "x" marks the location of the treasure.

But Arthur knew his classics and remembered Ariadne's technique to help Theseus escape from the Minotaur's labyrinth in Crete: Use a thread. He fixed

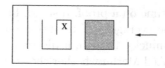

Fig. 1.9. A maze

the thread to the entrance position and started unrolling it. At a junction, he took the first unthreaded route counting counterclockwise which lay between the direction he came from and the direction the thread was pointing to. If there was no such direction, he backtracked by rolling up the thread to the previous junction. This strategy worked for all mazes. But Arthur had found out that it could take forever on some rather simple mazes. For example, it took about 2^k steps on the maze of Figure 1.10, which only had k junctions. He had tried several variants of Ariadne's trick but they are all seemed to have the same problem. So, Arthur asked Merlin for advice.

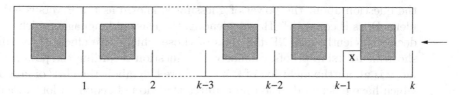

Fig. 1.10. Another maze

Merlin – being ahead of his time – told Arthur about the bread crumbs Hansel and Gretel would use. They would drop bread crumbs along the path they followed. When at a junction, they would first check whether there is a next junction that does not have bread crumbs yet. If so, they would go to the first such junction counting counterclockwise from where they came from. Otherwise, they would backtrack along the first bread crumbed path that came after the path last used, again counting counterclockwise. This strategy is now known as depth-first search. It always works, and is fast.

One problem Arthur had with all these nice strategies, though, was that they required some extra tools to keep track of where he had been: threads, bread crumbs, or a very good memory. Arthur asked Merlin whether he knew of an efficient technique that would only require him to keep a small number of junctions in mind. Merlin told him he could just, at each junction, flip a coin to pick the direction to follow next. That would not yield the shortest way to the treasure. The coin tosses may even dictate Arthur to go back and forth along the same path a couple of times. But Merlin claimed the odds were it would not take Arthur too long before he hit the treasure. Merlin even wanted to show Arthur a proof of his claim. Arthur, of course, did not want to waste his time on a proof. Instead, he tried the randomized strategy in practice, and the average performance seemed to confirm Merlin's claim.

When he was unlucky, though, it did take Arthur a while before he found the treasure. He asked Merlin whether there existed an efficient *deterministic* strategy that would only require him to keep track of a small number of junctions. To that question, Merlin did not know the answer. We still do not know, although we will shed some light on it in this work. It is a major open problem in computational complexity whether every problem which we can solve efficiently, has a solution with very modest memory requirements.

1.2 Contributions in This Dissertation

This thesis addresses all of the above issues, as well as some others. The questions we raised so far can be phrased in terms of relationships between classes of languages. The language corresponding to a decision problem is the set of all instances of the problem to which the answer is "yes." For example, the question about the power of guessing is known as the P versus NP problem: Does P equal NP? Here P denotes the class of languages which we can decide efficiently, and NP the class of those which have efficiently verifiable short membership proofs. Similarly, the question regarding the power of memory is about the inclusion of P in L, where L symbols the class of languages which have efficient decision procedures that do not require a lot of memory space. We refer to Chapter 2 for quantitative and more formal definitions.

From that perspective, the results in this dissertation divide into two categories:

- Simulations or inclusions: showing that all problems in one complexity class also belong to another one.
- Separations: showing that one complexity class contains a problem which the other does not.

1.2.1 Simulations

Chapter 3 presents our results on deterministic simulations of randomized processes. We focus on Arthur-Merlin games, randomized proof protocols like the one for the difference of molecules described above. We show how to derandomize these protocols and obtain deterministic relatively short proofs under a standard assumption in computational complexity, namely that the polynomial-time hierarchy does not collapse. The polynomial-time hierarchy is a tower of complexity classes the first two levels of which are P and NP. The assumption that it does not collapse is stronger than the hypothesis that P differs from NP but is also widely accepted. Thus our result provides the first strong evidence that the difference of molecules has relatively short proofs. Under a stronger assumption regarding the existence of hard computational problems, we can scale the proof size further down, putting the problem in the class NP.

Another way of looking at these results is as hardness versus randomness trade-offs: They show that either computationally hard problems exist or else randomness does not help much.

We also apply our derandomization technique to various randomized processes other than Arthur-Merlin games. In particular, we show that the randomized maze procedure described in Section 1.1.3 can be derandomized without increasing the memory need by much, provided some reasonable complexity theoretic assumption holds. So, modulo that assumption, we can answer Arthur's question affirmatively.

The work discussed in Chapter 3 was done jointly with A. Klivans. It was presented at the 31st ACM Symposium on Theory of Computing (Atlanta, May 1999) [75].

1.2.2 Separations

The other chapters of this thesis deal with techniques for separating complexity classes. One often tackles such questions by singling out the hardest problems in a complexity class, and concentrating on their properties. We consider a problem R hard for a complexity class if we can efficiently reduce every problem in the complexity class to R, i.e., if we can efficiently solve any problem in the class when given a black-box for R. If R itself also belongs to the class, we call R *complete* for the class. Several complexity classes, L, P and NP in particular, have complete problems under various reducibility notions.

Trying to separate complexity classes by isolating a structural difference between their complete languages, forms a unifying theme in Chapters 4 through 8. We looked at the following properties from this point of view:

Sparseness	–	the *density* of complete languages.
Autoreducibility	–	the *redundancy* of complete languages.
Resource-bounded measure	–	the *frequency* of complete languages.

Sparseness. Sparseness constitutes a candidate differentiating property that interests complexity theorists because of its connections to nonuniform complexity and to isomorphism questions. A language is sparse if it contains very few instances of each length. Showing that P has no sparse hard language under space efficient reductions would separate P from L. In Chapter 4, we will establish the logical completeness of this approach for reductions that can ask a bounded number of queries: If P differs from L then there exists no sparse hard language for P under space efficient reductions with a bounded number of black-box queries. The proof works for various other classes as well. Another instantiation states that no sparse hard language for NP exists under efficient randomized reductions with a bounded number of queries unless randomness is at least as powerful as guessing.

Most of the work in Chapter 4 was presented at the 11th IEEE Conference on Computational Complexity (Philadelphia, May 1996) [94]. The full version of the paper was published in the special issue of the Journal of Computer and System Sciences dedicated to selected papers of the conference [95].

Autoreducibility. Autoreducibility defines the most general type of efficient reduction of a problem to itself. A problem is autoreducible if we can solve a given instance efficiently when allowed to ask a black-box the solution to any other instance. Chapter 5 will establish that large complexity classes have complete languages that are not autoreducible, whereas the complete languages of smaller classes all share the property of autoreducibility. The specific results we get yield alternate proofs of known separations. We will also show that settling the question for certain intermediate classes either way would imply major new separations.

Chapter 5 is joint work with H. Buhrman, L. Fortnow, and L. Torenvliet. A precursor of the paper was presented at the 36th IEEE Symposium on Foundations of Computer Science (Milwaukee, October 1995) [33]. The full version was published in the SIAM Journal on Computing [34].

Resource-bounded measure. Resource-bounded measure formalizes the notions of scarceness and abundance within complexity classes. From the separation point of view, the theory seems particularly suited for showing that the complexity classes BPP and EXP differ. BPP consists of all languages which have efficient randomized decision procedures with a negligible error probability. EXP is the smallest deterministic complexity class like P known to contain BPP. The BPP versus EXP problem asks whether equality of these two classes holds. It would be truly amazing if it did, because randomness would allow us to speed up any computation by an exponential factor. Nevertheless, the question remains open as of today.

Within the formalism of resource-bounded measure, most languages turn out to be hard for BPP under relatively powerful reductions. On the other hand, we will prove in Chapter 7 that EXP and several other subclasses only have a few complete or hard languages under weaker reducibilities. A very narrow gap between the power of the reductions remains, and bridging it would separate BPP from EXP and from certain other classes.

Chapter 7 describes joint work with H. Buhrman. It was presented at the 13th IEEE Conference on Computational Complexity (Buffalo, June 1998) [36]. The full paper was published in the special issue of the Journal of Computer and System Sciences dedicated to selected papers of the conference [37].

Another approach for settling the BPP versus EXP problem, similar in spirit to the probabilistic method of combinatorics, tries to show that BPP is a small subclass of EXP. This seems like a more difficult task than just separating BPP from EXP but it may be easier to come up with a proof of it. Examples like that are well-known in combinatorics. We will establish in Chapter 6 that, in fact, the smallness statement is not stronger: if BPP differs from EXP then it is a small subclass of EXP. This result was published in Theoretical Computer Science [96].

One can view resource-bounded measure as a restriction of classical Lebesgue measure preserving several nice properties like additivity and monotonicity. Whether invariance under permutations also carries over, remains open. The issue comes up when investigating the resource-bounded measure of the class of autoreducible languages. In Chapter 8, we will show that a resource-bounded version of permutation invariance holds under a certain reasonable hypothesis, and that if it holds, then BPP differs from EXP – providing yet another way of tackling the BPP versus EXP problem. We will develop betting games as the basis for an alternate to resource-bounded measure, with permutation invariance built in, for quantifying the frequency of properties within complexity classes.

The work reported in Chapter 8 was done jointly with H. Buhrman, K. Regan, D. Sivakumar, and M. Strauss. It was presented at the 15th Symposium on Theoretical Aspects of Computer Science (Paris, February 1998) [38]. The final version of the paper was published in the SIAM Journal on Computing [39].

2. Preliminaries

In this chapter, we introduce basic concepts from computational complexity as well as terminology we will be using throughout the rest of the thesis.

Computational complexity delineates which problems computers can realistically solve. After describing the notion of a computational problem and giving some important examples, we will formalize the various computer models we will consider. We will introduce relevant resources for each of them and define classes of computational problems that can be solved efficiently on them, i.e., using few of these resources.

We will pay particular attention to randomized models and to the concept of completeness within complexity classes – the two main themes of this thesis. Finally, we will also give an introduction to resource-bounded measure, a tool we will use in the last three chapters.

2.1 Computational Problems

This section describes the notion of a computational problem. In the examples, we will review some terminology from graph theory and logic.

A *computational problem* is a relation $R \subseteq I \times O$ between inputs or instances, and outputs or solutions.

Example 2.1.1 (Graph Connectivity). A *graph* $G = (V, E)$ consists of a collection V of vertices or nodes, and a collection E of unordered pairs of vertices, called edges. Each of the edges describes an interconnection between two vertices, e.g., a chemical bond between two carbon atoms of a molecule. Vertices are often represented as points, and edges as lines between vertices. See Figure 2.1 for an example.

An instance of the GRAPH CONNECTIVITY problem consists of a graph G and two of its vertices s and t. The solution is the answer to the question whether there is a path in G connecting s and t. In Figure 2.1 the answer is "yes" for s and t; the heavy lines represent a path between s and t. The answer is "no" for vertices s and u.

Example 2.1.2 (Digraph Critical Path). A *digraph* $G = (V, A)$ consists of a collection V of vertices or nodes, and a collection A of ordered pairs of

D. van Mehlkebeek: Randomness and Completeness in Computational Complexity, LNCS 1950, pp. 13–52, 2000.

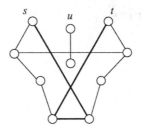

Fig. 2.1. A graph in which s and t are connected, but s and u are not

vertices, called arcs. It is a graph in which all edges have been given an orientation – "digraph" is short for "directed graph". A digraph is *acyclic* if it contains no directed cycle, i.e., no sequence of arcs that leads from a vertex to itself. Figure 2.2 represents a digraph which is not acyclic; the heavy arcs form a directed cycle. The acronym DAG stands for "directed acyclic graph."

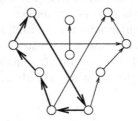

Fig. 2.2. A digraph with a directed cycle

An instance of the DIGRAPH CRITICAL PATH problem consists of a DAG $G = (V, A)$ and a weight function $w : A \to [0, \infty)$. A solution is a directed path in G of maximum weight, i.e., a sequence of arcs for which the sum of the weights is as large as possible. The heavy arcs in Figure 2.3 form a critical path.

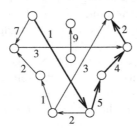

Fig. 2.3. A weighted DAG and a critical path

Example 2.1.3 (Graph Isomorphism). Two graphs $G_1 = (V_1, E_1)$ and $G_2 = (V_2, E_2)$ are *isomorphic* if they have the same structure, i.e., if there exists a one-to-one and onto function $f : V_1 \to V_2$ such that for any $v, w \in V_1$, $\{v, w\} \in E_1$ iff $\{f(v), f(w)\} \in E_2$. The two graphs in Figure 1.8 are isomorphic – they describe the same molecule. One of the possible correspondences f between their vertices, called an isomorphism, is presented.

An instance of the GRAPH ISOMORPHISM problem consists of two graphs, and the solution is the decision whether they are isomorphic or not.

Example 2.1.4 (Boolean Formula Satisfiability). A *Boolean formula* is an expression obtained from the constants TRUE and FALSE, and variables of the form p_i for $i \in \mathbb{N}$, by a finite number of applications of the following rules:

- Negating an expression: Transform ϕ into $\neg\phi$.
- Disjoining expressions: Combine ϕ and ψ into $(\phi \vee \psi)$.
- Conjoining expressions: Combine ϕ and ψ into $(\phi \wedge \psi)$.

The intended meaning of the operators $\neg$, $\vee$, and $\wedge$ is respectively "NOT", inclusive "OR" and "AND."

An instance of the BOOLEAN FORMULA SATISFIABILITY problem is a Boolean formula ϕ. The solution is whether ϕ has a satisfying truth-value assignment, i.e., a mapping $\sigma : \{p_i\}_i \to \{\text{TRUE, FALSE}\}$ that makes ϕ evaluate to TRUE after substituting $\sigma(p_i)$ for every occurrence of p_i and using the above logical meanings for the operators. For example, $(((p_1 \vee \neg p_2) \wedge (p_2 \vee \neg p_3)) \wedge (p_3 \vee \neg p_1))$ is a positive instance of BOOLEAN FORMULA SATISFIABILITY; $\sigma(p_1) = \sigma(p_2) = \sigma(p_3) = \text{FALSE}$ defines a satisfying assignment. The formula $(p_1 \wedge \neg p_1)$ is an example of a negative instance.

For future reference, we now introduce logical formulas, a generalization of Boolean formulas. The variables p_i in a Boolean formula are either TRUE or FALSE. We say that they range over the Boolean domain $\{\text{TRUE, FALSE}\}$. We can replace the variables p_i in a Boolean formula by arbitrary propositions, i.e., expressions in variables x_j, $j \in \mathbb{N}$, ranging over some domain D, such that any variable assignment $\sigma : \{x_j\}_j \to D$ makes the expression TRUE or FALSE. We call the resulting formula a *logical formula* over D. A Boolean formula is a logical formula over the Boolean domain. We will often use 0 and 1 to represent FALSE and TRUE respectively, and use $\{0, 1\}$ to denote the Boolean domain.

Example 2.1.5 (Graph Ramsey Triple). An instance of GRAPH RAMSEY TRIPLE is a triple (F, G, H) of graphs. The question is whether every coloring of the edges of F with red and blue contains a red copy of G or a blue copy of H.

For example, let F be the graph with 6 fully interconnected vertices, and G and H be triangles. Then (F, G, H) is a positive instance of GRAPH RAMSEY TRIPLE. This is because in any group of 6 people at least 3 of them know each other or 3 of them do not know each other.

Example 2.1.6 (Quantified Boolean Formula Validity). A *quantified logical formula* over a domain D is an expression obtained from a logical formula over D by a finite number of applications of the following transformations:

- Existential quantification: Transform ϕ into $(\exists x_i)\phi$ for some $i \in \mathbb{N}$.
- Universal quantification: Transform ϕ into $(\forall x_i)\phi$ for some $i \in \mathbb{N}$.

Without loss of generality, we will assume that a different variable x_i is used for each quantification step. The truth-value of $(\exists x_i)\phi$ is TRUE iff there is a setting of $x_i \in D$ making ϕ evaluate to TRUE; the truth-value of $(\forall x_i)\phi$ is TRUE iff every setting of $x_i \in D$ makes ϕ evaluate to TRUE. Note that these truth-values may depend on the setting of some variables other than x_i.

A *quantified Boolean formula* is a quantified logical formula over the Boolean domain. A quantified Boolean formula of the form $(\exists x_i)\phi$ is equivalent to the disjunction $(\phi|_{x_i \leftarrow \text{TRUE}} \lor \phi|_{x_i \leftarrow \text{FALSE}})$ where $\phi|_{x_i \leftarrow v}$ is obtained from ϕ by replacing every occurrence of x_i by v. Similarly, universal quantification corresponds to conjunction. So, quantified Boolean formulas have no more expressive power than Boolean formulas, but they may allow us to express the same statement more succinctly.

An instance of QUANTIFIED BOOLEAN FORMULA VALIDITY is a fully quantified Boolean formula, i.e., a quantified Boolean formula which has a quantifier for every variable occurring in the base Boolean formula. The solution is the decision whether the quantified Boolean formula has truth-value TRUE. The formula $(\forall x_1)(\exists x_2)((x_1 \lor \neg x_2) \land (\neg x_1 \lor x_2))$ is a positive instance of QUANTIFIED BOOLEAN FORMULA VALIDITY; changing the order of the quantifiers to $(\exists x_2)(\forall x_1)((x_1 \lor \neg x_2) \land (\neg x_1 \lor x_2))$ turns it into a negative instance.

Example 2.1.7 (Generalized Checkers). An instance of the problem GENERALIZED CHECKERS consists of an n by n checkerboard for an arbitrary $n \in \mathbb{N}$, and a configuration of white and black pieces on the board. The question is whether this is a valid configuration from which white can force a win.

To input an instance of a computational problem to a digital computer, we have to describe it as a finite sequence of symbols over some finite *alphabet* Σ. Similarly, the solution to an instance of a computational problem will be output in that format. This implies that both the set I of inputs and the set O of outputs must be countable. Usually, I is infinite but O may be finite. We call a finite sequence of symbols from Σ a *string* over Σ, and we denote the set of all strings over Σ by Σ^*: $\Sigma^* = \cup_{k \in \mathbb{N}}\Sigma^k$. We will also use $\Sigma^{\leqslant k}$ to represent $\cup_{\ell \leqslant k}\Sigma^\ell$. The *length* of a string $x \in \Sigma^k$ equals k and is denoted by $|x|$. We use the symbol λ to represent the empty string, the one and only string of length 0.

We will implicitly use the binary alphabet $\Sigma = \{0,1\}$ unless stated otherwise. However, we will not worry about the details of the encoding. Our results will be robust in the sense that they will hold for any reasonable encoding scheme.

We will sometimes need to combine several strings over Σ into a single string, and vice versa. A *pairing function* allows us to do that. It is a one-to-one and onto mapping $\langle \cdot, \cdot \rangle$ from $\Sigma^* \times \Sigma^*$ to Σ^*. We can extend its domain to an arbitrary number k of arguments by inductively defining $\langle x_1, x_2, \ldots, x_{k-1}, x_k \rangle$ as $\langle \langle x_1, x_2, \ldots, x_{k-1} \rangle, x_k \rangle$. We will use a pairing function that is efficiently computable and invertible, more specifically in polynomial time on a Turing machine (see Section 2.2 for the efficiency terminology). We will also refer to the *lexicographic ordering* $\leqslant_\ell$ of $\{0,1\}^*$: For $x, y \in \{0,1\}^*$, we write $x \leqslant_\ell y$ if $1x \leqslant 1y$ where $1x$ and $1y$ are interpreted as binary numbers.

An important class of computational problems are *decision problems*. In this case, the set of outputs equals $O = \{\text{yes}, \text{no}\}$: The solution to an instance of the problem is the answer "yes" or "no." All the example computational problems given above are decision problems except for DIGRAPH CRITICAL PATH. Equivalently, these problems can be viewed as deciding membership to the corresponding subset of Σ^* consisting of the encodings of the positive instances, those for which the answer is "yes." A subset of Σ^* is called a *language*. We will use the acronyms listed in Table 2.1 to denote the languages corresponding to some of the decision problems we introduced.

language:	decision problem:
U-STCON	GRAPH CONNECTIVITY
ISO	GRAPH ISOMORPHISM
SAT	BOOLEAN FORMULA SATISFIABILITY
TQBF	QUANTIFIED BOOLEAN FORMULA VALIDITY

Table 2.1. Languages and corresponding decision problems

The *complement* of a language L is the language $\Sigma^* \setminus L$, and we denote it by $\overline{L}$. For a class of languages $\mathcal{C}$, the class of the complements of the languages in $\mathcal{C}$ is denoted by $\text{co}\,\mathcal{C}$. The *characteristic function* of a language L is the function

$$\chi_L : \Sigma^* \to \{0,1\} : x \to \begin{cases} 1 & \text{if } x \in L \\ 0 & \text{otherwise.} \end{cases}$$

The *characteristic sequence* of L is the binary sequence $\chi_L(s_1)\chi_L(s_2)\ldots$, where $s_1, s_2, \ldots$ denotes the lexicographic ordering of Σ^* (in particular $s_1 = \lambda$). We will sometimes also denote the characteristic sequence by χ_L.

We say that a computer *solves* a computational problem $R \subseteq I \times O$ if it transforms any given input $x \in I$ into an output $y \in O$ satisfying $R(x, y)$. It does that by applying a sequence of elementary transformations prescribed by a program or algorithm. The available elementary transformations and the possible ways of combining them depend on the computer model. We will discuss several models in Section 2.2.

No computer can solve every problem. In particular, it cannot solve its halting problem: Deciding whether it will halt when executing a given program on a given input. The class of solvable computational problems turns out to be the same for all known general purpose computer models, including the ones we will consider next. However, some models do seem to differ in the *efficiency* with which they can solve these problems, and therefore in the class of computational problems they can *realistically* solve.

2.2 Models of Computation, Resource Bounds, and Complexity Classes

In this section, we will describe the various models of computation we will consider, introduce relevant resources for them, and define classes of computational problems which can be solved using few of these resources. The main open questions in computational complexity ask about the relationships between these classes, and we will state the most important ones. We defer the discussion of randomized models to Section 2.3.

We will measure resources as a function of the instance size and look at worst-case scenarios. We define the amount of *resources needed* for a given input size n as the maximum over all inputs x of size n, of the amount of resources needed for instance x. The *size of an instance x* is the length $|x|$ of the string that encodes it. A *resource bound* is a monotone nondecreasing function $f : \mathbb{N} \to [0, \infty)$. Because of the robustness of the resource bounds we will consider, more natural problem-specific measures for the input size than its length can also be used, e.g., the number of vertices in case of graph problems.

We usually look at infinite computation problems, and are mainly interested in how the resource need increases when the input size grows larger. We will make extensive use of the following notation in doing so. It allows us to compare the asymptotic growth rate of resource bounds up to constant factors. Let $f, g : \mathbb{N} \to [0, \infty)$ be functions.

- $f \in O(g)$ if there exists a constant $c > 0$ such that $f(n) \leqslant c \cdot g(n)$ for all sufficiently large $n \in \mathbb{N}$. This means that f does not grow faster than g.
- $f \subset \Omega(g)$ if there exists a constant $c > 0$ such that $f(n) \geqslant c \cdot g(n)$ for all sufficiently large $n \in \mathbb{N}$. So, f grows at least as fast as g does.
- $f \in \Theta(g)$ if both $f \in O(g)$ and $f \in \Omega(g)$, i.e., f and g have the same growth rate.
- $f \in o(g)$ if for any constant $c > 0$ and for large enough $n \in \mathbb{N}$ (depending on c), $f(n) \leqslant c \cdot g(n)$. This means that f grows slower than g.
- $f \in \omega(g)$ if for any constant $c > 0$ and for large enough $n \in \mathbb{N}$ (depending on c), $f(n) \geqslant c \cdot g(n)$. So, f grows faster than g.

The most frequently used resource bounds are listed in Table 2.2.

resource bound:	name:
$O(\log n)$	logarithmic
$n^{O(1)}$	polynomial
$2^{n^{o(1)}}$	subexponential
$2^{n^{O(1)}}$	exponential

Table 2.2. Commonly used resource bounds and their names

We now begin our discussion of the various computation models. They are all very elementary. For each one of them more involved alternatives exist but, for our purposes, these variants are all equivalent to the standard model we present. When we specify our algorithms, we will actually do it at a much higher level, relying on the fact that such higher-level descriptions can be cast in our standard elementary model.

2.2.1 Turing Machines

The Turing machine constitutes our standard model of a sequential computer.

Model. A *Turing machine* consists of a finite control, three semi-infinite tapes (the input tape, the work tape, and the output tape), and a read/write head for each of them. See Figure 2.4. At any point in time, the finite control is in one of a finite number of states S, each tape cell contains a symbol from the underlying alphabet Σ, and each of the tape heads is located on one of the cells of its tape. At the start of the computation, the finite control is in some designated state $s_o \in S$. The input is written on the leftmost part of the input tape, and the rest of the input tape, the work tape and the output tape are blank. The tape heads are positioned on the first cell of each tape. Then the computation starts. In each step, the finite control reads the symbols under the heads on the input and work tape. Based on the values of these symbols and its current state, it switches to a new state, writes a symbol on the cell of the work tape under the head, and can move the heads on these tapes to a neighboring cell. It may also write a symbol on the cell under the output tape head and move that head one position to the right. This process continues until the finite control enters the final state $s_f \in S$. The contents of the output tape to the left of the output head defines the result of the computation.

An *instantaneous description* of the Turing machine contains all the information about its current configuration except for the input and output: the state of the finite control, the contents of the work tapes, and the positions of the input tape and work tape heads. Note that at any point in time, only a finite portion of the tapes is non-blank, so each instantaneous description is finite. The sequence of instantaneous descriptions starting from the initial one forms a transcript of the computation on the given input.

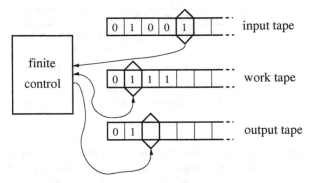

Fig. 2.4. Structure of a Turing machine

Resources. The most relevant resources are the time and space the Turing machine needs to compute the solution. We measure the *time* as the number of transformations until the machine reaches the final state s_f. The *space* needed is the number of different cells of the work tape that are accessed during the computation.

For bounding the allotted time and space we will typically use constructible functions. A function $t : \mathbb{N} \to [0, \infty)$ is *time-constructible* if there exists a Turing machine that runs in time exactly $t(n)$ on every input of size n. Similarly, we call $s : \mathbb{N} \to [0, \infty)$ *space-constructible* if there exists a Turing machine that runs in space exactly $s(n)$ on every input of size n. All explicit resource bounds we use in this thesis are space-constructible, and the superlinear ones among them are also time-constructible.

Complexity Classes. We define $\mathsf{DTIME}[t(n)]$ as the class of languages that can be decided in time $O(t(n))$ on a Turing machine. A bit more time allows us to solve more problems.

Theorem 2.2.1 (Time Hierarchy Theorem [62]). *Let $t_1, t_2 : \mathbb{N} \to [0, \infty)$ be such that t_2 is time-constructible, and $t_2 \in \omega(t_1 \log t_1)$. Then $\mathsf{DTIME}[t_1] \subsetneq \mathsf{DTIME}[t_2]$.*

We consider computations on a sequential machine time efficient if they take no more than polynomial time. GRAPH CONNECTIVITY and DIGRAPH CRITICAL PATH are examples of computational problems we know how to solve in polynomial time. We denote the corresponding class of languages by P: $\mathsf{P} \doteq \cup_{c>0} \mathsf{DTIME}[n^c]$. So, U-STCON belongs to P. Another commonly used time-bounded class is exponential time: $\mathsf{EXP} \doteq \cup_{c>0} \mathsf{DTIME}[2^{n^c}]$. All the decision problems discussed in Section 2.1 belong to EXP. We will sometimes also refer to $\mathsf{E} \doteq \cup_{c>0} \mathsf{DTIME}[2^{cn}]$, although this class is not as robust as EXP because membership of a decision problem to E may depend on the details of the encoding. The Time Hierarchy Theorem implies that $\mathsf{P} \subsetneq \mathsf{E} \subsetneq \mathsf{EXP}$.

DSPACE[$s(n)$] denotes the class of languages that can be decided in space $O(s(n))$ on a Turing machine. A little bit more space buys us more decision power.

Theorem 2.2.2 (Space Hierarchy Theorem [61]). *Let $s_1, s_2 : \mathbb{N} \to [0, \infty)$ be such that s_2 is space-constructible, and $s_2 \in \omega(s_1)$. Then* DSPACE[s_1] $\subsetneq$ DSPACE[s_2].

We consider computations space efficient if they use no more than logarithmic work space. We define L as the class of all decision problems that can be solved in space $O(\log n)$ on a Turing machine. Deciding whether a graph is acyclic can be done in logarithmic space. It is conjectured that U-STCON also belong to L; the most space efficient algorithm known to date runs in space $O(\log^{4/3} n)$ [12]. Other frequently encountered space-bounded complexity classes include PSPACE $\doteq \cup_{c>0}$DSPACE[n^c], and EXPSPACE $\doteq \cup_{c>0}$DSPACE[2^{n^c}]. All the example decision problems in Section 2.1 are known to lie in PSPACE except for GENERALIZED CHECKERS, which lies in EXPSPACE. TQBF is one of the hardest PSPACE languages in a sense we will clarify in Section 2.4. The Space Hierarchy Theorem yields that L $\subsetneq$ PSPACE $\subsetneq$ EXPSPACE.

Regarding the relationship between time and space, it is clear that the space requirement is never larger than the time requirement. The best we know about the converse is that DSPACE[$s(n)$] $\subseteq \cup_{c>0}$DTIME[$2^{c \cdot s(n)}$] for any space-constructible function $s(n) \geqslant \log n$. In particular, we know that

$$L \subseteq P \subseteq PSPACE \subseteq EXP \subseteq EXPSPACE. \qquad (2.1)$$

The hierarchy theorems tell us that some of these inclusions have to be strict, but for each individual one strictness is an unsolved conjecture.

2.2.2 Uniform Families of Boolean Circuits

Families of Boolean circuits form an alternate model for sequential computation equivalent to the Turing machine except for that we can use a different "program" for each input size. We call such a model *nonuniform*. We can make the model uniform and obtain genuine algorithms by generating the circuits using a Turing machine.

We will use uniformly generated families of Boolean circuits as our standard model of a parallel computer. The idea behind parallel computing is to speed up computations by using several processors that simultaneously work on parts of the problem, and cooperatively reach the solution. The gates of a Boolean circuit act in such a way.

Model. A *Boolean circuit* is a combination of NOT-, OR- and AND-gates built on top of input gates, with the structure of a DAG. Each of the input gates is labeled with a variable x_i for some $i \in \mathbb{N}$. Given a truth-value assignment $\sigma : \{x_i\}_i \to \{\text{TRUE}, \text{FALSE}\}$, we can inductively define a truth-value for each of the gates. The value of an input gate with label x_i is $\sigma(x_i)$, and each of the other gates gets the result of applying the corresponding Boolean function to the values of the incoming gates. See Figure 2.5 for an example of a Boolean circuit. All OR- and AND-gates in this thesis are binary, i.e., they have two incoming arcs, unless stated otherwise.

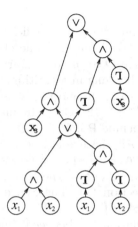

Fig. 2.5. A Boolean circuit

We note that a Boolean formula is a special case of a Boolean circuit, namely a circuit in which the underlying undirected graph contains no cycles. The example circuit in Figure 2.5 is not a formula.

If the labels of the input gates are all in $\{x_i\}_{i=1}^{n}$, each gate of the circuit defines a Boolean function on n variables, or equivalently, by our usual association, a function from $\{0,1\}^n$ to $\{0,1\}$. For example, the top gate of the Boolean circuit in Figure 2.5 determines the parity of its three inputs, i.e., their sum modulo 2.

So, we can use a Boolean circuit to solve a decision problem on a finite number of inputs I'. If I' contains all the inputs that we are interested in, that one circuit settles the problem. If we want to be able to compute a solution for any instance of an infinite problem, we need an infinite *family of circuits*. In order to decide a language L, we will use a family of circuits $\{C_n\}_n$, where circuit C_n computes the characteristic function of L on $\{0,1\}^n$. For this family to constitute an algorithm, we require that there is some generating Turing machine that on input 1^n outputs the circuit C_n. We call such a family of circuits *uniform* if the Turing machine runs in space $O(\log n)$.

Such a uniformly generated family of circuits represents a parallel algorithm in the following way. We can view the gates of the circuits as little processors that perform an easy computation using the values of their incoming gates. Each of the gates on the same level in Figure 2.5 can execute their computations in parallel, provided some synchronization.

Resources. We will primarily look at the size and the depth of circuits. We define the *size* as the number of connections, which essentially equals the number of gates – the size and the number of gates differ by at most a factor of 2. The *depth* is the length of a longest path in the underlying DAG and corresponds to the time the parallel computation takes. The size and depth of the circuit in Figure 2.5 are 16 and 6 respectively.

Complexity Classes. For any language L we denote by $C_L(n)$ the size of a smallest circuit that decides L on $\{0,1\}^n$. We define $\mathsf{SIZE}[s(n)]$ as the class of languages L for which $C_L(n) \in O(s(n))$. Note that because of nonuniformity, these classes may contain noncomputable languages like the halting problem.

Every Boolean function $f : \{0,1\}^n \to \{0,1\}$ on n variables can be computed by a circuit of size $\frac{2^n}{n} \cdot (1 + \Theta(\frac{\log n}{n}))$, and most functions actually require circuits of that size. A very tight hierarchy theorem holds for circuit size.

Theorem 2.2.3 (Size Hierarchy Theorem [108]). *Let γ_n denote the maximum circuit size required for Boolean functions on n variables. For any $s < \gamma_n$, there exists a Boolean function on n variables that can be computed by a circuit of size*

$$\begin{cases} s+1 & \text{if } s < \gamma_{n-1} \\ s+n & \text{if } \gamma_{n-1} \leqslant s < \gamma_n, \end{cases}$$

but not by a circuit of size s.

We consider a family of circuits $\{C_n\}_n$ small if the size of C_n is bounded by a polynomial in n. The class of languages with small circuits is denoted by $\mathsf{P/poly}$. This notation refers to an alternate characterization as an advice class. In general, for any complexity class $\mathcal{C}$ and any function $h : \mathbb{N} \to \mathbb{N}$, we say that a language L is in the class $\mathcal{C}/h$ if there exists a language L' in $\mathcal{C}$ and an "advice" function $a : \mathbb{N} \to \Sigma^*$ with $|a(n)| \leqslant h(n)$ such that $x \in L$ iff $\langle x, a(|x|)\rangle \in L'$. Note that the advice only depends on the length of the input. It could be the description of a circuit deciding the language on inputs of that length. Along these lines one can show that $\mathsf{P/poly} \doteq \cup_{c>0}\mathsf{P}/n^c$ coincides with the class of languages with small circuits.

Theorem 2.2.4 ([109]). $\mathsf{P/poly} = \cup_{c>0}\mathsf{SIZE}[n^c]$.

We define the class $\mathsf{DEPTH}[d(n)]$ as the class of languages which can be decided by a family $\{C_n\}_n$ of circuits such that the depth of C_n is at most $d(n)$. Any Boolean function f on n variables can be decided by circuits of depth $n - \log\log n + o(1)$ and most functions require that depth. The hierarchy theorem for circuit depth is as tight as it can get.

Theorem 2.2.5 (Depth Hierarchy Theorem [93]). *Let δ_n be the maximum circuit depth required for Boolean functions on n variables, and let $d < \delta_n$. There is a Boolean function on n variables that can be computed by a circuit of depth $d + 1$, but not by a circuit of depth d.*

Like $\mathsf{SIZE}[s(n)]$, $\mathsf{DEPTH}[d(n)]$ is a nonuniform class. Regarding *uniform* circuit classes, we define the NC-hierarchy as follows: For any $k \in \mathbb{N}$, NC^k denotes the class of languages that can be decided by a uniform family of circuits $\{C_n\}_n$ of polynomial size and depth $O(\log^k n)$. The union of the classes NC^k forms "Nick's class" NC, called after Nicholas Pippenger. It is clear that $\mathsf{NC}^k \subseteq \mathsf{NC}^{k+1}$. For $k = 0$ strictness holds; for $k > 0$ it is conjectured. NC^1 represents the class of problems that are efficiently solvable on parallel computers, namely in logarithmic time with a polynomial number of processors. A typical problem in NC^1 is addition – given a list of numbers in binary notation and an index i, decide the i-th bit of their sum.

There is a strong connection with efficient space-bounded computation on sequential machines:

Theorem 2.2.6 ([120]). $\mathsf{NC}^1 \subseteq \mathsf{L} \subseteq \mathsf{NC}^2$.

For both inclusions strictness is conjectured.

As we hinted at before, circuits can efficiently simulate Turing machines.

Theorem 2.2.7 ([123, 28]). *Let L be a language that can be decided by a Turing machine running in time $t(n)$ and space $s(n) \geqslant \log n$. Then L can be decided by a family of circuits of size $O(t(n) \log s(n))$, as well as by a family of circuits of depth $O(s(n) \log t(n))$.*

Conversely, given a circuit of size s and depth d with n inputs, we can evaluate it on a given input in time polynomial in $(s+n)$ as well as in space $O(d+\log n)$.

Similar to the relationships between time and space on Turing machines, we know that $\mathsf{SIZE}[s] \subseteq \mathsf{DEPTH}[s]$ and that $\mathsf{DEPTH}[d] \subseteq \mathsf{SIZE}[2^d]$. If we restrict ourselves to formulas, there is a tight relationship between the two measures: The required depth and the logarithm of the required size differ by at most a factor of 2 [127]. In particular, families of formulas of polynomial size and families of circuits of logarithmic depth are equivalent.

2.2.3 Nondeterministic Turing Machines

A nondeterministic Turing machine does not represent a real computing device. However, it allows us to capture the following complexity pattern that several important decision problems share: It may be hard to decide whether a given input belongs to the language or not, but if if does, by making the right guesses, we can come up with a membership proof the validity of which is easy to check. In that sense a nondeterministic Turing machine should be viewed as a formalization of a proof system rather than as a computer model. Nondeterministic computations can be cast as interactions between an all-powerful prover and a computationally limited verifier where the prover tries to convince the verifier of some fact, namely that the input belongs to the language in question.

Nondeterministic Turing machines also lend themselves to characterize the complexity of more general computational problems, but we will restrict our attention to decision problems.

Model. The model of a *nondeterministic Turing machine* is the same as that of a "classical" Turing machine (also known as a "deterministic" Turing machine) except for that there may be several possible transitions given the current state of the finite control and the symbols under the heads of the input and work tapes. Each time this happens during the computation, we say that the machine makes a nondeterministic choice. A nondeterministic Turing machine decides a language L if for every input $x \in L$ there is a sequence of transitions that leads to an accepting configuration, i.e., a configuration in the final state s_f and such that the output tape contains the encoding for "yes." In that case, we say that the machine has an *accepting computation* on input x. There is no such sequence for an input $x \notin L$.

We can view a computation of a nondeterministic Turing machine M as a path in its configuration digraph G_M. The vertices of G_M are all possible configurations of M, and arcs correspond to allowed transitions between configurations. In principle, G_M can contain a directed cycle but a simple modification of M then makes the configuration digraph acyclic. We will always assume that G_M is a DAG. M accepts an input x if there is a path in G_M from the initial configuration on input x to an accepting configuration.

In terms of proof systems, the nondeterministic choices are the information provided by the prover. The guarantee is that there is a way for the prover to make the verifier accept iff $x \in L$ – the proof system is sound and complete.

Resources. As in the case of deterministic Turing machines, the most relevant resources are *time* and *space*. For a given input x, they are defined as the maximum over all possible computation paths on input x of the time respectively space needed along that path.

A secondary resource is the amount of nondeterminism the machine needs, but we will not consider that measure.

Complexity Classes. NTIME$[t(n)]$ denotes the class of languages that can be decided by a nondeterministic Turing machine in time $O(t(n))$. Similar to the deterministic case, some more time allows us to decide more languages.

Theorem 2.2.8 (Nondeterministic Time Hierarchy Theorem [140]). *Let $t_1, t_2 : \mathbb{N} \to [0, \infty)$ be such that t_2 is time-constructible, and $t_2(n) \in \omega(t_1(n+1))$. Then NTIME$[t_1] \subsetneq$ NTIME$[t_2]$.*

NP $\doteq \cup_{c>0}$ NTIME$[n^c]$ represents the class of languages with short efficiently verifiable membership proofs. ISO and SAT are typical NP languages. For ISO, an isomorphism constitutes and efficiently verifiable short proof; for SAT a satisfying truth-value assignment does the job. SAT is in fact one of the hardest languages in NP. See Section 2.4 for more details.

We will also use NE $\doteq \cup_{c>0}$ NTIME$[2^{cn}]$ and NEXP $\doteq \cup_{c>0}$ NTIME$[2^{n^c}]$. It follows from the Nondeterministic Time Hierarchy Theorem that NP $\subsetneq$ NE $\subsetneq$ NEXP.

NTIME$[t(n)]$ contains its deterministic counterpart DTIME$[t(n)]$. As for the converse inclusion, the best we know for an arbitrary time-constructible function $t(n)$ is that NTIME$[t(n)] \subseteq \cup_{c>0}$DTIME$[2^{c \cdot t(n)}]$ – exhaustively try all possible proofs of length $O(t(n))$. In particular, the smallest deterministic time-bounded class known to contain NP is EXP. The big open problem in computational complexity theory is to prove the conjecture that P $\neq$ NP – that coming up with a proof is harder than checking one.

A relevant question for nondeterministic complexity classes is whether they are closed under complementation. Exhaustively ruling out all possible proofs as above shows that coNTIME$[t(n)] \subseteq \cup_{c>0}$ NTIME$[2^{c \cdot t(n)}]$, and that is the best we know in general. For example, we do not know of subexponential size membership proofs for $\overline{\text{SAT}}$. Complexity theorists conjecture that polynomial size proofs for coNP languages do not exist, i.e., that NP $\neq$ coNP. Note that this is a stronger conjecture than that P $\neq$ NP.

We defer the discussion of the relationship between nondeterministic time and circuit size to section 2.2.4. We now turn to space-bounded nondeterminism. NSPACE$[s(n)]$ denotes the class of languages that can be decided by a nondeterministic Turing machine using $O(s(n))$ space. The same hierarchy theorem as in the deterministic case holds.

Theorem 2.2.9 (Nondeterministic Space Hierarchy Theorem [67]). *Let $s_1, s_2 : \mathbb{N} \to [0, \infty)$ be such that s_2 is space-constructible, and $s_2 \in \omega(s_1)$. Then* NSPACE$[s_1] \subsetneq$ NSPACE$[s_2]$.

NL $\doteq$ NSPACE$[\log n]$ represents the class of languages for which a space efficient verifier can check membership of the input while interacting with a prover that tries to convince him/her of this fact. An example of a language in NL is U-STCON: The prover can tell the verifier how to get from s to t; the verifier only has to keep track of which vertex s/he is at and check that the moves the prover suggests are valid. In fact, the same strategy works for checking that there is a path from s to t in a digraph. The corresponding language D-STCON is one of the hardest in NL.

Nondeterministic polynomial space coincides with PSPACE. This is a consequence of Savitch's Theorem, which shows how to deterministically simulate nondeterministic computations with a quadratic overhead in space:

Theorem 2.2.10 (Savitch's Theorem [120]). *Let $s : \mathbb{N} \to [0, \infty)$ be space-constructible and such that $s(n) \geqslant \log n$. Then* NSPACE$[s(n)] \subseteq$ DSPACE$[s^2(n)]$.

Obviously, DSPACE$[s] \subseteq$ NSPACE$[s]$ for any s. Instantiating Savitch's Theorem for logarithmic s yields that NL $\subseteq$ DSPACE$[\log^2 n]$. In fact, the proof shows that NL $\subseteq$ NC^2. Strictness of this inclusion is conjectured.

Another interesting property of nondeterministic space-bounded computations is their closure under complementation.

Theorem 2.2.11 (Immerman-Szelepcsényi [67, 130]). *Let* $s : \mathbb{N} \to [0, \infty)$ *be space-constructible and such that* $s(n) \geqslant \log n$. *Then* coNSPACE$[s] =$ NSPACE$[s]$.

As for the connection between nondeterministic space and circuit depth, the relevant part of Theorem 2.2.7 can be extended to the nondeterministic setting.

Theorem 2.2.12 ([28]). *Let* L *be a language that can be decided by a nondeterministic Turing machine running in time* $t(n)$ *and space* $s(n) \geqslant \log n$. *Then* L *can be decided by a family of circuits of depth* $O(s(n) \log t(n))$.

Conversely, we can evaluate a depth d circuit with n inputs on a nondeterministic Turing machine in space $O(d + \log n)$ – no better than on a deterministic Turing machine.

Regarding nondeterministic time versus space, we only know the same trivial relations as in the deterministic case. We can refine the sequence of inclusions (2.1) as follows:

$$\text{L} \subseteq \text{NL} \subseteq \text{P} \subseteq \text{NP} \subseteq \text{PSPACE} \subseteq \text{EXP} \subseteq \text{NEXP} \subseteq \text{EXPSPACE}.$$

By the hierarchy theorems, we know that some of the inclusions are strict but we do not know which ones exactly. The conjecture is that all of them are.

2.2.4 Alternating Turing Machines

An alternating Turing machine is a generalization of a nondeterministic Turing machine intended to capture the complexity of languages like GRAPH RAMSEY TRIPLE. Such languages can be defined using quantified logical formulas with alternating existential and universal quantifiers. Nondeterministic Turing machines can handle formulas with only existential quantifiers; alternating Turing machines can cope with any sequence of quantifiers.

Alternating Turing machines are only used for decision problems: They only accept or reject an input.

Model. An *alternating Turing machine* is a nondeterministic Turing machine with an additional labeling of the non-final states $S \setminus \{s_f\}$ of the finite control with $\exists$ or $\forall$. States labeled with $\exists$ and $\forall$ are called "existential" and "universal" respectively.

An alternating Turing machine M decides the membership of an input x as follows. Recall that we always assume that the configuration digraph G_M is acyclic. Consider the circuit obtained by restricting G_M to the configurations with input x and reversing the arcs. The final configurations are the input gates of the circuit. The configurations in an existential state are (non-binary) OR-gates; the ones in a universal state are (non-binary) AND-gates. We set the value of an input to TRUE iff the corresponding final configuration is accepting. The alternating Turing machine M accepts x iff the value of the gate corresponding to the initial configuration on input x is TRUE.

Another way of looking at this is the following. Suppose that the circuit is leveled, i.e., each gate is assigned a level $\ell \in \mathbb{N}$ such that the inputs to gates at level ℓ are at level $\ell + 1$. The gate corresponding to the initial configuration is at level 0. Suppose also that all gates at the same level have the same type: OR, AND or input (bottom level). Then we can express the acceptance criterion as a quantified logical formula over the configurations of M on input x:

$$(Q_0 \, y_0)(Q_1 \, y_1) \ldots (Q_k \, y_k) \, \phi(x, y_0, y_1, \ldots, y_k), \tag{2.2}$$

where Q_ℓ denotes an existential quantifier $\exists$ if level ℓ contains OR-gates, and a universal quantifier $\forall$ otherwise, and $\phi(x, y_0, y_1, \ldots, y_k)$ is some proposition involving x and $y_0, y_1, \ldots, y_k$. We will be more specific about the structure of ϕ later on.

A nondeterministic Turing machine is equivalent to an alternating Turing machine with only existential states. All quantifiers in (2.2) are $\exists$ and the acceptance criterion is whether ϕ is satisfiable.

Resources. *Time* and *space* consumption on a given instance are defined in the same way as for nondeterministic Turing machines, namely as the maximum consumption over all computation paths on the given input.

An additional resource for alternating Turing machines is the number of times the state of the machine switches from $\exists$ to $\forall$ or vice versa along a computation path. Such a switch is called an *alternation* and corresponds to a quantifier alternation in (2.2).

Complexity Classes. ATIME$[t(n)]$ contains all languages that alternating Turing machines can decide in time $O(t(n))$. A very tight hierarchy theorem holds for alternating time.

Theorem 2.2.13 (Alternating Time Hierarchy Theorem [44]). *Let $t_1, t_2 : \mathbb{N} \to [0, \infty)$ be such that t_2 is time-constructible, and $t_2 \in \omega(t_1)$. Then* ATIME$[t_1] \subsetneq$ ATIME$[t_2]$.

Alternating polynomial time coincides with deterministic polynomial space. This is a corollary to the following theorem that shows how to simulate space-bounded (non)-deterministic computations by time-bounded alternating computations and vice versa, with a quadratic overhead in each direction.

Theorem 2.2.14 ([44]). *Let $t : \mathbb{N} \to [0, \infty)$ be space-constructible and such that $t(n) \geqslant n$. Then* NSPACE$[(t(n))^{1/2}] \subseteq$ ATIME$[t(n)] \subseteq$ DSPACE$[t^2(n)]$.

Another corollary is that alternating exponential time coincides with deterministic ¡exponential space.

Note that the number of alternations of an alternating machine can be of the order of its running time. Interesting subclasses of alternating polynomial time are obtained by restricting the number of alternations to some

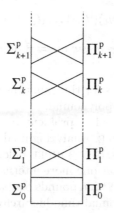

Fig. 2.6. The polynomial-time hierarchy

constant k. We let Σ_0^{p} and Π_0^{p} denote P. For any integer $k \geqslant 0$, we define $\Sigma_{k+1}^{\mathrm{p}}$ as the class of languages accepted by an alternating Turing machine that runs in polynomial time, has no more than k alternations, and has an existential initial state s_o. Similarly, using machines with a universal instead of an existential initial state s_o, we obtain the class Π_{k+1}^{p}. These classes form two intertwined hierarchies with the following properties. See also Figure 2.6.

- $\Sigma_k^{\mathrm{p}} = \mathrm{co}\Pi_k^{\mathrm{p}}$
- $\Sigma_k^{\mathrm{p}} \cup \Pi_k^{\mathrm{p}} \subseteq \Sigma_{k+1}^{\mathrm{p}} \cap \Pi_{k+1}^{\mathrm{p}}$
- $\Sigma_k^{\mathrm{p}} = \Pi_k^{\mathrm{p}} \Rightarrow \cup_\ell \Sigma_\ell^{\mathrm{p}} = \Sigma_k^{\mathrm{p}}$

The last two properties imply that the hierarchy

$$\Sigma_0^{\mathrm{p}} \subseteq \Sigma_1^{\mathrm{p}} \subseteq \Sigma_2^{\mathrm{p}} \subseteq \ldots$$

has the upward *collapse* property: If two subsequent levels Σ_k^{p} and $\Sigma_{k+1}^{\mathrm{p}}$ coincide, then the whole hierarchy collapses to Σ_k^{p}.

This hierarchy is called the *polynomial-time hierarchy*. We denote the union of the classes in the polynomial-time hierarchy by PH. Using exponential-time alternating machines instead of polynomial-time ones, we similarly obtain the *exponential-time hierarchy*. It consists of the classes Σ_k^{exp} and Π_k^{exp} for $k \in \mathbb{N}$, the union of which is denoted by EXPH. The first two properties above also hold for the exponential-time hierarchy. Note that $\Sigma_0^{\mathrm{p}} = \Pi_0^{\mathrm{p}} = $ P, $\Sigma_1^{\mathrm{p}} = $ NP, and $\Pi_1^{\mathrm{p}} = $ coNP. Similarly, $\Sigma_0^{\mathrm{exp}} = \Pi_0^{\mathrm{exp}} = $ EXP, $\Sigma_1^{\mathrm{exp}} = $ NEXP, and $\Pi_1^{\mathrm{exp}} = $ coNEXP.

The other view (2.2) of the acceptance criterion of alternating Turing machines formalizes into the following characterization of the classes in the polynomial-time hierarchy.

Theorem 2.2.15 ([128, 44]). *Let $k \in \mathbb{N}$. A language L belongs to Σ_k^{p} iff there exist a polynomial p and a language $R \in $ P such that for any $x \in \Sigma^*$:*

$$x \in L \Leftrightarrow (\exists\, y_1)(\forall\, y_2) \dots (Q_k\, y_k)\, [\langle x, y_1, y_2, \dots, y_k \rangle \in R],$$

where $Q_k = \forall$ if k is even and $Q_k = \exists$ otherwise, and all quantifiers are over $\Sigma^{p(|x|)}$.

A similar theorem holds for the exponential-time hierarchy, allowing p to be exponential instead of polynomial.

A typical example of a problem in the polynomial-time hierarchy is GRAPH RAMSEY TRIPLE. Analyzing its definition and using Theorem 2.2.15 shows that GRAPH RAMSEY TRIPLE belongs to $\Pi_2^{\mathrm{p}} = \mathrm{co}\Sigma_2^{\mathrm{p}}$.

It is conjectured that one more alternation allows us to decide more languages within the same time bounds. In particular, complexity theorists conjecture that the polynomial-time hierarchy does not collapse. Note that this is a stronger assumption than that $\mathsf{NP} \neq \mathsf{coNP}$; $\mathsf{NP} = \mathsf{coNP}$ would imply a collapse of the polynomial-time hierarchy at its first level.

The properness of the polynomial-time hierarchy is a standard assumption in computational complexity, and a whole body of results have been established using it. One example deals with the relationship between nondeterministic time and circuit size. The interesting direction is the simulation of nondeterministic time-bounded computations by small circuits. Trivially, $\mathsf{NTIME}[t(n)] \subseteq \cup_{c>0}\mathsf{SIZE}[2^{c \cdot t(n)}]$. The question is whether we can do better, e.g., whether nondeterministic polynomial time has polynomial-size circuits. The latter is impossible unless the polynomial-time hierarchy collapses to its second level.

Theorem 2.2.16 (Karp-Lipton [74]). *If $\mathsf{NP} \subseteq \mathsf{P/poly}$ then $\Sigma_2^{\mathrm{p}} = \Pi_2^{\mathrm{p}}$.*

If we allow a couple alternations and superpolynomial time, polynomial size provably does not suffice [72]. The same technique yields that exponential time with two alternations requires exponential-size circuits.

Theorem 2.2.17. *There exists a language $L \in \Sigma_3^{2^n}$ such that $C_L(n) \in 2^{\Omega(n)}$.*

Since $\mathsf{NP} = \mathsf{P}$ implies that $\Sigma_3^{2^n} \subseteq \mathsf{E}$, and $\mathsf{NP} = \mathsf{L}$ that $\Sigma_3^{2^n} \subseteq \mathsf{DSPACE}[n]$, we have:

Corollary 2.2.1. *If $\mathsf{NP} = \mathsf{P}$ there exists a language $L \in \mathsf{E}$ such that $C_L(n) \in 2^{\Omega(n)}$. If $\mathsf{NP} = \mathsf{L}$ there exists such a language L in $\mathsf{DSPACE}[n]$.*

We now turn to space-bounded alternating computations. $\mathsf{ASPACE}[s(n)]$ is defined as the class of all languages that alternating Turing machines can decide in space $O(s(n))$. The same tight space hierarchy theorem as for deterministic and nondeterministic Turing machines holds:

Theorem 2.2.18 (Alternating Space Hierarchy Theorem [44]). *Let $s_1, s_2 : \mathbb{N} \to [0, \infty)$ be such that s_2 is space-constructible, and $s_2 \in \omega(s_1)$. Then $\mathsf{ASPACE}[s_1] \subsetneq \mathsf{ASPACE}[s_2]$.*

Alternating space turns out to be equivalent to deterministic time one exponential level up.

Theorem 2.2.19 ([44]). *Let* $s : \mathbb{N} \to [0, \infty)$ *be space-constructible and such that* $s(n) \geqslant \log n$. *Then* $\mathsf{ASPACE}[s(n)] = \cup_{c>0}\mathsf{DTIME}[2^{c \cdot s(n)}]$.

In particular, alternating logarithmic space coincides with deterministic polynomial time, and alternating polynomial space with deterministic exponential time.

Bounding the number of alternations in space-bounded computations does not yield interesting new classes. As a corollary to Theorem 2.2.11, for robust space bounds like logarithmic, linear, and polynomial, the resulting classes all coincide with the corresponding nondeterministic space classes.

By Theorems 2.2.14 and 2.2.19, questions about the relationships between alternating time and space translate into similar questions about deterministic time and space, which we discussed in Section 2.2.1.

2.3 Randomness

In this section we discuss the role of randomness in computational complexity. The ability to take decisions based on the outcome of coin tosses seems to simplify both computing solutions and verifying proofs. In each case there will be some probability of error. That may seem disconcerting but we will always be able to make the error probability much smaller than the odds of a hardware failure. Therefore, provided we have access to a random bit source, these randomized procedures are as reliable as deterministic ones.

Several problems turn out to have simple randomized solutions that require much less time or space than the known deterministic solutions. However, it remains an open question whether random bits can really reduce the need for resources like time and space. Some researchers believe randomness cannot help much in that respect. They try to construct efficient pseudorandom generators: deterministic procedures that stretch seeds containing a few random bits into much longer bit sequences that look random to the randomized process in question. This allows them to reduce the amount of randomness needed and, in some cases, eliminate the need for random bits completely without increasing the need for other resources by much.

We will first introduce models of randomized computation and corresponding complexity classes, as we did in the previous section. Then we will do the same for randomized proof checking. Finally, we will give an overview of known approaches for the construction of time and space efficient pseudorandom generators and their implications for deterministic simulations of randomized computations.

2.3.1 Randomized Computations

We will consider randomized versions of the models we introduced in Section 2.2: Randomized Turing machines will be the sequential model of computation and uniform randomized circuits the parallel one.

In each case we will distinguish between two types of algorithms, depending on the kind of error they can make. A *Monte Carlo* algorithm always returns an answer but has a small probability of giving an incorrect answer. A *Las Vegas* algorithm never errs but has a small probability of not returning an answer. Las Vegas algorithms are therefore superior to Monte Carlo algorithms. We will mostly be dealing with decision problems. For them, we can make a further distinction between Monte Carlo algorithms, and we end up with the following three types:

- *Two-sided error* algorithms. This is the most general type of algorithm. It can err on both sides of the language, i.e., both for inputs in and out the language it has a small probability of outputting the wrong decision. The corresponding complexity classes are indicated with the prefix BP, which stands for "bounded probabilistic". The "bounded" refers to the fact that the probability of error is bounded away from $\frac{1}{2}$, say at most $\frac{1}{3}$.
- *One-sided error* algorithms. These are algorithms that can only err on the language side: If the input does not belong to the language, they always say so, but if the input is in the language, there is a bounded probability (say at most $\frac{1}{2}$) that the algorithm outputs "no." The corresponding complexity classes get the prefix R, which stands for "randomized." An interesting question is whether these classes are closed under complementation.
- *Zero-sided error* algorithms. These are the Las Vegas algorithms. They never err but may say "I don't know" with a bounded probability (say at most $\frac{1}{2}$). We will denote the corresponding complexity classes with the prefix ZP for "zero error probabilistic." A language has an efficient zero-error algorithm iff both the language and its complement have efficient one-sided error algorithms.

Once we have an algorithm with bounded error, we can increase our confidence by running it several times on the same input and combining the outcomes in a straightforward way. If we run a zero-sided error algorithm k times, the probability that none of the runs gives us an answer is at most 2^{-k}. The same bound holds for the probability that none of k runs of a one-sided error algorithm detect that an input belongs to the language (the case in which the algorithm can make an error). For two sided error, taking the majority vote of k runs also decreases the error probability exponentially. Suppose the original algorithm errs with probability at most $\frac{1}{2} - \delta$. Then we can bound the probability that the majority vote is wrong by:

$$\sum_{i=0}^{k/2} \binom{k}{i} (\frac{1}{2}+\delta)^i (\frac{1}{2}-\delta)^{k-i} \leqslant (\frac{1}{4}-\delta^2)^{k/2} . \sum_{i=0}^{k/2} \binom{k}{i} \leqslant (1-4\delta^2)^{k/2} \leqslant \exp(-2\delta^2 k),$$

where we used the inequality $1 - x \leqslant \exp(-x)$ in the last step. This shows that even if δ is as small as one over some fixed polynomial, a polynomial number k of runs suffices to make the error probability exponentially small.

Another way to obtain this result is by using Chernoff bounds, an indispensable tool in the context of randomized algorithms. Several variants exist; we state two of them.

Theorem 2.3.1 (Chernoff Bounds [7]). *Let x_i, $i \in [k]$, be independent random variables and let p_i denote the expected value of x_i.*

- *If every $x_i \in \{0, 1\}$, then for any $0 \leqslant a \leqslant 2\sigma^2$,*

$$\Pr\left[\sum_{i=1}^{k} x_i - \mu \geqslant a\right] \leqslant \exp\left(-\frac{a^2}{4\sigma^2}\right),$$

where $\mu = \sum_{i=1}^{k} p_i$ and $\sigma^2 = \sum_{i=1}^{k} p_i(1 - p_i)$.
- *If every $x_i \in [-1, 1]$ and $p_i = 0$, then for any $a \geqslant 0$,*

$$\Pr\left[\sum_{i=1}^{k} x_i \geqslant a\right] \leqslant \exp\left(-\frac{a^2}{2k}\right).$$

Randomized Turing Machines. In the Turing machine model we give the computer the ability to flip coins by allowing it access to an additional tape that contains the outcomes of independent fair coin tosses. So, a *randomized Turing machine* is a Turing machine with such a "random bit tape." The tape is read-only and the tape head can only move to the right. Reading a bit from this tape and moving the tape head correspond to flipping a coin.

The *time* and *space* usage of a randomized Turing machine are defined as the maximum over all possible contents for the random bit tape of the usage given that random bit tape.

BPP, RP, and ZPP denote the classes of languages that can be decided by randomized Turing machines in polynomial time with two-sided error, one-sided error, and zero-sided error respectively.

Note that RP is a subset of NP. RP can be seen as the class of languages with time efficiently verifiable proof systems that have the additional property that membership proofs are abundant. ZPP equals RP $\cap$ coRP. BPP lies in the second level of the polynomial-time hierarchy.

Theorem 2.3.2 ([125, 80]). BPP $\subseteq \Sigma_2^{\mathrm{p}} \cap \Pi_2^{\mathrm{p}}$.

Another interesting property is that BPP languages have small circuits.

Theorem 2.3.3 ([1]). BPP $\subseteq$ P/poly.

A typical example of a language in ZPP is the set of prime numbers in binary notation [112, 126, 2].

As for space-bounded randomized computations, we only consider randomized machines that *always* halt, i.e., for every sequence of coin flips. The latter condition is equivalent to the requirement that the machine always halt within $2^{O(s(n))}$ steps, where $s(n)$ denotes the space bound. In particular, randomized logspace machines that always halt do so after a polynomial number of steps. If a space $s(n)$ bounded randomized machine is not required to always halt, it may have an expected running time which is doubly exponential in $s(n)$.

BPL, RL, and ZPL denote the classes of languages that can be decided by randomized Turing machines that use logarithmic work space, always halt, and have two-sided error, one-sided error, and zero-sided error respectively.

A typical example of a language in RL is U-STCON. In order to check whether two vertices s and t are connected in a graph G with n vertices, we can perform a random walk starting from s. In each step, we pick one of the neighbors of the current vertex at random as the next vertex. If s and t are not connected, we will never reach t. On the other hand, if they are connected, then we will almost surely hit t in n^3 steps [3]. We only have to keep track of the current vertex and of a constant number of counters, each of logarithmic size. This is the randomized maze strategy of Section 1.1.3. It shows that U-STCON lies in RL. In fact, it lies in ZPL [103].

Sometimes, we will consider a variant of our model with two-way instead of one-way access to the random bit tape, i.e., the head on that tape can move both to the right and to the left instead of only to the right. This allows us to reuse random bits without storing them in memory. For the time-bounded randomized complexity classes we consider, the difference is irrelevant, but the two-way variant seems to be have more power than the standard one-way model in the space-bounded setting. We define BPSPACE$^*[s(n)]$ as the class of languages that can be decided by a two-sided error randomized Turing machine with *two-way read access* to its random bit tape that uses no more than $O(s(n))$ work space and always halts. We define RSPACE$^*[s(n)]$ and ZPSPACE$^*[s(n)]$ analogously. For $s(n) = \log n$, we obtain BPL*, RL*, and ZPL* respectively.

Uniform Families of Randomized Boolean Circuits. We give circuits access to a random bit source by providing them with additional input gates that represent the outcomes of independent fair coin tosses. We label such a gate with r_i for $i \in \mathbb{N}$. Each r_i equals 0 or 1 with probability 50/50, independent of the r_j's for $j \neq i$. So, a *randomized Boolean circuit* is a Boolean circuit in which there are two types of input gates: those corresponding to actual input bits (labeled x_i for some $i \in \mathbb{N}$) and those corresponding to random bits (labeled r_i for some $i \in \mathbb{N}$). The output of the circuit on a given input x is a random variable depending on the r_i's. As in the case of Turing machines, we will only consider circuits that have bounded error. Again, we will distinguish between two-sided, one-sided, and zero-sided error.

In particular, we define RNC^k for $k \in \mathbb{N}$ as the class of languages for which there exists a uniform family $\{C_n\}_n$ of randomized Boolean circuits of polynomial size and depth $O(\log^k n)$ that decide it with one-sided error. A well-known problem in RNC^2 is deciding whether a given graph has a perfect matching [85], i.e., a collection of disjoint edges that covers every vertex. In fact, this problem lies in ZPNC^2 [73].

Note that randomized circuits inherently have the ability to use the same random bit r_i multiple times for free. Randomized Turing machines in the natural one-way model have to store these bits on their work tape if they want to reuse them later on during the computation. Because of this, it is an open problem whether RNC^1 is contained in RL. We do know that $\mathsf{RNC}^1 \subseteq \mathsf{RL}^*$.

2.3.2 Randomized Proof Checking

Proof checking constitutes another area where coin flips seem beneficial from a complexity theoretic point of view. We can think of a randomized proof system as a protocol between two parties, Arthur and Merlin. Merlin is a wise man who is computationally unlimited and tries to convince Arthur of some fact, say that a given input belongs to some language. Arthur is computationally limited. He does not trust Merlin and cross-examines him by asking randomized questions.

As in the case of randomized computations, we could distinguish between two-sided error, one-sided error and zero-sided error. In the context of proof checking we typically use the one-sided error paradigm: If the input belongs to the language, then Merlin can always convince Arthur of that fact; otherwise Merlin only has a small chance of tricking Arthur into believing that the input belongs to the language. In the settings we will consider, we can always eliminate the error on one side of two-sided error proof systems.

We will focus on time efficient verification, i.e., Arthur runs in polynomial time. We will refer to such processes as *Arthur-Merlin protocols*; they are also known as *interactive proof systems*. In the absence of randomness, the class of languages with time efficiently verifiable membership proofs equals NP. In that case, a very limited amount of interaction between Arthur and Merlin suffices to obtain the full power of the model: For every language in NP there exists a protocol in which Merlin gives Arthur a proof which he subsequently checks on his own, without asking Merlin any further questions. In the randomized setting, the amount of interaction between Arthur and Merlin does seem to matter.

The class MA contains all languages for which there exists an Arthur-Merlin protocol in which Merlin provides a membership proof which Arthur subsequently checks on his own – using coin flips but without asking Merlin any questions. The acronym MA refers to a two-round protocol in which Merlin moves first and then Arthur moves. Formally, a language L is in MA if there exists a deterministic polynomial-time Turing machine N and a polynomial p such that for any input x,

$$x \in L \Rightarrow \exists y \in \{0,1\}^{p(n)} : \Pr_{|z|=p(n)} [N \text{ accepts } \langle x, y, z \rangle] = 1$$

$$x \notin L \Rightarrow \forall y \in \{0,1\}^{p(n)} : \Pr_{|z|=p(n)} [N \text{ accepts } \langle x, y, z \rangle] \leqslant \frac{1}{2},$$

where n denotes $|x|$ and the probabilities are with respect to the uniform distribution.

We know that MA lies within the second level of the polynomial-time hierarchy.

Theorem 2.3.4 ([21]). MA $\subseteq \Sigma_2^p \cap \Pi_2^p$.

Related to Theorem 2.2.16, the following result suggests that exponential time does not have small circuits.

Theorem 2.3.5 ([18]). *If* EXP $\subseteq$ P/poly *then* EXP = MA.

Note that by Theorem 2.3.4, the hypothesis that EXP = MA implies that the polynomial-time hierarchy collapses to the second level. From Theorem 2.2.16 we already knew that the latter collapse occurred under the hypothesis of Theorem 2.3.5.

The class AM contains all languages for which there exists an Arthur-Merlin protocol with a bounded number of rounds. It turns out that every such protocol can be transformed into an equivalent one in which Arthur first flips some coins, presents the outcomes to Merlin, who then replies to this question, and finally Arthur performs a deterministic consistency check based on his previous coin flips and Merlin's answer [21, 59]. We will call an Arthur-Merlin protocol of that type an *Arthur-Merlin game*. The acronym AM refers to this normal form: Arthur moves first and then Merlin makes one move. Formally, a language L is in AM if there exists a deterministic polynomial-time Turing machine N and a polynomial p such that for any input x,

$$x \in L \Rightarrow \Pr_{|y|=p(n)} [\exists z \in \{0,1\}^{p(n)} : N \text{ accepts } \langle x, y, z \rangle] = 1$$

$$x \notin L \Rightarrow \Pr_{|y|=p(n)} [\exists z \in \{0,1\}^{p(n)} : N \text{ accepts } \langle x, y, z \rangle] \leqslant \frac{1}{2},$$

where $n = |x|$ and the probabilities are with respect to the uniform distribution.

In particular, MA-protocols can be brought into the above normal form of an Arthur-Merlin game, since MA $\subseteq$ AM. In Arthur-Merlin games, Arthur shows the outcomes of his coin flips to Merlin. This makes the protocol *public coin*. In a *private coin* protocol Arthur keeps his coin flips secret. He uses the coin flips to determine the questions he will ask Merlin but the questions don't reveal all of the coin flips.

Although the class AM is conjectured to be more powerful than MA, it still is not high up in the polynomial-time hierarchy.

Theorem 2.3.6 ([21]). $\mathsf{AM} \subseteq \Pi_2^{\mathrm{p}}$.

A typical example of a language in AM is $\overline{\mathsf{ISO}}$, graph nonisomorphism. Suppose that Merlin presents Arthur two graphs which he claims are not isomorphic, and Arthur wants to verify this claim. We can use the protocol described in Section 1.1.1 in order to do so. Arthur picks one of the two graphs at random, applies a random permutation to its vertices, and shows the result to Merlin, asking him which of the two given graphs he started out with. In case the given graphs are indeed not isomorphic, Merlin can figure out which one of the two Arthur's graph is isomorphic with, and that is the one Arthur started out with. So, in that case Merlin can always find the correct answer. However, in case the given graphs are isomorphic, Merlin has no clue which of the two given graphs Arthur picked. No matter what strategy Merlin uses, his odds of getting the answer right are 50/50. This is because the probability that Arthur ends up with a certain graph is not affected by the condition that he started out with the first input graph or with the second one. Note that it is crucial in this protocol that Arthur keeps his coin flips private. However, it is possible to transform the protocol into an equivalent one in which it is safe for Arthur to flip his coins in public.

Without any explicit bound on the number of rounds, the class of languages for which there exists an Arthur-Merlin protocol coincides with PSPACE [86, 124].

2.3.3 Pseudo-Random Generators

Several applications, e.g., in cryptography, need a lot of random bits. However, independent fair coin tosses are hard to obtain in large quantities. In that sense, random bits form a scarce resource like time and space, and we would like to use as few as possible of them. Pseudo-random generators allow us to reduce the number of random bits we need.

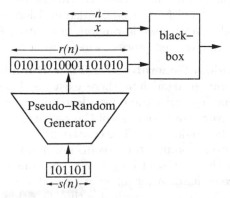

Fig. 2.7. A pseudo-random generator

Let us model a randomized process as a black-box that takes an input x to the process, say of size n, as well as a string ρ of $r(n)$ bits, and outputs the result of the process on input x when using ρ as the random bit sequence. A *pseudo-random generator* is a deterministic procedure G that transforms a seed σ of $s(n)$ truly random bits into a longer pseudo-random bit sequence of length $r(n)$, as needed by the randomized process on inputs of size n. See Figure 2.7. We say that G *fools* the randomized process if, on any input x, the statistical behavior of the process is the same when presented with uniformly at random chosen bit sequences of length $r(n)$ and when presented with the output of G on a uniformly at random chosen seed of length $s(n)$. We will specify below more precisely what "same statistical behavior" means. The relevant characteristics of a pseudo-random generator are its *seed length* $s(n)$ and its *computational complexity*, i.e., the complexity of computing the i-th bit of $G(\sigma)$ given i (in binary) and σ.

We can simulate the original randomized process using fewer random bits as follows: Pick a seed at random, expand it by applying G, and run the original process on the resulting pseudo-random bit sequence. This way, we reduce the number of random bits needed to the seed length of the pseudo-random generator. Depending on the complexity of G, the time and space requirements for the simulated process may be only slightly larger than for the original process.

Apart from economizing a scarce resource, efficient pseudo-random generators with short seed lengths also allow us to obtain efficient deterministic simulations of randomized processes. At least if we are able to reset the process to its initial state. Then we can just run the process from its initial state on all seeds and keep track of the statistics. This will be our main focus: the construction of pseudo-random generators for general classes of randomized processes that result in time and/or space efficient deterministic simulations of these processes. As a result we obtain limits on the time and space gains randomness can buy us.

In the remainder of this section, we will discuss pseudo-random generators for time-bounded and for space-bounded decision procedures with two-sided error. We will develop pseudo-random generators for Arthur-Merlin games and for other randomized processes in Chapter 3.

Pseudo-Random Generators for Time-Bounded Computations. For several randomized algorithms there exist good pseudo-random generators that fool them. Typically these pseudo-random generators are based on the fact that the correctness analysis of the algorithm only requires limited independence of the random bits. The construction of pseudo-random generators that fool *arbitrary* computations seems much more difficult. Even outputting one more bit than the seed length, i.e., the construction of pseudo-random *extenders*, seems hard. After all, every pseudo-random generator G will fail to fool some algorithm, in particular the algorithm that checks whether the string ρ lies in the range of G. Note, though, that the latter test may require many more resources than the algorithms we are trying to fool. There may be more clever ways to check the range of an extender G, but exhaustively trying the seeds σ and verifying whether $G(\sigma) = \rho$ takes exponential time.

In general, whether a distribution looks random to us, really depends on our computational power. If we are computationally restricted, even the output of a deterministic procedure like a pseudo-random generator, which generates a long string out of a much shorter uniformly at random chosen string, can look like a uniformly at random chosen sequence to us, because we do not have the computational power to make the distinction. This observation lies at the heart of the known constructions of pseudo-random generators fooling arbitrary resource-bounded computations.

For time-bounded computations no unconditional constructions are known. In fact, the smallest deterministic time-bounded complexity class known to contain BPP is exponential time. The BPP *versus* EXP *problem* asks whether this inclusion is strict. It is conjectured to be the case but the question remains open.

We do know how to construct good pseudo-random generators for arbitrary time-bounded computations based on computational problems with certain hardness and easiness properties. The hardness properties guarantee that the pseudo-random generator fools any algorithm running within a certain time bound, like linear time or polynomial time; the easiness properties make the pseudo-random generator efficiently computable. For any given level of complexity of the pseudo-random generator, the results take the form of *hardness versus randomness tradeoffs*: the stronger the hardness property, the shorter the seed length of the pseudo-random generator, the more time efficient the deterministic simulations we obtain. The strongest conditions yield polynomial-time deterministic simulations of BPP; the weaker ones yield superpolynomial but still subexponential simulations. However, it is an open problem whether computational problems exist that meet any of these sets of hardness and easiness conditions. We do have explicit candidates of "easy" problems that satisfy the hardness requirements, but the question is whether they really meet the hardness conditions and, if so, at which level.

Two constructions of pseudo-random generators based on the above approach have been developed over the years: the Blum-Micali-Yao construction and the Nisan-Wigderson construction.

The *Blum-Micali-Yao* construction transforms any one-way function into a pseudo-random generator. A *one-way function* is a polynomial-time computable function f that is hard to invert on average: No small circuit that, given $y \doteq f(x)$, tries to find a string x' such that $f(x') = y$, succeeds on a non-negligible fraction of the strings x of length n.

Blum and Micali [26] constructed a pseudo-random generator based on the conjectured one-wayness of exponentiation modulo a prime. Yao [138] generalized their approach to work for any one-way permutation, i.e., a one-way function that is one-to-one and length-preserving. Håstad, Impagliazzo,

Levin, and Luby [63] eventually showed that a one-way function suffices. In fact, they showed the equivalence of one-way functions and polynomial-time computable pseudo-random extenders: There are efficient transformations of one into the other, where the strength of the extender, i.e., how complex procedures it fools, is related to the hardness of inverting the one-way function. Out of a polynomial-time computable pseudo-random extender, one can construct a pseudo-random generator with larger expansion at the cost of some loss in strength. The pseudo-random generators obtained this way are computable in time polynomial in the output length. The expansion actually achievable depends on the hardness of inverting the original one-way function and on the required strength of the pseudo-random generator.

The fact that the pseudo-random sequence is computable in time polynomial in its length is a must in several applications, e.g., in cryptography. Another property of the Blum-Micali-Yao type generators is that they may fool procedures of much higher complexity than themselves. This is also interesting in a cryptographic setting because there the bad guys may well have many more resources than the good guys. However, these properties are overkill for obtaining efficient deterministic simulations of randomized computations. Since the simulation will cycle over all $2^{s(n)}$ seeds of length $s(n)$ anyway, there is no reason to require that the pseudo-random generator runs in time polynomial in $r(n)$: Running in time about $2^{s(n)}$ is equally good. Note that the range check discussed on page 38, a procedure which the pseudo-random generator fails to fool, runs in about the same amount of time.

The *Nisan-Wigderson* construction allows us to build pseudo-random generators of such computational complexity out of any exponential-time decision problem f that requires large circuits. The larger the circuit complexity of f, the stronger the pseudo-random generator we obtain. Hence, one gets the best results for EXP-complete decision problems f.

Nisan and Wigderson [104] showed that their construction worked under a stronger hardness condition, namely that f requires large circuits even if the circuit is only supposed to decide f correctly on slightly more than half of its inputs. This was an average-case condition, similar to the one-wayness required for the Blum-Micali-Yao construction. Later work [18, 68, 69] showed how to transform an arbitrary exponential-time decision problem that requires large circuits to be computed *exactly* into another exponential-time decision problem which requires circuits of comparable size to be even *approximated* in the above sense. Thus the average-case hardness condition was relaxed to a worst-case one. In the Blum-Micali-Yao setting it is open whether such a relaxation is possible.

The Nisan-Wigderson approach will be used in Chapter 3, and we will say more about it there. For now, we just state two results that will be applied in the other chapters. They use the technical notion of security to measure the strength of a pseudo-random generator. The *security* $S_G(n)$ of a pseudo-random generator G at length n is the largest integer t such that for any circuit C of size at most t with $r(n)$ inputs

$$| \Pr_{\rho}[C(\rho) = 1] - \Pr_{\sigma}[C(G(\sigma)) = 1]| < \frac{1}{t},$$

where ρ is uniformly distributed over $\{0,1\}^{r(n)}$ and σ over $\{0,1\}^{s(n)}$. The larger the security, the larger circuits the pseudo-random generator fools and the better a job it does in fooling them.

The first result is essentially due to Babai, Fortnow, Nisan and Wigderson [18]. It yields a weak pseudo-random generator but only needs a weak assumption.

Theorem 2.3.7 ([18]). *If* MA $\neq$ EXP, *there is a pseudo-random generator G computable in* E *with seed length $s(n) = n$ and output length $r(n) \in n^{\theta(\log n)}$ such that for any integer k, $S_G(n) \geqslant n^k$ for infinitely many n.*

At the other end of the spectrum, Impagliazzo and Wigderson [69] constructed a pseudo-random generator which would be strong enough to show that BPP = P. It takes a strong assumption, though.

Theorem 2.3.8 ([69]). *If there is a language $L \in$ E such that $C_L(n) \in 2^{\Omega(n)}$, then there is a pseudo-random generator G computable in* E *with seed length $s(n) = n$, output length $r(n) \in 2^{\Omega(n)}$ and security $S_G(n) \in 2^{\Omega(n)}$.*

Observe that for an E-computable extender G with seed length n and security $2^{\Omega(n)}$, the range of G is a language L in E satisfying $C_L(n) \in 2^{\Omega(n)}$. Since a pseudo-random generator defines an extender with the same characteristics, Theorem 2.3.8 implies that we can blow up the output length of an E-computable pseudo-random generator of security $2^{\Omega(n)}$ to $2^{\Omega(n)}$ without significantly reducing the security.

Corollary 2.3.1. *If there exists an* E-*computable pseudo-random generator G with seed length $s(n) = n$ and security $S_G(n) \in 2^{\Omega(n)}$, then there exists an* E-*computable pseudo-random generator with seed length n and both output length and security in $2^{\Omega(n)}$.*

Note that by Theorem 2.3.5, the hypothesis of Theorem 2.3.7 implies a similar statement as the hypothesis of Theorem 2.3.8, namely that there is a language $L \in$ EXP such that for any integer k, $C_L(n) \geqslant n^k$ for infinitely many n.

Pseudo-Random Generators for Space-Bounded Computations. The Nisan-Wigderson approach also works in the space-bounded setting, yielding similar hardness versus randomness trade-offs as in the time-bounded setting. We will detail them in Chapter 3. One instance (Theorem 3.5.10) shows that if a certain hardness assumption holds, space-bounded randomized decision procedures with bounded two-sided error can be simulated deterministically without increasing the space need by more than a constant factor. The validity of the hardness condition is again an open question.

However, somewhat weaker pseudo-random generators for space-bounded computation are known to exist unconditionally. For any space-constructible function $s(n) \geqslant \log n$, Nisan [101] constructed a pseudo-random generator computable in space $O(s(n))$ and with seed length $O(s(n) \log r(n))$ that fools any randomized decision procedure with bounded two-sided error that runs in space $s(n)$ and uses no more than $r(n)$ random bits. It follows that $\mathsf{BPSPACE}[s(n)] \subseteq \mathsf{DSPACE}[(s(n))^2]$. Nisan's pseudo-random generator is currently the best known. Saks and Zhou [119] did manage to improve the deterministic simulation of space-bounded randomized computation to $\mathsf{BPSPACE}[s(n)] \subseteq \mathsf{DSPACE}[(s(n))^{3/2}]$ without constructing a pseudo-random generator with seed length $o(s^2(n))$. Since the random walk algorithm puts graph connectivity, U-STCON, in RL, their result implies that U-STCON can be solved in deterministic space $O(\log^{3/2} n)$. Currently the most space efficient algorithm for U-STCON runs in space $O(\log^{4/3} n)$ [12]. It is based on a more economical derandomization of the random walk algorithm than provided by the Saks-Zhou result.

2.4 Reductions and Completeness

One way to assess the computational complexity of a problem R is to determine which problems we can solve easily if we are allowed to use a "black-box" or "oracle" for R. We say that each of these problems reduces to R. Conversely, several complexity classes can be described as the class of problems that reduce to some problem R. In that case, R characterizes the complexity of that class and is called a complete problem for the class. Depending on the reducibility notion used, various properties of the complexity class can be traced back to properties of R. In this section, we will discuss several reducibility notions from that point of view.

First we will formalize the concept of computation with the help of a black-box or oracle. This will lead to the notion of relativization, an important technique in computational complexity. Among other things, it allows us to give yet another characterization of the polynomial-time hierarchy. Once we have oracle computations in place, we will define various reductions and associated completeness notions. Finally, we will see that several of the problems we introduced in Section 2.1 are complete for some complexity class under a natural reducibility, and therefore capture the complexity of that class.

2.4.1 Relativization

We now define computations that can get help from a black-box for a given computational problem R, both in the Turing machine model and in the

Boolean circuit model. We say that these computations are relative to the *oracle R.*

Oracle Turing Machines. We allow Turing machines access to the black-box in the form of an oracle tape. An *oracle Turing machine* is a deterministic/nondeterministic/alternating/randomized Turing machine with an additional one-way read/write tape and two distinguished states: the query state s_q and the answer state s_a. The computation of the machine is dictated by the same rules as before, except for when it is in the query state s_q. In that case, the contents of the oracle tape is interpreted as an instance of R, and is replaced in one step by a solution for that instance. The oracle tape head is moved to the leftmost position and the machine switches to the answer state s_a. The rest of the configuration remains the same. In effect, we obtain a solution to an instance of R at the cost of a single computation step. We denote the output of an oracle Turing machine M on input x given the oracle R by $M^R(x)$.

The running *time* and *space* need of an oracle Turing machine with a given oracle R are defined in the same way as for Turing machines without oracle access. In particular, the oracle tape is *not* taken into account for the space consumption – only the work tape matters.

All the Turing machine based complexity classes defined in Section 2.2 can be relativized. For any fixed oracle R, we denote the corresponding complexity class by writing R as an exponent to the original class. For example, P^R denotes the class of languages that can be decided by polynomial-time deterministic oracle Turing machines with access to R.

Oracle Circuits. We only describe how we provide circuits access to oracles for decision problems R. We do so by introducing an additional type of gate, namely oracle gates. The inputs to an oracle gate are ordered, and the output is the single bit that represents the solution to the instance of R described by the string formed by the ordered input bits. We call the resulting circuits *oracle circuits.* We denote the output of oracle circuit C on input x given the oracle R by $C^R(x)$. We will sometimes refer to C^R as an R-oracle circuit.

The *size* of an oracle circuit is its number of connections. The contribution of a NOT-gate to the size of the circuit is 1, for binary AND- and OR-gates it is 2, and for oracle gates it equals the length of the query. The *depth* of an oracle circuit is the largest weight of a path in the underlying DAG. The weight of a path is the sum of the weights of the gates on the path. Input gates have weight zero, and all other gates have a weight equal to the logarithm of the number of incoming edges.

The above definitions allow us to consider relativized versions of circuit based complexity classes. In case of uniform classes like NC^1, we only provide the circuits themselves with access to the oracle, not the generating Turing machine. For any language L and Boolean oracle R, we denote by $C_L^R(n)$ the size of a smallest oracle circuit with oracle R that decides L on $\{0,1\}^n$.

Relativizing Theorems. Most theorems in computational complexity have the property that they remain true if, for any oracle R, we give all Turing machines and circuits involved access to R. We say that these theorems *relativize*. An example is the theorem that BPP is contained in $\Sigma_2^p \cap \Pi_2^p$. Its relativized version states that the inclusion $\mathsf{BPP}^R \subseteq (\Sigma_2^p)^R \cap (\Pi_2^p)^R$ holds for any oracle R. One of the rare examples of a result that does not relativize is Theorem 2.3.5: There exists an oracle R such that $\mathsf{EXP}^R \subseteq \mathsf{P}^R/\mathsf{poly}$, but $\mathsf{MA}^R \neq \mathsf{EXP}^R$ [32].

The reason why most *theorems* relativize is that almost all known *proof techniques* relativize, i.e., they remain valid when we give all programs access to the same oracle. This is the case for diagonalization arguments and for simulations. On the other hand, for many of the open separation questions we can construct an oracle relative to which the separation holds and another one relative to which it fails. An example is the separation of P from NP: There exists an oracle A such that $\mathsf{P}^A \neq \mathsf{NP}^A$ but there also exists an oracle B such that $\mathsf{P}^B = \mathsf{NP}^B$. Therefore, settling these questions requires non-relativizing proof techniques. Hence the importance of such proof techniques in computational complexity.

Relativization allows us to give another characterization of the polynomial-time and exponential-time hierarchies.

Theorem 2.4.1 ([97, 44]). *For any integer $k \geqslant 0$, $\Sigma_{k+1}^p = \mathsf{NP}^{\Sigma_k^p}$ and $\Sigma_{k+1}^{\exp} = \mathsf{NEXP}^{\Sigma_k^p}$.*

Within this framework, we define the Δ-levels of the hierarchies as follows: $\Delta_{k+1}^p \doteq \mathsf{P}^{\Sigma_k^p}$ and $\Delta_{k+1}^{\exp} \doteq \mathsf{EXP}^{\Sigma_k^p}$ for any integer $k \geqslant 0$. $\Delta_0^p \doteq \mathsf{P}$ and $\Delta_0^{\exp} \doteq \mathsf{EXP}$.

2.4.2 Reductions

A *reduction* of a computational problem A to a computational problem B is an oracle program for A with B as the oracle. We write $A \leqslant B$, indicating that A is computationally no harder than B modulo the power of the reduction. Various types of reductions can be distinguished based on the *model of computation*, the *resource bounds*, and the *kind of oracle access* allowed.

In Section 2.4.3, we will argue the need for reductions with different computational models and resource bounds. We will use both deterministic and randomized reductions with two-sided error. In each case, we will consider reductions that are computable in polynomial time, in logarithmic space, and in parallel logarithmic time. The combination of the model of computation and the resource bounds is indicated by mentioning the corresponding complexity class as a superscript to the $\leqslant$-sign. For example, $\leqslant^{\mathsf{P}}$, $\leqslant^{\mathsf{L}}$, and $\leqslant^{\mathsf{NC}^1}$ denote deterministic reducibilities running in polynomial time, logarithmic space, and parallel logarithmic time respectively. Similarly, $\leqslant^{\mathsf{BPP}}$, $\leqslant^{\mathsf{BPL}}$, and $\leqslant^{\mathsf{BPNC}^1}$ denote the corresponding randomized reductions with two-sided error. We say that a two-sided error reduction has *confidence* $\delta(n)$ if for any input of size n the probability of a correct answer is at least $\frac{1}{2} + \delta(n)$. We will sometimes also refer to the one-sided error randomized reductions $\leqslant^{RP}$, $\leqslant^{RL}$, and $\leqslant^{RNC^1}$. Note that $A \leqslant^{NC^1} B$ implies $A \leqslant^{L} B$, which on its turn implies $A \leqslant^{P} B$. The same implications hold for the corresponding one- and two-sided error randomized reductions.

Often the reduction only needs a very restricted type of oracle access. This makes the reductions easier to analyze, and that is why we typically make these oracle access restrictions explicit. We will consider four types of oracle access: many-one (m), bounded truth-table (btt), truth-table (tt) and Turing (T). The names stem from computability theory and we refer to a textbook on that topic for their origin. The type of oracle access is indicated as a subscript to the $\leqslant$-sign: $\leqslant_m$, $\leqslant_{btt}$, $\leqslant_{tt}$, and $\leqslant_T$ respectively.

A *many-one* reduction is a reduction which makes only one oracle query and outputs the answer to that oracle query. In case of languages A and B, a many-one reduction from A to B can be thought of as a mapping $f : \Sigma^* \to \Sigma^*$ such that for any $x \in \Sigma^*$, $x \in A$ iff $f(x) \in B$. This is the most restrictive type of oracle access we will consider. It turns out to be powerful enough in a lot of cases. As an example, SAT can be $\leqslant_m^{NC^1}$-reduced to the problem whether a given 3-CNF formula is satisfiable. A CNF formula is a Boolean formula which is the conjunction of clauses, where a clause is a disjunction of literals and a literal is either a variable or the negation of a variable. The acronym CNF stands for Conjunctive Normal Form – every Boolean formula can be rewritten in this form (but the formula may become much larger while doing so). A 3-CNF formula is a CNF formula in which every clause contains 3 literals.

A *bounded truth-table* reduction is a reduction which can ask only a bounded number of oracle queries. That is to say, there exists a constant k such that on any input the reduction makes no more than k oracle queries. The answers can be combined in an arbitrary way to obtain the result of the reduction. For example, the language consisting of all Boolean formulas with exactly one satisfying assignment $\leqslant_{btt}^{NC^1}$-reduces to SAT. In fact, two queries suffice: We first ask whether the given formula is satisfiable, and then we ask whether it has more than one satisfying assignment. The latter question is an NP-problem and, as we will see in the next section on completeness, can be transformed in parallel logarithmic time into the question whether some other formula is satisfiable. The input is accepted iff the answer to the first query is positive and the answer to the second one is negative.

A *truth-table* reduction is a reduction which can ask any number of queries but in a nonadaptive way, i.e., no query can depend upon the answers to previous queries. Another way to think of it is that first all the queries to the oracle are computed, then they are all asked at once in parallel, and then the computation proceeds using the answers to these queries but without any further oracle access. If the reduction makes no more than $f(n)$ queries on inputs of size n, we may indicate that by writing $\leqslant_{f(n)\text{-tt}}$ instead of $\leqslant_{tt}$.

Given a list of Boolean formulas, deciding whether an odd number of them are satisfiable $\leqslant_{\mathrm{tt}}^{\mathrm{NC}^1}$-reduces to SAT.

A *Turing* reduction is the most general type of reduction. There is no restriction on the oracle access whatsoever. If the number of queries on inputs of size n is bounded by $f(n)$, we may write $\leqslant_{f(n)\text{-}\mathrm{T}}$ instead of $\leqslant_{\mathrm{T}}$. An example of a situation where the full adaptive power seems necessary – at least at first glance (see Corollary 3.5.1) – is the construction of a satisfying assignment for a Boolean formula given a black-box for SAT. The problem $\leqslant_{\mathrm{T}}^{\mathrm{P}}$-reduces to SAT. We fix, one by one, the values of the variables in the formula in such a way that the formula remains satisfiable.

The notation "$\leqslant$" suggests that the reducibility relation is transitive, i.e., if $A \leqslant B$ and $B \leqslant C$ then $A \leqslant C$. Most of the reductions we will consider have this property. In particular, all the reductions $\leqslant_r^{\mathrm{P}}$, $\leqslant_r^{\mathrm{L}}$, $\leqslant_r^{\mathrm{NC}^1}$, $\leqslant_r^{\mathrm{BPP}}$, $\leqslant_r^{\mathrm{BPL}}$, and $\leqslant_r^{\mathrm{BPNC}^1}$ for any $r \in \{\mathrm{m}, \mathrm{btt}, \mathrm{tt}, \mathrm{T}\}$ are transitive. The same is true of $\leqslant_{\mathrm{m}}^{\mathrm{RP}}$, $\leqslant_{\mathrm{m}}^{\mathrm{RPL}}$, and $\leqslant_{\mathrm{m}}^{\mathrm{RPNC}^1}$.

2.4.3 Complete Problems

We call a computational problem R *hard* for a complexity class $\mathcal{D}$ under a reducibility $\leqslant$ if every problem in $\mathcal{D}$ $\leqslant$-reduces to R. If in addition R itself belongs to $\mathcal{D}$, we call R *complete* for $\mathcal{D}$ under $\leqslant$.

Most of the reducibilities $\leqslant^{\mathcal{C}}$ we introduced in Section 2.4.2 have the property of downward closure, i.e., if $A \leqslant^{\mathcal{C}} B$ and $B \in \mathcal{C}$ then $A \in \mathcal{C}$. This is the case for all of the deterministic and 2-sided error randomized reductions as well as for $\leqslant_{\mathrm{m}}^{\mathrm{RP}}$. Therefore, studying the inclusion $\mathcal{D} \subseteq \mathcal{C}$ is equivalent to trying to answer the question whether a $\leqslant^{\mathcal{C}}$-complete problem for $\mathcal{D}$ belongs to $\mathcal{C}$, provided such a problem exists. In the context of the P versus NP question, $\leqslant^{\mathrm{P}}$-reductions will be used; for the L versus NP and L versus P question $\leqslant^{\mathrm{L}}$-reductions are appropriate; for the NC^1 versus NP or NC^1 versus P or NC^1 versus L problems $\leqslant^{\mathrm{NC}^1}$-reductions will be considered.

The type of reduction is often implicitly understood. The term "NP-completeness" refers to completeness for NP under $\leqslant_{\mathrm{m}}^{\mathrm{P}}$-reductions. Similarly, "P-complete" means complete for P under $\leqslant_{\mathrm{m}}^{\mathrm{L}}$-reductions, and "L-complete" means complete for L under $\leqslant_{\mathrm{m}}^{\mathrm{NC}^1}$-reductions.

NP-completeness is arguably the single most pervasive concept of computational complexity. A first example of an NP-complete language is the "standard" complete language K consisting of all triples $\langle M, x, 0^t \rangle$, where M is the description of a nondeterministic Turing machine, x is a string, and t is a nonnegative integer such that machine M has an accepting computation on input x of length at most t. Similar artificial complete languages exist for all classical time- and space-bounded deterministic, nondeterministic and alternating complexity classes. For each of the randomized complexity classes we discussed, it is an open question whether they have complete languages. The first natural problem shown to be NP-complete was the BOOLEAN FORMULA

SATISFIABILITY problem SAT . This result is known as Cook's Theorem [47]. In fact, SAT is $\leqslant_m^{NC^1}$-complete for NP.

The class NP contains a vast number of practically relevant computational problems. Almost all the ones for which no polynomial-time algorithm is known, have been shown to be NP-complete and therefore intractable unless every problem in NP is tractable. Ladner [78] proved that if P $\neq$ NP then there are languages in NP that are not in P but are not NP-complete either. In fact, he showed that there is a whole hierarchy of such problems under that assumption. However, only a handful natural candidates are known. The GRAPH ISOMORPHISM problem ISO is one of them. Given the fact that $\overline{\text{ISO}}$ lies in AM, the following theorem gives strong evidence that ISO is not NP-complete.

Theorem 2.4.2 ([27]). *If* coNP $\subseteq$ AM *then* $\Sigma_2^p = \Pi_2^p$.

We end this section by describing some natural complete problems for various complexity classes, from small to large.

A *tree* is a connected graph without cycles. A *forest* is a graph without cycles. The connected components of forests are trees. The graph connectivity problem for forests is L-complete [49]. We denote the corresponding language by F-STCON; an element of F-STCON is the description of a forest and two of its vertices that are connected. The connectivity problem for digraphs, D-STCON, as well as the connectivity problem for DAG's, DAG-STCON, are complete for NL under $\leqslant_m^{NC^1}$-reductions [121].

The CIRCUIT VALUE PROBLEM CVP is the language consisting of pairs $\langle C, x \rangle$ where C is the description of a Boolean circuit, say on n inputs, and x is a bit string of length n such that C accepts the input x. The problem is complete for P under $\leqslant_m^{NC^1}$-reductions [77].

GRAPH RAMSEY TRIPLE is complete for Π_2^p under $\leqslant_m^{NC^1}$-reductions [122]. The QUANTIFIED BOOLEAN FORMULA VALIDITY problem TQBF is complete for PSPACE under $\leqslant_m^{NC^1}$-reductions [44]. GENERALIZED CHECKERS is EXP-complete [117].

2.5 Resource-Bounded Measure

This section provides an introduction to resource-bounded measure, a technical tool we will use in Chapters 6, 7, and 8.

2.5.1 Motivation

Separations of complexity classes $\mathcal{C} \subsetneq \mathcal{D}$, although they may be very hard to obtain, are in some sense not very pleasing. In principle, they only establish the existence of a single language L in $\mathcal{D}$ which is not a member of $\mathcal{C}$. A more convincing argument would be to show that $\mathcal{D}$ is much larger than $\mathcal{C}$, i.e., that languages like L are frequent.

In the case of the P versus NP question, the above objection does not really hold. Separating P from NP would prove that none of the hundreds of NP-complete languages can be solved in polynomial time. But how can we formalize a statement like "most languages in NP are NP-complete?" More generally, we would like to have a measure for the frequency with which a given property Q occurs within a complexity class.

If we forget for a moment about the complexity class restriction and consider all possible languages, then we can use the Lebesgue measure on $\{0,1\}^\infty$ as a tool by associating a language with its characteristic sequence. A reader unfamiliar with Lebesgue measure can think of the Lebesgue measure of a subset $\mathcal{A}$ of $\{0,1\}^\infty$ as the probability that we end up with a sequence in $\mathcal{A}$ when we flip an unbiased coin to determine each of the bits of the sequence independently. We would say that a property Q is frequent if the Lebesgue measure of the class of characteristic sequences of languages that satisfy Q is large. This approach is used in so-called "random oracle results." For example, the statement that P differs from NP relative to a random oracle means that the Lebesgue measure of the class of oracles R such that $P^R \neq NP^R$ equals 1.

We could also try to use this approach to measure the frequency of a property Q within a complexity class $\mathcal{C}$. But there are some drawbacks. First, as in the case of random oracle results, we should not expect too much quantitative information. Membership to a complexity class $\mathcal{C}$ and the validity of Q are typically invariant under finite changes in the characteristic sequence, and Kolmogorov's zero-one law then states that the Lebesgue measure of the subclass of $\mathcal{C}$ satisfying Q is either 0 or 1 or else undefined. But this still tells us whether Q occurs rarely in $\mathcal{C}$, very often or with intermediate frequency. More seriously, however, our classes $\mathcal{C}$ are countable, so the Lebesgue measure of any subclass will always be zero.

One way to remedy the situation is to consider a restriction of Lebesgue measure in the mathematical sense: We restrict the domain of the measure function and only consider a class "small" if it lies in the domain and has Lebesgue measure zero. At the same time, we would like to keep some of the nice properties of Lebesgue measure, like the fact that a subclass of a small class is small, and that the union of two small classes is small. Lutz [88] proposed a solution that interacts nicely with complexity classes. The idea is to only consider a class small if we can prove that its Lebesgue measure is zero in some resource-bounded way. Lutz based his approach on a characterization of having Lebesgue measure zero using martingales.

2.5.2 Martingales

A *martingale* is abstractly defined as a function $d : \{0,1\}^* \to [0,\infty)$ satisfying the following "average law": for all $w \in \{0,1\}^*$,

$$d(w) = \frac{d(w0) + d(w1)}{2}. \tag{2.3}$$

A *supermartingale* is a function $d : \{0,1\}^* \to [0, \infty)$ satisfying the inequality

$$d(w) \geqslant \frac{d(w0) + d(w1)}{2} \tag{2.4}$$

for every $w \in \{0,1\}^*$. A (super)martingale *succeeds* on a sequence $\omega \in \{0,1\}^\infty$ if $d(\omega) \doteq \limsup_{w \sqsubseteq \omega,\, w \to \omega} d(w) = \infty$.

A martingale d describes a strategy for an infinite one-person betting game. At the beginning of the game, an infinite bit sequence ω is fixed but not revealed. The player starts with initial capital $d(\lambda)$, and in each round guesses the next bit of ω and bets some of his capital on that outcome. Then the actual value of the bit is revealed. On a correct guess, the player earns the amount of money he bet; otherwise he loses it. The value of $d(w)$ equals the capital of the player after being revealed the bit sequence w. The player wins on ω if he manages to make his capital arbitrarily high during the game. A supermartingale describes a similar game, but now the player is allowed to throw away some of his capital in every round.

The interpretation in Lutz's theory is that a string $w \in \{0,1\}^*$ stands for an initial segment of the characteristic sequence of a language A over an alphabet Σ. We say that a (super)martingale d succeeds on a language A if it succeeds on its characteristic sequence χ_A. We denote the class of languages on which d succeeds by $S^\infty[d]$, and say that d *covers* a class $\mathcal{C}$ of languages if $\mathcal{C} \subseteq S^\infty[d]$.

Martingales yield the following characterization.

Theorem 2.5.1. *A class $\mathcal{C}$ has Lebesgue measure zero iff it can be covered by a martingale iff it can be covered by a supermartingale.*

Lutz obtained a resource-bounded variant by putting resource bounds on the martingales. He originally defined the complexity of a martingale d in terms of computing fast-converging rational approximations to d. Subsequently he showed that for certain classes of complexity bounds one loses no generality by requiring that martingales themselves have rational values a/b such that the integers a and b can be computed within the complexity bound. We adopt this requirement throughout Chapters 6, 7 and 8, and specify that integers are represented in standard binary notation.

Definition 2.5.1. *Let Δ be a complexity class of functions. A class $\mathcal{C}$ of languages has Δ-measure zero, written $\mu_\Delta(\mathcal{C}) = 0$, if there is a martingale d computable in Δ such that $\mathcal{C} \subseteq S^\infty[d]$.*

Lutz measured the resources to compute $d(w)$ in terms of the length N of w. However, one can also work in terms of the length n of the last string the martingale has bet on. For $N > 0$, n equals $\lfloor \log_2 N \rfloor$; all we care about is that $n = \Theta(\log N)$ and $N = 2^{\Theta(n)}$. We will adopt the latter convention, and express martingale complexities in terms of n. In particular, we will refer to E-measure as the measure defined by martingales computable in time $2^{O(n)} = N^{O(1)}$, and to EXP-measure as the one defined by martingales computable in time $2^{n^{O(1)}} = 2^{(\log N)^{O(1)}}$. Note that we are abusing E and EXP here to denote classes of functions as opposed to decision problems. Abusing notation similarly, we define:

Definition 2.5.2 ([88]). *A class C has Δ-measure one, written $\mu_\Delta(C) = 1$, if $\mu_\Delta(\Delta \setminus C) = 0$.*

2.5.3 Properties

As with Lebesgue measure, the property of having resource-bounded measure zero is monotone and closed under union ("finite unions property"). The property that becomes crucial in resource-bounded measure is that the whole space Δ does not have measure zero, which Lutz calls the "measure conservation" property. With a slight abuse of meaning for "$\neq$," this property is written $\mu_\Delta(\Delta) \neq 0$. In particular, $\mu_E(E) \neq 0$ and $\mu_{EXP}(EXP) \neq 0$. μ_E is an adequate tool to measure the size of subsets of E in the following way: We say that a subset A of E is small if $\mu_E(A) = 0$ and that it is large if $\mu_E(A) = 1$. The above properties guarantee that a subset of E cannot be small and large at the same time, since this would imply that $\mu_E(E) = 0$. It is possible for a subset of E to be neither small nor large with respect to E-measure. In a similar way we can use μ_{EXP} to measure the size of subsets of EXP.

Subclasses of Δ that require substantially fewer resources, do have Δ-measure zero. For example, P has E-measure zero. Indeed, for any fixed $c > 0$, DTIME$[2^{cn}]$ has E-measure zero, and DTIME$[2^{n^c}]$ has EXP-measure zero. These results follow from the next resource-bounded version of closure under countable union of the smallness concept, which we only state for E. We say that a system $(d_i)_i$ of martingales d_i is E-*uniform* if we can compute $d_i(w)$ in time $i^c \cdot 2^{cn}$ for some constant c.

Theorem 2.5.2 ([88]). *Let $(d_i)_i$ be an E-uniform system of martingales such that d_i covers the class C_i. Then $\cup_i C_i$ has E-measure zero.*

A similar theorem using EXP-uniform systems holds for EXP-measure.

The concept of resource-bounded measure is known to be robust under several changes. In particular, if does not matter whether we use martingales or supermartingales in the definitions, and whether the success criterion is the capital having a limes superior or an actual limit of ∞.

Lemma 2.5.1. *Let d be a supermartingale computable in time $t(n)$. Then there is a martingale d' computable in time $O(2^n t(n))$ such that $S^\infty[d] \subseteq S^\infty[d']$.*

Proof. Define $d' : \{0,1\}^* \to [0, \infty)$ as follows:

$$d'(\lambda) = d(\lambda)$$
$$d'(wb) = d(wb) + d'(w) - \frac{d(w0) + d(w1)}{2}.$$

The proof that d' is a martingale as well as the analysis of its complexity is straightforward. By induction on $|w|$, we can show that $d'(w) \geqslant d(w)$. Consequently, $S^\infty[d] \subseteq S^\infty[d']$.

The following lemma says that we can assume a martingale grows almost monotonically (sure winnings) and not too fast (slow winnings).

Lemma 2.5.2 (Slow-but-Sure-Winnings Lemma). *Let d be a martingale. Then there is a martingale d' with $d'(\lambda) = d(\lambda)$ and $S^\infty[d] \subseteq S^\infty[d']$ such that*

$$(\forall w)(\forall u) : d'(wu) > d'(w) - 2d'(\lambda) \tag{2.5a}$$
$$(\forall w) : d'(w) < 2(|w| + 1)d(\lambda). \tag{2.5b}$$

If d is computable in time $t(n)$, then d' is computable in time $(2^n t(n))^{O(1)}$.

The idea is to play the strategy of d, but in a more conservative way. Say we start with an initial capital of \$1. We will deposit a part c of our capital in a bank and only play the strategy underlying d on the remaining liquid part e of our capital. We start with no savings and a liquid capital of \$1. If our liquid capital reaches or exceeds \$2, we deposit an additional \$1 or \$2 to our savings account c so as to keep the liquid capital in the range \$$[1, 2)$ at all times. If d succeeds, it will push the liquid capital infinitely often to \$2 or above, so c grows to infinity, and d' succeeds too. Since we never take money out of our savings account c, and the liquid capital e is bounded by \$2, once our total capital $d' = c + e$ has reached a certain level, it will never go more than \$2 below that level anymore, no matter how bad the strategy underlying d is. On the other hand, since we add at most \$2 to c in each step, $d'(w)$ cannot exceed $2(|w| + 1)$ either.

We now give the formal proof.

Proof (of Lemma 2.5.2). Define $d' : \{0, 1\}^* \to [0, \infty)$ by

$$d'(w) = (c(w) + e(w))d(\lambda),$$

where $c(\lambda) = 0$ and $e(\lambda) = 1$, and

$$
\begin{cases}
c(wb) = c(w) + 2 \\
e(wb) = \frac{d(wb)}{d(w)}e(w) - 2
\end{cases}
\text{if } d(w) \neq 0 \text{ and } \frac{d(wb)}{d(w)}e(w) \geqslant 3,
$$

$$
\begin{cases}
c(wb) = c(w) + 1 \\
e(wb) = \frac{d(wb)}{d(w)}e(w) - 1
\end{cases}
\text{if } d(w) \neq 0 \text{ and } 2 \leqslant \frac{d(wb)}{d(w)}e(w) < 3,
$$

$$
\begin{cases}
c(wb) = c(w) \\
e(wb) = \frac{d(wb)}{d(w)}e(w)
\end{cases}
\text{if } d(w) \neq 0 \text{ and } \frac{d(wb)}{d(w)}e(w) < 2,
$$

$$
\begin{cases}
c(wb) = c(w) \\
e(wb) = e(w)
\end{cases}
\text{otherwise.}
$$

To see that the recursion does not excessively blow up the time complexity or size of the answer, note that owing to cancelation of values of d, as long as $d(w) \neq 0$ every value $e(w)$ is given by a sum of the form

$$\sum_{k=0}^{N} a_k \frac{d(w)}{d(w[1 \ldots k])}$$

where each a_k is in $\{-2, -1, 0, 1\}$, $N = |w|$, and $w[1 \ldots k]$ stands for the first k bits of w. Each term in the sum is computable in time $O(t(n)^{O(1)} N)$. It follows that we can sum the $N + 1$ terms in time $(Nt(n))^{O(1)}$.

By induction on $|w|$ we observe that

$$0 \leqslant e(w) < 2, \tag{2.6}$$

and that

$$d'(wb) = \begin{cases} \left[c(w) + \frac{d(wb)}{d(w)} e(w) \right] d(\lambda) & \text{if } d(w) \neq 0 \\ d'(w) & \text{otherwise,} \end{cases}$$

from which it follows that d' is a martingale.

Now let ω be an infinite 0-1 sequence denoting a language on which d succeeds. Then $e(w)$ will always remain positive for $w \sqsubseteq \omega$, and $\frac{d(wb)}{d(w)} e(w)$ will become 2 or more infinitely often. Consequently, $\lim_{w \sqsubseteq \omega, |w| \to \infty} c(w) = \infty$. Since $d'(w) \geqslant c(w) d(\lambda)$, it follows that $S^\infty[d] \subseteq S^\infty[d']$. Moreover, by Equation (2.6) and the fact that c does not decrease along any sequence, we have that

$$d'(wu) \geqslant c(wu)d(\lambda) \geqslant c(w)d(\lambda) = d'(w) - e(w)d(\lambda) > d'(w) - 2d(\lambda).$$

Since c can increase by at most 2 in every step, $c(w) \leqslant 2|w|$. Together with Equation (2.6), this yields that

$$d'(w) = (c(w) + e(w))d(\lambda) < 2(|w| + 1)d(\lambda).$$

One can also show that $S^\infty[d'] \subseteq S^\infty[d]$ in Lemma 2.5.2, so the success set actually remains intact under the above transformation.

3. Derandomizing Arthur-Merlin Games

In this chapter, we study the construction of efficient pseudo-random generators for randomized proof systems known as Arthur-Merlin games. Our main tool is relativization: We will show that known hardness versus randomness trade-offs relativize. As a corollary, we obtain that graph nonisomorphism has subexponential size proofs unless the polynomial-time hierarchy collapses. Applications of the same technique to various randomized processes other than Arthur-Merlin games also follow.

3.1 Introduction

The power of randomness in computation is a fundamental area of study in the theory of computing. We know of many examples where "flipping a coin" facilitates algorithm design. From a complexity theoretic point of view, however, the merits of randomization remain unclear. Can we always eliminate the use of random bits without substantially increasing the need for other resources?

Blum and Micali [26] and Yao [138] gave a partial answer to this question. They realized that if some of the seemingly hard algorithmic problems really are computationally intractable then, in certain settings, randomness cannot help much. Nisan and Wigderson [104] established a range of hardness versus randomness trade-offs. They showed how to use any language in exponential time that is nonuniformly hard in an average-case sense to construct a pseudorandom generator that fools circuits of polynomial size. They obtained nontrivial derandomizations of polynomial-time randomized decision algorithms under average-case hardness assumptions and even deterministic polynomial-time simulations under the strongest of their hypotheses. Babai, Fortnow, Nisan, and Wigderson [18] and Impagliazzo and Wigderson [69] relaxed the hardness condition from average-case to worst-case. As a corollary, they showed how to simulate every polynomial-time randomized decision algorithm deterministically in subexponential time for infinitely many input lengths unless exponential time collapses to the second level of the polynomial-time hierarchy (and in fact to the class MA) [18].

The authors of these papers [104, 18, 69] used their techniques to derandomize traditional models of randomized computation, most notably BPP. We

D. van Mehlkebeek: Randomness and Completeness in Computational Complexity, LNCS 1950, pp. 53–76, 2000.
© Springer-Verlag Berlin Heidelberg 2000

show how to apply them to more general models of randomized computation. The key observation we make is that the reductions proved in these articles are "black-box", i.e., they relativize. More specifically, the above papers show how to transform any small circuit that distinguishes the output of a certain pseudo-random generator from the uniform distribution into a small circuit that computes a function used to build the pseudo-random generator. We observe that these reductions work for *any* nonuniform model of computation that satisfies certain closure properties, and in particular for oracle circuits given any fixed oracle. Thus, in order to build a pseudo-random generator that looks random to any small B-oracle circuit, we need only assume the existence of a function that cannot be computed by small B-oracle circuits.

The above observations allow us to apply the classical hardness versus randomness results to various settings, in particular to the nondeterministic setting of Arthur-Merlin games [16]. The class AM of languages with bounded round Arthur-Merlin games forms a randomized extension of NP. The most notable problem in AM not known to be in NP is GRAPH NONISOMORPHISM [57, 59, 21]. Derandomizing AM requires security against nondeterministic adversaries. Rudich [118] pointed out that pseudo-random generators in the traditional cryptographic setting where an adversary has more resources than the generator cannot hope to have this property because the adversary can always guess the seed and check. In particular, the Blum-Micali-Yao type of generator does not fool every Arthur-Merlin game. Merlin can convince Arthur that a pseudo-random bit sequence is produced by the pseudo-random generator by telling Arthur which seed was used. Since the pseudo-random generator is efficiently computable, Arthur can easily check that the seed does produce the pseudo-random sequence. From a derandomization perspective, however, the Nisan-Wigderson type of pseudo-random generator does not suffer from this drawback, as adversaries in this setting do not have the resources to run the generator — even if they correctly guess the seed.

We give evidence that AM coincides with NP. More specifically, we show that the existence of an exponential-time decidable language with high worst-case nonuniform SAT-oracle complexity implies nontrivial derandomizations of AM. The trade-offs are presented in Table 3.1, where we use C^B to denote circuit complexity given access to oracle B. See Section 3.2 for precise definitions, and Section 3.3 for the general trade-off statement.

hardness assumption:	derandomization consequence:
$\exists f \in \mathsf{NEXP} \cap \mathsf{coNEXP} : C_f^{\mathrm{SAT}}(n) \in n^{\omega(1)}$	$\mathsf{AM} \subseteq \cap_{\epsilon > 0} \mathsf{NTIME}[2^{n^\epsilon}]$
$\exists f \in \mathsf{NEXP} \cap \mathsf{coNEXP} : C_f^{\mathrm{SAT}}(n) \in 2^{n^{\Omega(1)}}$	$\mathsf{AM} \subseteq \cup_{c > 0} \mathsf{NTIME}[2^{(\log n)^c}]$
$\exists f \in \mathsf{NE} \cap \mathsf{coNE} : C_f^{\mathrm{SAT}}(n) \in 2^{\Omega(n)}$	$\mathsf{AM} = \mathsf{NP}$

Table 3.1. Hardness versus randomness trade-offs for AM

If the hardness condition on the left-hand side of Table 3.1 holds for infinitely many input lengths, then the corresponding derandomization on the right-hand side works for infinitely many input lengths. We refer to the *weak* version of Table 3.1 when we assume the above hardness conditions only hold for infinitely many input lengths. As in previous papers [104, 18, 69], we typically state our theorems assuming the hardness conditions are true for every input length. However, both interpretations hold for all of our results.

We can view the assumptions in Table 3.1 as statements concerning the relationships among computation, nonuniformity, and nondeterminism. For example, the third entry in the table states that if nonuniformity and nondeterminism cannot significantly speed up computation then we can derandomize AM. We point out that if the hardness assumption in the first row of the weak version of Table 3.1 fails, then exponential time collapses to the third level of the polynomial-time hierarchy.

Arvind and Köbler [14] obtained similar results to those in Table 3.1 using nondeterministic circuits, but needed average-case hardness assumptions instead of worst-case. As opposed to oracle circuits with access to SAT, nondeterministic circuits do not seem to have the closure properties that allow us to relax the hardness hypothesis from average-case to worst-case. Bridging this gap is crucial. It lets us conclude from the weak version of Table 3.1 that every language in AM, and graph nonisomorphism in particular, has subexponential size proofs for infinitely many input lengths unless the polynomial-time hierarchy collapses. Without any unproven hypothesis, the smallest proofs known for the nonisomorphism of two graphs on n vertices are of size $2^{O(\sqrt{n\log n})}$, namely the transcripts of the deterministic graph isomorphism algorithm by Luks and Zemlyachenko [20, 19].

Our simulations of AM are a special case of a general derandomization tool which applies to any randomized process for which we can efficiently check the successfulness of a given random bit sequence. We formally define the notion of a success predicate in Section 3.4. If we can decide the success predicate of a randomized process with polynomial size B-oracle circuits, then the hardness assumption on the left-hand side of Table 3.2 provides a pseudo-random generator G with the characteristics on the right-hand side of Table 3.2 for derandomizing the process. The symbol $\mathcal{A}$ in Table 3.2 represents an arbitrary class of oracles.

hardness assumption:	complexity of G:	seed length:
$\exists f \in \mathsf{EXP}^{\mathcal{A}} : C_f^B(n) \in n^{\omega(1)}$	$\mathsf{EXP}^{\mathcal{A}}$	$O(n^\epsilon)$ for every $\epsilon > 0$
$\exists f \in \mathsf{EXP}^{\mathcal{A}} : C_f^B(n) \in 2^{n^{\Omega(1)}}$	$\mathsf{EXP}^{\mathcal{A}}$	$(\log n)^{O(1)}$
$\exists f \in \mathsf{E}^{\mathcal{A}} : C_f^B(n) \in 2^{\Omega(n)}$	$\mathsf{E}^{\mathcal{A}}$	$O(\log n)$

Table 3.2. Overview of pseudo-random generator constructions

We apply our framework to the following randomized processes from different areas of theoretical computer science.

- The Valiant-Vazirani random hashing procedure which prunes the number of satisfying assignments of a Boolean formula to one [137].
- Exact learning of circuits using equivalence queries and access to an NP oracle [30].
- The construction of matrices with high rigidity [136].
- The construction of polynomial-size universal traversal sequences [3].

Elaborating on the first application, given a Boolean formula ϕ, we can construct in subexponential time a collection of polynomial-size formulas with the Valiant-Vazirani property with respect to ϕ unless the polynomial-time hierarchy collapses. If there exists a language in E with nonuniform SAT-oracle complexity $2^{\Omega(n)}$ we achieve a polynomial time deterministic procedure. It follows that, under the same hypothesis, we can find in polynomial time a satisfying assignment for a Boolean formula given nonadaptive access to SAT as opposed to the standard adaptive method described at the end of Section 2.4.2. We obtain derandomization results of a similar kind for our other examples. See Section 3.5 for the precise statements.

Regarding universal traversal sequences, we obtain polynomial-time constructions under the assumption that there exists a language in E with nonuniform complexity $2^{\Omega(n)}$. We also show that if there is a language in linear space that requires circuits of size $2^{\Omega(n)}$, then BPL = L. This answers a question raised by Clementi, Rolim, and Trevisan [46]. As a corollary to the proof, under the same hypothesis, we can generate universal traversal sequences in logspace.

This chapter is organized as follows. Section 3.2 introduces some notation. In Section 3.3 we generalize the techniques used to derandomize BPP and establish how to use them in the Arthur-Merlin setting. Section 3.4 defines a broad class of randomized processes and shows how our approach allows us to reduce the randomness of any process that fits within this class. In Section 3.5 we apply this framework to the four examples mentioned above. We give some conclusions in Section 3.6.

3.2 Notation

Recall that for a given Boolean function $f : \{0,1\}^* \to \{0,1\}$ and oracle B, the *circuit complexity* $C_f^B(n)$ of f at length n relative to B is the smallest integer t such that there is a B-oracle circuit of size t that computes f on inputs of length n. The *hardness* $H_f^B(n)$ of f at length n relative to B is the largest integer t such that for any oracle circuit D of size at most t with n inputs

$$| \Pr_x[D^B(x) = f(x)] - \frac{1}{2}| < \frac{1}{t},$$

where x is uniformly distributed over $\{0,1\}^n$.

We will implicitly fix some of the parameters of pseudo-random generators. In this chapter, a pseudo-random generator will always output $r(n) = n$ bits at length n. So, a *pseudo-random generator* G can be viewed as a sequence of functions $(G_n)_n$ such that G_n maps $\{0,1\}^{s(n)}$ to $\{0,1\}^n$ for some function $s : \mathbb{N} \to \mathbb{N}$ with $s(n) < n$. The function s is called the *seed length* of G. We say that G is *computable in* $\mathcal{C}$ if the problem of deciding the i-th bit of $G_n(\sigma)$ given $\langle n, \sigma, i \rangle$ belongs to $\mathcal{C}$. Given an oracle B, G_n is said to be *secure against* B if for any oracle circuit D of size at most n

$$|\Pr_\rho[D^B(\rho) = 1] - \Pr_\sigma[D^B(G_n(\sigma)) = 1]| < \frac{1}{n}, \tag{3.1}$$

where ρ is uniformly distributed over $\{0,1\}^n$ and σ over $\{0,1\}^{s(n)}$. In other words, we fix the security parameter at length n to n. G is said to be secure against B if G_n is secure against B for almost all n.

3.3 Derandomizing Arthur-Merlin Games

In this section, we develop methods for derandomizing Arthur-Merlin games and give evidence that the class AM of languages with bounded round Arthur-Merlin games is not much larger than NP and may even coincide with it.

As is customary in the area of derandomization, our approach will be to construct pseudo-random generators with appropriate security properties. The following lemma states that to derandomize AM, the pseudo-random generator need only be secure against SAT.

The lemma uses the following notation. For any function $t : \mathbb{N} \to \mathbb{N}$, AM-TIME$[t(n)]$ represents the class of languages L for which there exists a deterministic Turing machine N that runs in time $O(t(n))$ on inputs of the form $\langle x, y, z \rangle$ where $x \in \{0,1\}^n$ and $y, z \in \{0,1\}^{t(n)}$, such that for any input x,

$$x \in L \Rightarrow \Pr_{|y|=t(n)}[\exists z \in \{0,1\}^{t(n)} : N(\langle x, y, z \rangle) \text{ accepts }] = 1 \tag{3.2a}$$

$$x \notin L \Rightarrow \Pr_{|y|=t(n)}[\exists z \in \{0,1\}^{t(n)} : N(\langle x, y, z \rangle) \text{ accepts }] \leqslant \frac{1}{2}, \tag{3.2b}$$

where $n = |x|$ and the probabilities are with respect to the uniform distribution. AM coincides with $\cup_{c>0}$ AM-TIME$[n^c]$.

Lemma 3.3.1. *Let $s : \mathbb{N} \to \mathbb{N}$ be a space constructible function, and $t, \tau : \mathbb{N} \to \mathbb{N}$ be time-constructible functions. If there is a pseudo-random generator G computable in* NTIME$[\tau(n)] \cap$ coNTIME$[\tau(n)]$ *and with seed length s that is secure against SAT, then*

$$\text{AM-TIME}[t(n)] \subseteq \text{NTIME}[2^{s(t'(n))} \cdot \tau(s(t'(n))) \cdot t(n)], \tag{3.3}$$

where $t'(n) \in O(t(n) \log^2 t(n))$.

We give a proof of Lemma 3.3.1 in Section 3.3.1.

In order to build such a pseudo-random generator, we will extend previous work [104, 18, 69, 129] to the nondeterministic setting of Arthur-Merlin games. The main construction in these papers is a reduction from a circuit that distinguishes the output of a pseudo-random generator based on f from the uniform distribution to a circuit capable of computing f. We argue that this construction works for any nonuniform model of computation satisfying certain closure properties, and in particular for B-oracle circuits for any fixed oracle B. In this way, we obtain pseudo-random generators secure against B from functions which small B-oracle circuits cannot compute.

We begin with a generalized version of the main result of Nisan and Wigderson [104]. Their construction works for any nonuniform model which is closed under precomputation and complementation. In particular, it carries through for oracle circuits. See Section 3.3.2 for a more detailed argument.

Theorem 3.3.1. *Let B be any oracle, g a Boolean function and $\ell : \mathbb{N} \to \mathbb{N}$ a space constructible function. If*

$$H_g^B(m(n)) \geqslant n^2$$

then there exists a pseudo-random generator G which is secure against B and has space constructible seed length $s(n) \in O(\ell^2(n)/\log n)$. Computing any bit of $G(\sigma)$ for $\sigma \in \{0,1\}^{s(n)}$ takes time $2^{O(s(n))}$ plus one evaluation of g on an input of length $\ell(n)$.

The worst-case to average-case hardness transformation of Babai et al. [18] only needs closure of the model of computation under majority, complementation, and certain arithmetic field operations. Since oracle circuits have these closure properties, the transformation also works for that model. This observation would enable us to establish the first two lines of derandomization results for Arthur-Merlin games in Table 3.1 but falls short in establishing the last line. The reduction of Impagliazzo and Wigderson [69] also carries through for oracle circuits and is powerful enough to establish all of Table 3.1. An alternate to the Impagliazzo-Wigderson construction is described by Sudan et al. [129]. In Section 3.3.3 we provide the details on how to generalize the latter. We obtain the following result.

Theorem 3.3.2. *There exist positive constants γ and δ such that for any oracle B, Boolean function f, and space constructible function $h : \mathbb{N} \to \mathbb{N}$ the following holds. Provided*

$$h(n) \leqslant (C_f^B(\gamma n))^\delta / n$$

there exists a Boolean function g such that $H_g^B(n) \geqslant h(n)$. Computing g on an input of length n takes time $2^{O(n)}$ plus evaluating f on all inputs of length γn.

Combining Theorems 3.3.1 and 3.3.2 yields our main derandomization tool. Some instantiations are given in Table 3.2.

Theorem 3.3.3. *There exists a positive constant c such that the following holds for any class $\mathcal{A}$ of oracles, oracle B, Boolean function $f \in \mathsf{E}^{\mathcal{A}}$, and space constructible function $\ell : \mathbb{N} \to \mathbb{N}$. If*

$$C_f^B(\ell(n)) \geqslant n^c$$

then there exists a pseudo-random generator G computable in $\mathsf{E}^{\mathcal{A}}$ which is secure against B and has space constructible seed length $s(n) \in O(\ell^2(n)/\log n)$. The same holds if E is replaced by EXP.

In this section, we will apply Theorem 3.3.3 with $\mathcal{A} = \mathsf{NP} \cap \mathsf{coNP}$ and $B = \mathsf{SAT}$. Note that $\mathsf{EXP}^{\mathsf{NP} \cap \mathsf{coNP}} = \mathsf{NEXP} \cap \mathsf{coNEXP}$. Together with Lemma 3.3.1, Theorem 3.3.3 yields the following result.

Theorem 3.3.4. *If there is a Boolean function $f \in \mathsf{NEXP} \cap \mathsf{coNEXP}$ such that $C_f^{\mathsf{SAT}}(n) \in n^{\omega(1)}$, then*

$$\mathsf{AM} \subseteq \cap_{\epsilon > 0} \mathsf{NTIME}[2^{n^{\epsilon}}].$$

We can rephrase the weak version of Theorem 3.3.4 as follows.

Theorem 3.3.5. *If $\mathsf{NEXP} \cap \mathsf{coNEXP} \not\subseteq \mathsf{P}^{\mathsf{NP}}/\mathsf{poly}$, then for every $L \in \mathsf{AM}$, and every $\epsilon > 0$ there exists a language $L' \in \mathsf{NTIME}[2^{n^{\epsilon}}]$ such that L and L' agree on infinitely many input lengths.*

So, if the conclusion of Theorem 3.3.5 fails to hold, then $\mathsf{NEXP} \cap \mathsf{coNEXP} \subseteq \mathsf{P}^{\mathsf{NP}}/\mathsf{poly}$, which implies that $\mathsf{EXP} = \Sigma_3^{\mathsf{p}} \cap \Pi_3^{\mathsf{p}}$. Therefore, we obtain:

Theorem 3.3.6. *If exponential time does not collapse to the third level of the polynomial-time hierarchy, then every language in AM, and graph nonisomorphism in particular, has subexponential size proofs for infinitely many lengths.*

More generally, Theorem 3.3.3 yields the following derandomization result for Arthur-Merlin games. Note that $\mathsf{E}^{\mathsf{NP} \cap \mathsf{coNP}} = \mathsf{NE} \cap \mathsf{coNE}$.

Theorem 3.3.7. *If there is a Boolean function $f \in \mathsf{NE} \cap \mathsf{coNE}$, and a space constructible function $\ell : \mathbb{N} \to \mathbb{N}$ such that*

$$C_f^{\mathsf{SAT}}(\ell(n)) \in \Omega(n),$$

then

$$\mathsf{AM} \subseteq \cup_{c > 0} \mathsf{NTIME}[2^{\ell^2(n^c)/\log n}].$$

Theorem 3.3.7 yields a range of hardness versus randomness trade-offs for the various choices of the parameter ℓ. Since $C_f^B(n) \in O(2^n/n)$ always holds, the hypothesis of Theorem 3.3.7 cannot be met for ℓ sublogarithmic. On the other hand, the conclusion becomes trivial in the case where ℓ is polynomial. Therefore, the interesting range for ℓ lies between logarithmic and subpolynomial.

For example, for ℓ polylogarithmic, Theorem 3.3.7 (combined with some padding) yields the second line in Table 3.1.

Theorem 3.3.8. *If there is a Boolean function $f \in$ NEXP $\cap$ coNEXP such that $C_f^{\mathrm{SAT}}(n) \in \Omega(2^{n^\epsilon})$ for some $\epsilon > 0$, then every language in AM has quasipolynomial size proofs.*

In case of logarithmic ℓ, Theorem 3.3.7 achieves complete derandomizations of Arthur-Merlin games.

Theorem 3.3.9. *If there is a Boolean function $f \in$ NE $\cap$ coNE such that $C_f^{\mathrm{SAT}}(n) \in 2^{\Omega(n)}$, then AM $=$ NP. In particular, the same hypothesis implies that graph nonisomorphism has polynomial size proofs.*

Finally, we note that for derandomizing AM it is actually sufficient to construct efficient pseudo-random generators that are secure against SAT-oracle circuits with *parallel* access to the oracle. All theorems in this section also hold for oracle circuits with such restricted access.

3.3.1 Proof of Lemma 3.3.1

Let L be a language satisfying (3.2a) and (3.2b), and consider

$$L' = \{\langle x, y \rangle \mid y \in \{0,1\}^{t(|x|)} \text{ and } \exists z \in \{0,1\}^{t(|x|)} : M(\langle x, y, z \rangle) = 1\}.$$

By Cook's Theorem [48], since $L' \in$ NTIME$[n]$, there exists a circuit of size $t'(n) \in O(t(n) \log^2 t(n))$ that many-one reduces L' to SAT on inputs $\langle x, y \rangle$ with $x \in \{0,1\}^n$ and $y \in \{0,1\}^{t(n)}$. For any fixed value of $x \in \{0,1\}^n$, let C_x denote the corresponding oracle circuit obtained by hardwiring x. Note that C_x makes a single oracle query and outputs the answer to that query. Since G is a pseudo-random generator secure against SAT, conditions (3.2a) and (3.2b) imply that

$$\Pr_\sigma[C_x^{\mathrm{SAT}}(G_{t'(n)}(\sigma)) = 1] \begin{array}{l} > 1/2 \text{ if } x \in L \\ < 1/2 \text{ if } x \notin L, \end{array} \tag{3.4}$$

where the probability is with respect to the uniform distribution of σ over $\{0,1\}^{s(t'(n))}$.

Since G is computable in NTIME$[\tau(n)] \cap$ coNTIME$[\tau(n)]$, there exists a nondeterministic Turing machine N running in time τ that accepts the language $\{\langle n, \sigma, i, b \rangle \mid i\text{-th bit of } G_n(\sigma) \text{ equals } b\}$. Now, consider the nondeterministic algorithm in Figure 3.1.

```
counter ← 0
for every σ ∈ {0,1}^{s(t'(n))}
    for  i ← 1,...,t(n)
        guess ρ_i ∈ {0,1}
        guess a computation path p for N(⟨n,σ,i,ρ_i⟩)
        if N(⟨n,σ,i,ρ_i⟩) rejects along p
            then reject and abort
        guess z ∈ {0,1}^{t(n)}
        counter ← counter + M(⟨x,ρ,z⟩)
    if counter > 2^{t'(n)-1} then accept
```

Fig. 3.1. Nondeterministic algorithm for deciding L

Figure 3.1 describes a nondeterministic Turing machine that runs in time $2^{s(t'(n))} \cdot \tau(s(t'(n))) \cdot t(n)$. The largest possible value of counter at the end of the outer loop over all possible nondeterministic choices in the algorithm of Figure 3.1, equals $2^{s(t'(n))} \cdot \Pr_\sigma[C_x^{\mathrm{SAT}}(G_{t'(n)}(\sigma)) = 1]$. It follows from (3.4) that the machine accepts L. This finishes the proof of Lemma 3.3.1.

3.3.2 Proof of Theorem 3.3.1

Nisan and Wigderson use the following notion of a combinatorial design in their construction of a pseudo-random generator.

Definition 3.3.1 ([104]). *An (m,ℓ) design of size k over a universe Ω is a collection $S = (S_1, S_2, \ldots, S_k)$ of subsets of Ω, each of size ℓ, such that for any $1 \leqslant i < j \leqslant k$, the intersection $S_i \cap S_j$ has size at most m.*

In particular, in order to construct G_n, Nisan and Wigderson need a $(\log n, \ell)$ design of size n for a given value of $\ell \geqslant \log n$. The size of the design universe will be the seed length $s(n)$ of G_n and therefore should be small. Nisan and Wigderson [104] show that the greedy approach works and that it yields a $(\log n, \ell)$ design of size n over a universe of size $O(\ell^2/\log n)$. See [135, Lemma 7] for a detailed analysis.

Lemma 3.3.2 ([104]). *A $(\log n, \ell)$ design of size n can be constructed over a universe of size $s \in O(\ell^2/\log n)$ in time $2^s \cdot n^{O(1)}$.*

Given a function $g : \{0,1\}^\ell \to \{0,1\}$ and a $(\log n, \ell)$ design $S = (S_1, S_2, \ldots, S_n)$ over $\{1, 2, \ldots, s\}$, Nisan and Wigderson define their pseudo-random generator G_n as follows:

$$G_n : \{0,1\}^s \to \{0,1\}^n : \sigma \to g(\sigma|_{S_1}) g(\sigma|_{S_2}) \ldots g(\sigma|_{S_n}), \qquad (3.5)$$

where $\sigma|_{S_i}$ denotes the substring of σ consisting of the bits indexed by the elements from S_i.

The following theorem, combined with Lemma 3.3.2, finishes the proof of Theorem 3.3.1.

Theorem 3.3.10. *Let B be any oracle, $g : \{0,1\}^\ell \rightarrow \{0,1\}$, and $\mathcal{S} = (S_1, S_2, \ldots, S_n)$ a $(\log n, \ell)$ design over $\{1, 2, \ldots, s\}$. If $H_g^B \geqslant n^2$ then G_n as defined by (3.5) is secure against B.*

The proof goes along the lines of the one by Nisan and Wigderson [104]. It is an application of Yao's observation that distinguishability from the uniform distribution implies predictability [138], and uses the so-called *hybrid argument* [58].

Proof. We proceed by contradiction. Assume that G_n is not secure against B. This means that there exists an oracle circuit D of size at most n such that either

$$\Pr_\sigma[D^B(G_n(\sigma)) = 1] - \Pr_\rho[D^B(\rho) = 1] > \frac{1}{n}, \tag{3.6}$$

or else $\Pr_\rho[D^B(\rho) = 1] - \Pr_\sigma[D^B(G_n(\sigma)) = 1] > \frac{1}{n}$, where ρ is uniformly distributed over $\{0,1\}^n$ and σ over $\{0,1\}^s$. We will assume that (3.6) holds. The other case is similar.

Consider the following sequence of "hybrid" distributions $\mathcal{D}_0, \ldots, \mathcal{D}_n$:

$$
\begin{array}{lllllll}
\mathcal{D}_0 & = & g(\sigma|_{S_1}) & g(\sigma|_{S_2}) & \cdots & g(\sigma|_{S_{n-1}}) & g(\sigma|_{S_n}) \\
\mathcal{D}_1 & = & \rho_1 & g(\sigma|_{S_2}) & \cdots & g(\sigma|_{S_{n-1}}) & g(\sigma|_{S_n}) \\
\vdots & & & & \vdots & & \\
\mathcal{D}_i & = & \rho_1 & \rho_2 & \cdots \rho_{i-1} \rho_i \, g(\sigma|_{S_{i+1}}) \cdots & g(\sigma|_{S_{n-1}}) & g(\sigma|_{S_n}) \\
\vdots & & & & \vdots & & \\
\mathcal{D}_{n-1} & = & \rho_1 & \rho_2 & \cdots & \rho_{n-1} & g(\sigma|_{S_n}) \\
\mathcal{D}_n & = & \rho_1 & \rho_2 & \cdots & \rho_{n-1} & \rho_n
\end{array}
$$

As before, ρ is uniformly distributed over $\{0,1\}^n$ and σ over $\{0,1\}^s$.

Since the left-hand side of (3.6) can be written as

$$\Pr_{y \in \mathcal{D}_0}[D^B(y) = 1] - \Pr_{z \in \mathcal{D}_n}[D^B(z) = 1]$$

$$= \sum_{i=1}^n \Pr_{y \in \mathcal{D}_{i-1}}[D^B(y) = 1] - \Pr_{z \in \mathcal{D}_i}[D^B(z) = 1],$$

there must exist an index i, $1 \leqslant i \leqslant n$, such that

$$\Pr_{y \in \mathcal{D}_{i-1}}[D^B(y) = 1] - \Pr_{z \in \mathcal{D}_i}[D^B(z) = 1] \geqslant \frac{1}{n^2}. \tag{3.7}$$

The only difference between $\mathcal{D}_{i-1}$ and $\mathcal{D}_i$ is the way the ith bit is generated: In $\mathcal{D}_{i-1}$ it is set to $g(\sigma|_{S_i})$ whereas in $\mathcal{D}_i$ it is a random bit. Equation (3.7) says that in the former case the B-oracle circuit D^B is more likely to accept than in the latter case. This suggests the following randomized predictor $P(x)$ for $g(x)$:

– Pick $\rho_1, \rho_2, \ldots, \rho_i \in \{0, 1\}$ uniformly at random.
– Set $\sigma|_{S_i}$ equal to x and pick the other bits of σ uniformly at random.
– If $D^B(\rho_1, \rho_2, \ldots, \rho_i, g(\sigma|_{S_{i+1}}), \ldots, g(\sigma|_{S_n}))$ accepts then output ρ_i; otherwise output $\overline{\rho_i}$ (the complement of ρ_i).

Claim 3.3.1. Let x denote $\sigma|_{S_i}$. Then

$$\Pr_{\rho,\sigma}[P(x) = g(x)] - \frac{1}{2} = \Pr_{y \in \mathcal{D}_{i-1}}[D^B(y) = 1] - \Pr_{z \in \mathcal{D}_i}[D^B(z) = 1]. \qquad (3.8)$$

Proof. We argue the claim by conditioning on all of ρ and σ except ρ_i. Let $\tilde{y}$ denote y with the ith bit flipped.

– Case $D^B(y) = D^B(\tilde{y})$.
  Since the value of the ith component doesn't affect D^B, the right-hand side of (3.8) vanishes. $P(x)$ is a random bit in this case so the left-hand side also vanishes.
– Case $D^B(y) \neq D^B(\tilde{y})$.
  Then $D^B(z)$ accepts with probability $\frac{1}{2}$, and $P(x)$ equals $g(x)$ precisely when $D^B(y) = 1$.

This finishes the proof of Claim 3.3.1.

Note that $x \doteq \sigma|_{S_i}$ is uniformly distributed over $\{0,1\}^m$. By an averaging argument, (3.7) and (3.8) imply that we can fix ρ and all of σ outside of S_i such that

$$\Pr_x[P(x) = g(x)] \geqslant \frac{1}{2} + \frac{1}{n^2}. \qquad (3.9)$$

Note that

$$P(x) = D^B(\rho_1, \rho_2, \ldots, \rho_i, g(\sigma|_{S_{i+1}}), \ldots, g(\sigma|_{S_n})) \oplus \overline{\rho_i}. \qquad (3.10)$$

Since $|S_j \cap S_i| \leqslant \log n$ for $j \neq i$, each of the components $g(\sigma|_{S_j}), i < j \leqslant n$, only depend on $\log n$ bits of x and therefore can be computed by circuits of size at most n with input x. There are at most $n-1$ such components. As ρ is fixed and the size of D if at most n, it follows that the right-hand side of (3.10) can be evaluated by a B-oracle circuit C^B of size at most $(n-1)n + n = n^2$. In combination with (3.9) this leads to the contradiction that $H_g^B < n^2$.

3.3.3 Proof of Theorem 3.3.2

Sudan et al. showed the following list decoding result [129, Definition 21 and Lemma 25].

Theorem 3.3.11 ([129]). *There exists a family of mappings $(\mathcal{C}_{N,\epsilon})_{N \in \mathbb{N}, \epsilon > 0}$ where $\mathcal{C}_{N,\epsilon} : \{0,1\}^N \to \{0,1\}^{N'(N,\epsilon)}$ such that the following hold.*

- $\mathcal{C}_{N,\epsilon}$ is computable in time polynomial in N and $1/\epsilon$. In particular, $N' \doteq N'(N, \epsilon)$ is polynomial in N and $1/\epsilon$.
- There exists a randomized algorithm that, on input N and ϵ and given oracle access to a string $y \in \{0,1\}^{N'}$, runs in time polynomial in $\log N$ and $1/\epsilon$ and outputs with high probability a list of randomized oracle machines M_j with the next properties:
  - For every $x \in \{0,1\}^N$ such that $(\mathcal{C}_{N,\epsilon}(x))_i = y_i$ for at least $(\frac{1}{2} + \epsilon)N'$ of the positions i, $1 \leqslant i \leqslant N'$, there exists an index j such that for any position i, $1 \leqslant i \leqslant N$, $M_j^y(i)$ outputs x_i with high probability.
  - Each machine M_j runs in time polynomial in $\log N$ and $1/\epsilon$.

By Adleman's argument [1] we can transform the randomized procedures in the second bullet of Theorem 3.3.11 into circuits. This yields the following corollary.

Corollary 3.3.1. *There exists a constant c such that for any $N \in \mathbb{N}$, $x \in \{0,1\}^N$ and $y \in \{0,1\}^{N'}$ satisfying $(\mathcal{C}_{N,\epsilon}(x))_i = y_i$ for at least $(\frac{1}{2} + \epsilon)N'$ of the positions i, $1 \leqslant i \leqslant N'$, there exists an oracle circuit D of size $(\frac{1}{\epsilon} \log N)^c$ such that $D^y(i) = x_i$ for every $1 \leqslant i \leqslant N$.*

We define g such that its truth-table at length $n' \doteq \log N'$ equals the encoding $\mathcal{C}_{N,\epsilon}$ of the truth-table of f at length $n \doteq \log N$. We set $\epsilon = 1/h(n')$ where $h(n')$ is the hardness level we want to achieve. Since $h(n') \in O(2^{n'}/n')$, the first bullet in Theorem 3.3.11 implies that N and N' are polynomially related, so we can set $n = \gamma \cdot n'$ for some positive constant γ.

Now, suppose that there exists a B-oracle circuit of size at most $h(n')$ that computes g correctly on at least $(\frac{1}{2} + \frac{1}{h(n')})N'$ of the inputs of length n'. By plugging in this circuit as the oracle y in Corollary 3.3.1, we obtain a B-oracle circuit that computes f at length $n = \gamma \cdot n'$ correctly and has size at most $(\frac{1}{\epsilon} \log N)^c \cdot h(n') = (\gamma n')^c \cdot (h(n'))^{c+1}$. In other words,

$$C_f^B(\gamma n') \leqslant (\gamma n')^c \cdot (h(n'))^{c+1}. \tag{3.11}$$

For $\delta < 1/(c+1)$, (3.11) contradicts the upper bound on $h(n')$ in the hypothesis of Theorem 3.3.2. Therefore, $H_g^B(n') \geqslant h(n')$.

3.4 A General Framework for Derandomization

In the previous section, we showed that an Arthur-Merlin protocol can be viewed as a SAT-oracle distinguisher for a pseudo-random generator, and if a Boolean function f exists with sufficient hardness against SAT-oracle circuits we can construct a pseudo-random generator based on f that will look random to our Arthur-Merlin protocol. Still, we have only applied our results to randomized *decision* algorithms. In this section, we show how to relax this condition and obtain hardness versus randomness trade-offs for a broader class of randomized processes. Under a sufficient hardness condition depending upon the particular randomized algorithm, we are able to reduce the algorithm's randomness to a logarithmic factor and, in some cases, provide a complete derandomization. Weaker hardness conditions yield partial derandomizations.

We first describe the notion of a *randomized process* to which our approach applies. We formalize a process that uses $r(n)$ random bits on inputs of length n as a pair (F, π), where:

- F is a function that takes a string x and a string ρ of length $r(|x|)$, and outputs the outcome of the process on input x using ρ as the random bit sequence.
- π is a predicate with the same domain as F that indicates whether the process succeeds on input x using ρ, i.e., whether ρ is a "good" choice of random bits for the given input x. We call π the success predicate of the randomized process.

In the case of Arthur-Merlin games F is Boolean. More specifically, for the game defined by (3.2a) and (3.2b) in Section 3.3, $F(x, \rho)$ coincides with the predicate $\exists z \in \{0,1\}^{t(n)} : N(\langle x, \rho, z \rangle) = 1$; the success predicate $\pi(x, \rho)$ equals $F(x, \rho)$ if $x \in L$ and the complement of $F(x, \rho)$ otherwise. In the specific randomized processes we will consider in Section 3.5, F will be non-Boolean.

What matters for our derandomization results is the complexity of the success predicate π and, more precisely, the property stated in the following lemma.

Lemma 3.4.1. *Let B be any oracle, and (F, π) a randomized process using $r(n)$ random bits such that for any fixed input x of length n, the predicate $\pi_x : \{0,1\}^{r(n)} \to \{0,1\}$ where $\pi_x(\rho) \doteq \pi(x, \rho)$ can be decided by a B-oracle circuit of size $t(n) \geqslant r(n)$. If G is a pseudo-random generator with seed length $s(n)$ which is secure against B, then for any input x of length n*

$$| \Pr_{\rho}[\pi(x, \rho) = 1] - \Pr_{\sigma}[\pi(x, G_{t(n)}(\sigma)[1..r(n)]) = 1]| \in O(1/t(n)),$$

where ρ is uniformly distributed over $\{0,1\}^{r(n)}$ and σ over $\{0,1\}^{s(t(n))}$.

In our applications we will be concerned with randomized processes that use a polynomial number of random bits. We will choose the oracle B in Lemma 3.4.1 powerful enough so that it can check the process efficiently in the following sense.

Definition 3.4.1. *Let B be an oracle, and (F, π) a randomized process using a polynomial number $r(n)$ of random bits. We say that B can* efficiently *check (F, π) if there is a polynomial p such that for any fixed input x of length n, the predicate $\pi_x : \{0,1\}^{r(n)} \to \{0,1\}$ where $\pi_x(\rho) \doteq \pi(x, \rho)$ can be decided by a B-oracle circuit of size $p(n)$.*

Using the success predicate as a distinguisher as in Lemma 3.4.1, Theorem 3.3.3 yields our general derandomization result.

Theorem 3.4.1. *Let $\mathcal{A}$ be a class of oracles, B an oracle, d a positive constant, and $\ell : \mathbb{N} \to \mathbb{N}$ a space constructible function. Let (F, π) be a randomized process using a polynomial number of random bits such that B can efficiently check (F, π). If there exists a Boolean function $f \in \mathsf{E}^{\mathcal{A}}$ such that $C_f^B(\ell(n)) \in \Omega(n)$, then there exists a function G computable in $\mathsf{E}^{\mathcal{A}}$ and a space constructible function $s(n) \in O(\ell^2(n^{O(1)})/\log n)$ such that for any input x of length n*

$$|\Pr_{\rho}[\pi(x, \rho) = 1] - \Pr_{\sigma}[\pi(x, G(\sigma)) = 1]| \in O(1/n^d),$$

where ρ is uniformly distributed over $\{0,1\}^{r(n)}$ and σ over $\{0,1\}^{s(n)}$. The same holds if E is replaced by EXP.

See Table 3.2 for some interesting instantiations of Theorem 3.4.1.

In order to reduce the randomness of a randomized process, we will first analyze the complexity of an oracle B capable of efficiently checking the associated success predicate and then construct a pseudo-random generator secure against B based on a function with presumed hardness against B.

3.5 More Applications

We will now apply the general framework of Section 3.4 to various other constructions in computational complexity. As customary, we only state our results in terms of the strongest of the assumptions in Table 3.2, yielding polynomial time deterministic simulations. It should be noted, however, that weaker assumptions can be taken (e.g., that the polynomial-time hierarchy does not collapse) in order to achieve weaker, but still subexponential, deterministic simulations.

3.5.1 Valiant-Vazirani

Our first example is the randomized Boolean hashing protocol developed by Valiant and Vazirani [137]. They give a method for pruning the satisfying assignments of a propositional formula to one.

Theorem 3.5.1 (Valiant-Vazirani [137]). *There exists a randomized polynomial time algorithm that, on input a propositional formula ϕ, outputs a list of propositional formulas such that:*

- *Every satisfying assignment to any of the formulas in the list also satisfies ϕ.*

– *If ϕ is satisfiable, then with high probability at least one of the formulas in the list has exactly one satisfying assignment.*

Let $F(x, \rho)$ denote the list of formulas the Valiant-Vazirani algorithm produces on input x using coin flips specified by ρ. We define the success predicate $\pi(x, \rho)$ to hold unless x is a satisfiable formula and none of the formulas in $F(x, \rho)$ has a unique satisfying assignment. It is clear that (F, π) corresponds to a formalization of the Valiant-Vazirani process and fits within our framework.

Theorem 3.5.2. *If there is a Boolean function $f \in \mathsf{E}$ such that $C_f^{\mathrm{SAT}}(n) \in 2^{\Omega(n)}$, then, given a propositional formula ϕ, we can generate in polynomial time a list of propositional formulas such that:*

– *Every satisfying assignment to any of the formulas in the list also satisfies ϕ.*
– *If ϕ is satisfiable, then at least one of the formulas in the list has exactly one satisfying assignment.*

Proof. Let (F, π) be the formalization as described above. Notice that checking whether a given propositional formula has at least two satisfying assignments is an NP question. Hence, we can check, in polynomial time, whether a propositional formula has a unique satisfying assignment using two queries to SAT. It follows that SAT can efficiently check (F, π). Applying theorem 3.4.1 to (F, π) yields a pseudo-random generator G computable in E that looks random to the Valiant-Vazirani process. Enumerating over all seeds and collecting all formulas produces the desired list of formulas in polynomial time.

We now have the following corollary about computing satisfying assignments nonadaptively.

Corollary 3.5.1. *If there is a Boolean function $f \in \mathsf{E}$ such that $C_f^{\mathrm{SAT}}(n) \in 2^{\Omega(n)}$, then, given a satisfiable propositional formula ϕ, we can find a satisfying assignment for ϕ in polynomial time given nonadaptive oracle access to SAT.*

Proof. A satisfying assignment to a uniquely satisfiable propositional formula ψ can be found in polynomial time using nonadaptive oracle queries to SAT: We set a variable v of ψ iff the formula obtained from ψ by substituting TRUE for v is satisfiable.

We run the latter procedure on each formula ψ of the list produced by Theorem 3.5.2 on input ϕ, and output the first satisfying assignment we obtain.

We also obtain interesting structural observations. The class #P (read "sharp P") contains by definition all functions $f : \Sigma^* \to \mathbb{N}$ for which there exists a nondeterministic polynomial-time Turing machine M such that $f(x)$

equals the number of accepting computations of M on input x. A language L belongs to $\oplus$P (read "parity P") if there exists a #P function f such that an input x belongs to L iff $f(x)$ is odd. In other words, $L \in \oplus$P if there exists a nondeterministic polynomial-time Turing machine M such that $x \in L$ iff M has an odd number of accepting computations on input x. A GapP function is defined to be the difference of two #P functions, and SPP denotes the class of all languages whose characteristic function is a GapP function. SPP contains $\oplus$P (as well as PP). We refer the reader to the survey by Fortnow [54] for background on these counting classes. Theorem 3.5.2 implies:

Corollary 3.5.2. *If there is a Boolean function $f \in$ E such that $C_f^{\mathrm{SAT}}(n) \in 2^{\Omega(n)}$, then* NP *is contained in* SPP.

Proof. Let $h(\phi, i)$ denote the #P function that gives the number of satisfying assignments to the ith formula of the list produced by Theorem 3.5.2 on input ϕ. Then

$$1 - \prod_i (1 - h(\phi, i)) \tag{3.12}$$

equals the characteristic function of SAT. By the closure properties of GapP [52], (3.12) belongs to GapP.

Similarly, we can conditionally derandomize the result by Toda and Ogiwara [132] that the polynomial-time hierarchy does not add power to GapP in a randomized setting. Applying our techniques to their main lemma yields:

Lemma 3.5.1. *Let B be any oracle. If there is a Boolean function $f \in$ E such that $C_f^{\mathrm{SAT}^B}(n) \in 2^{\Omega(n)}$, then* GapP$^{\mathrm{NP}^B}$ *is contained in* GapP^B.

This allows us to show:

Theorem 3.5.3. *For any integer $k \geqslant 1$ the following holds. If there is a Boolean function $f \in$ E such that $C_f^{\mathrm{TQBF}_k}(n) \in 2^{\Omega(n)}$, then Σ_k^{p} is contained in* SPP.

Here TQBF$_k$ denotes the language of all true fully quantified propositional formulas with at most $k - 1$ quantifier alternations.

Proof. Corollary 3.5.2 relativizes and, under the given assumption, implies that the characteristic function of any language in Σ_k^{p} is contained in GapP$^{\mathrm{TQBF}_{k-1}}$. The successive application of Lemma 3.5.1 with $B = \mathrm{TQBF}_{k-2}$, $B = \mathrm{TQBF}_{k-3}$, ..., $B = \mathrm{TQBF}_1$, and $B = \varnothing$ yields under the given assumption that GapP$^{\mathrm{TQBF}_k}$ is contained in GapP.

Corollary 3.5.3. *Let B be any oracle hard for the polynomial-time hierarchy under polynomial-time Turing reductions. If there is a Boolean function $f \in$ E such that $C_f^B(n) \in 2^{\Omega(n)}$, then the polynomial-time hierarchy is contained in* SPP.

Corollary 3.5.3 is strongly related to Toda's Theorem [131] that the polynomial-time hierarchy lies in $\mathsf{BP} \cdot \oplus \mathsf{P}$. Applying our derandomization technique directly to Toda's Theorem yields:

Theorem 3.5.4. *If there is a Boolean function $f \in \mathsf{E}$ such that $C_f^{\oplus \mathrm{SAT}}(n) \in 2^{\Omega(n)}$, then the polynomial-time hierarchy is contained in $\oplus \mathsf{P}$.*

3.5.2 Learning Circuits

Learning theory represents another area where we can apply our techniques. We will focus on exact *concept learning with equivalence queries* [11, 83], in which the learner presents hypotheses to a teacher, who then tells the learner whether the hypothesis agrees with the concept in question. If it does, the learner has succeeded; otherwise the teacher provides a counterexample and the learner continues.

A fundamental question is whether we can efficiently learn Boolean circuits in this model. If $\mathsf{P} = \mathsf{NP}$, we can; if one-way functions exist, we cannot [110]. Without any complexity theoretic assumption, Bshouty et al. [30] showed that access to an NP oracle and to a source of randomness suffice to efficiently learn Boolean circuits. We give evidence that we may be able to dispense with the source of randomness.

Theorem 3.5.5. *If there is a Boolean function $f \in \mathsf{NE} \cap \mathsf{coNE}$ such that $C_f^{\mathrm{TQBF}_2}(n) \in 2^{\Omega(n)}$, then we can perform the following task in deterministic polynomial time given access to an NP oracle: exactly learn Boolean circuits of size t using equivalence queries with hypotheses that are circuits of size $O(tn + n \log n)$.*

As before, TQBF_2 denotes the language of all true fully quantified propositional formulas with at most one quantifier alternation.

Proof. We apply Theorem 3.4.1 to a randomized process (F, π) underlying the algorithm of Bshouty et al. [30]. We define F in the obvious way, namely as the candidate equivalent circuit the learner outputs. The specification of the success predicate π is somewhat more involved than in the examples we have seen so far. We only want to consider a random seed as "good" if the learner, when using this seed, finds an equivalent circuit no matter how the teacher picks the counterexamples. Therefore, we define $\pi(x, \rho)$ to indicate whether for every choice of candidate counterexamples, either one of them fails to be a valid counterexample on input x and random seed ρ, or else the learner ends up with an equivalent circuit to x. It follows from the construction of Bshouty et al. that π is a Π_2^{p} predicate, and their analysis shows that for any input x, $\pi(x, \rho)$ holds with high probability.

Using the derandomization provided by Theorem 3.4.1, we end up with a polynomial number of candidate circuits at least one of which is equivalent to x. So, we just present each of these to the teacher and will succeed.

Bshouty et al. used their learning theory result to improve the known collapse of the polynomial-time hierarchy in case NP would have polynomial size circuits: They showed that the latter implies that the polynomial-time hierarchy is contained in ZPP^{NP}. Along the same lines, we obtain:

Corollary 3.5.4. *If* NP *has polynomial size circuits and there is a Boolean function* $f \in$ NE $\cap$ coNE *such that* $C_f(n) \in 2^{\Omega(n)}$, *then the polynomial-time hierarchy is contained in* P^{NP}.

3.5.3 Rigid Matrices

Several researchers have studied the problem of finding explicit constructions of combinatorial objects that have been proven to exist non-constructively (by using the probabilistic method, for example). In many cases, an explicit construction of some combinatorial object yields an interesting complexity theoretic result. One of the notable examples of this is the problem of *matrix rigidity*. The rigidity of a matrix M over a ring S, denoted $R_M^S(r)$, is the minimum number of entries of M that must be changed to reduce its rank to r or below (an entry can be changed to any element of S). Valiant [136] proved that an explicit construction of an infinite family of highly rigid matrices yields a circuit lower bound.

Theorem 3.5.6 ([136]). *Let* $\epsilon, \delta > 0$ *be constants. For any positive integer* n, *let* M_n *be an* $n \times n$ *matrix over a ring* S_n. *If* $R_{M_n}^{S_n}(\epsilon n) \geqslant n^{1+\delta}$ *for infinitely many values of* n, *then the linear transformation defined by* M_n *cannot be computed by linear size, log-depth circuits consisting of gates computing binary linear operators on* S_n.

Valiant also proved that almost all matrices over an infinite field have rigidity $(n - r)^2$ and almost all matrices over a fixed finite field have rigidity $\Omega((n - r)^2 / \log n)$. The best known explicit constructions achieve rigidity $\Omega(n^2/r)$ over infinite fields [111, 114] and $\Omega(\frac{n^2}{r} \log(\frac{n}{r}))$ [55] over finite fields. These are not sufficient to obtain circuit lower bounds using Theorem 3.5.6. Under a hardness assumption, our derandomization technique will give an explicit construction to which Theorem 3.5.6 applies: a family of matrices M_n over $S_n = \mathbb{Z}_{p(n)}[x]$ such that $R_{M_n}^{S_n}(r) \in \Omega((n - r)^2 / \log n)$, where $p(n)$ is polynomially bounded.

We will use the following lemma, which follows directly from Valiant's paper [136].

Lemma 3.5.2 ([136]). *Let* S *be a ring with at least 2 elements, and* n *a positive integer. All but at most a* $\frac{1}{n}$ *fraction of the* $n \times n$ *matrices* M *over* S *satisfy*

$$R_M^S(r) \geqslant \frac{(n - r)^2 - 2n - 2\log n}{1 + 2\log n}. \tag{3.13}$$

We can use our technique to achieve the nonconstructive rigidity bounds by noticing that there exist polynomial-sized SAT-oracle circuits which can check if a matrix is rigid.

Theorem 3.5.7. *If there exists a Boolean function $f \in \mathsf{E}$ such that $C_f^{\mathrm{SAT}}(n) \in 2^{\Omega(n)}$, then given integers $n \geqslant 1$ and $p \geqslant 2$, we can construct in time polynomial in $n + \log p$ a list of $n \times n$ matrices M over $S = \mathbb{Z}_p$ most of which satisfy (3.13).*

Proof. Let ρ be a string of length $n^2 \cdot \lceil \log p \rceil$. We will view ρ as the concatenation of n^2 blocks of $\lceil \log p \rceil$ bits each. Let $F(\langle 1^n, p \rangle, \rho)$ denote the matrix whose ij-th entry is the $(n(i-1)+j)$-th block of ρ interpreted as a number in binary and taken modulo p. We define the predicate $\pi(\langle 1^n, p \rangle, \rho)$ to be true if $M = F(\langle 1^n, p \rangle, \rho)$ satisfies (3.13). Note that the latter is a coNP predicate: If (3.13) is violated for some r, we can guess modified values for fewer than the right-hand side of (3.13) many entries of M and verify that the rank of the modified matrix over S is at most r. So, we can decide π by one query to an oracle for SAT. Moreover, Lemma 3.5.2 states that for most sequences ρ, the predicate holds. By applying theorem 3.4.1 to (F, π) we obtain a pseudo-random generator which on most seeds outputs a matrix with the required rigidity property. Enumerating over all seeds gives us the desired list of matrices in polynomial time. $\qquad\square$

Now we need to combine this list of matrices into a single matrix with similarly high rigidity. We can do so by switching to the ring of univariate polynomials over $\mathbb{Z}_p$.

Lemma 3.5.3. *Given $n \times n$ matrices $M_0, M_1, \ldots, M_k$ over $\mathbb{Z}_p$ where p is a prime larger than k, we can construct in time polynomial in $n + k + \log p$ an $n \times n$ matrix N over $\mathbb{Z}_p[x]$ such that*

$$R_N^{\mathbb{Z}_p[x]}(r) \geqslant \max_{0 \leqslant i \leqslant k} R_{M_i}^{\mathbb{Z}_p}(r), \tag{3.14}$$

where the entries of N are polynomials of degree at most k.

Proof. Let $q_{ij}(x)$ be the polynomial of degree at most k such that $q_{ij}(\ell)$ equals the ij-th entry of M_ℓ, $0 \leqslant \ell \leqslant k$, i.e., q_{ij} interpolates the ij-th entries of all $k+1$ matrices. Note that the q_{ij}'s exist and that each coefficient can be computed in time polynomial in $k + \log p$. Let N be the matrix whose ij-th entry is q_{ij}. We now argue that (3.14) holds.

Let $m = R_N^{\mathbb{Z}_p[x]}(r)$, and let N' be a matrix obtained by changing m entries of N such that the rank of N' is at most r. Then every $(r+t) \times (r+t)$ minor of N' has determinant 0 for $0 < t \leqslant n - r$. Thus the determinant of any $(r+t) \times (r+t)$ minor of N' can be viewed as an identically 0 polynomial in its entries. Let $\phi_a(N')$ be the matrix obtained by substituting $a \in \mathbb{Z}_p$ for x in every entry of N' (recall N' has entries from $\mathbb{Z}_p[x]$). Every $(r+t) \times (r+t)$

minor of $\phi_a(N')$ has determinant 0 for $0 < t \leqslant n-r$. We conclude by noticing that changing m or fewer entries of $\phi_a(N)$ has reduced its rank to a value less than or equal to r. But $\phi_a(N)$ equals M_a for $a \in \{0, 1, \ldots, k\}$. Therefore, $R^{\mathbb{Z}_p}_{M_i}(r) \leqslant m$ for any $0 \leqslant i \leqslant k$, i.e., (3.14) holds.

Given this construction of rigid matrices we can conclude the following relationship among circuit lower bounds.

Theorem 3.5.8. *If there exists a function $f \in \mathsf{E}$ such that $C^{\mathrm{SAT}}_f(n) \in 2^{\Omega(n)}$ then there exists a polynomially bounded function $p(n)$ and a polynomial-time computable family $\{M_n\}_n$ of matrices where M_n is an $n \times n$ matrix over $\mathbb{Z}_{p(n)}[x]$ such that the linear transformation defined by M_n cannot be computed by log-depth linear size circuits which have special gates that can compute binary linear operators over $\mathbb{Z}_{p(n)}[x]$.*

Proof. For any polynomial time computable function $p(n)$, Theorem 3.5.7 allows us to efficiently compute a list of $(n + \log p(n))^c$ matrices M over $\mathbb{Z}_{p(n)}$ for some constant c, most of which are rigid. Provided $p(n)$ is a prime satisfying

$$p(n) \geqslant (n + \log p(n))^c, \tag{3.15}$$

Lemma 3.5.3 efficiently combines them into a single matrix N over $\mathbb{Z}_{p(n)}[x]$ which satisfies a rigidity condition sufficient for Theorem 3.5.6. The smallest prime value for $p(n)$ that satisfies (3.15) is polynomially bounded in n, and we can compute it in time polynomial in n.

3.5.4 Universal Traversal Sequences

Universal traversal sequences, introduced by Cook, form another example where explicit constructions have important complexity theoretic implications. A *universal traversal sequence* for size n is a sequence σ of labels from $\{1, 2, \ldots, n-1\}$ such that for any undirected connected graph G with n vertices in which the incident edges at every vertex have been assigned distinct labels from $\{1, 2, \ldots, n-1\}$, the following process always visits every vertex of G: Pick an arbitrary start vertex, and in subsequent steps, go along the edge with the label matching the next symbol of σ; in case of no match, stay put during that step and continue with the next symbol of σ.

If we can construct universal traversal sequences in logspace, then we can solve undirected graph connectivity in logspace, and symmetric logspace equals logspace [81]. However, we do not know how to generate universal traversal sequences in logspace or even in polynomial time. Aleliunas et al. [3] showed that most sequences of length $O(n^3)$ over $\{1, 2, \ldots, n-1\}$ are universal traversal sequences for size n, but as of now the best explicit construction, due to Nisan [101], yields universal traversal sequences of length $n^{O(\log n)}$. We give evidence supporting the belief that explicit universal traversal sequences of polynomial size can be generated efficiently.

A straightforward application of our technique would yield a polynomial-time construction under the assumption that E requires exponential size SAT-oracle circuits. Since being a universal traversal sequence is a coNP predicate, Theorem 3.4.1 applied to the Aleliunas et al. process and oracle $B = \text{SAT}$ would efficiently generate under that hypothesis a collection of sequences most of which are universal traversal sequences. Concatenating all of them would yield the desired universal traversal sequence of polynomial size. However, we can do better and dispense with the oracle B.

Theorem 3.5.9. *If there is a Boolean function $f \in E$ such that $C_f(n) \in 2^{\Omega(n)}$, then we can construct universal traversal sequences in polynomial time.*

Proof. Let G encode a graph with n vertices with edge labels as above. For any sequence σ over $\{1, 2, \ldots, n-1\}$, let $\tau(G, \sigma)$ indicate whether for every vertex v of G, the walk in G starting from v and dictated by σ visits every vertex of G. Let $F(G, \rho)$ denote the sequence of length $c \cdot n^3$ over $\{1, 2, \ldots, n-1\}$ (where c is some sufficiently large constant) as specified by the successive bits of ρ. Let $\pi(G, \rho)$ equal $\tau(G, F(G, \rho))$. Note that π is a P predicate, so $B = \varnothing$ can efficiently check the randomized process (F, π). Since every universal traversal sequence σ satisfies $\tau(G, \sigma)$, the result of Aleliunas et al. [3] shows that for any graph G, $\pi(G, \rho)$ holds for most ρ. Therefore, Theorem 3.4.1 allows us to generate in polynomial time a collection of sequences σ most of which satisfy $\tau(G, \sigma)$. Their concatenation forms a single sequence σ' satisfying $\tau(G, \sigma')$. Since the σ's are independent of G, so is their concatenation σ'. Hence, we have constructed a sequence σ' which satisfies $\tau(G, \sigma')$ for every edge labeled graph G with n vertices, i.e., we have found a universal traversal sequence σ'.

Under the stronger assumption that linear space requires exponential size circuits, we can actually construct universal traversal sequences in logspace. In fact, that assumption allows us to build logspace computable pseudo-random generators for logspace, and hence to derandomize BPL, the class of languages accepted by logspace randomized Turing machines with bounded two-sided error.

Theorem 3.5.10. *If there is a Boolean function $f \in \text{DSPACE}[n]$ such that $C_f(n) \in 2^{\Omega(n)}$, then $\text{BPL} = \text{L}$.*

We provide a proof below. Along the lines of Babai et al. [22], the pseudorandom generators behind Theorem 3.5.10 let us conclude:

Corollary 3.5.5. *If there is a Boolean function $f \in \text{DSPACE}[n]$ such that $C_f(n) \in 2^{\Omega(n)}$, then we can construct universal traversal sequences in logspace.*

Proof (of Theorem 3.5.10). In order to establish Theorem 3.5.10 it suffices to show the following: If the function f in Theorem 3.3.3 is in linear space, and

$\ell(n) \in \Theta(\log n)$, then we can make the pseudo-random generator G provided by Theorem 3.3.3 computable in linear space. This is because the seed length $s(n)$ of G in Theorem 3.3.3 is logarithmic for logarithmic $\ell(n)$.

The proof of Theorem 3.3.3 consists of two steps:

- Converting the worst-case hard function f into an average-case hard function g using Theorem 3.3.2.
- Applying Theorem 3.3.1 to the average-case hard function g to obtain the pseudo-random generator G.

First we argue that if the function f in Theorem 3.3.2 is in linear space then so is the function g. This is because the code $\mathcal{C}_{N,\epsilon}$ in Theorem 3.3.11 is actually computable in space $O(\log N + \log 1/\epsilon)$, as follows from a straightforward analysis of the paper by Sudan et al. [129].

We next apply Theorem 3.3.1 to the function g in order to obtain the pseudo-random generator G. Computing the ith bit of $G(\sigma)$ for $\sigma \in \{0,1\}^{s(n)}$ amounts to computing the set S_i of a $(\log n, \ell)$ design $\mathcal{S} = (S_1, S_2, \ldots, S_n)$ over $\{1, 2, \ldots, s(n)\}$, and evaluating g on input $\sigma|_{S_i}$. The latter can be done in space $O(s(n))$ since g is in linear space.

The greedy design construction of Lemma 3.3.2 requires too much space, namely $\Theta(n)$. However, the next lemma describes a different approach which only needs $O(s(n)) = O(\log n)$ space. The construction goes along the lines of Impagliazzo and Wigderson [69]. Allender informed us that Wigderson showed him the same construction [4]. For any $\ell(n) \in \Theta(\log n)$, it yields a $(\log n, \ell(n))$ design of size n^δ over $\{1, 2, \ldots, s(n)\}$ for some positive δ and $s(n) \in O(\log n)$. Note that this design is smaller than the one obtained through the greedy construction, which yields $\delta = 1$. However, designs of the former type are good enough for Theorem 3.3.10 (with appropriately modified parameters) and Theorem 3.3.1 to carry through. So, the next lemma finishes the proof of Theorem 3.5.10.

Lemma 3.5.4. *For any positive constant c, there are positive constants α and γ such that we can generate an $(\alpha s, c\alpha s)$ design of size $2^{\gamma s}$ over $\{1, 2, \ldots, s\}$ in space $O(s)$.*

Proof (of Lemma 3.5.4). We will show that the following process has a positive probability of generating an (m, ℓ) design of size $k \doteq 2^{\gamma s}$ over $\Omega = \{1, 2, \ldots, s\}$ for sufficiently small positive constants α and γ, where $m \doteq \alpha s$ and $\ell \doteq \beta s$ with $\beta \doteq c\alpha$: Pick k subsets of Ω of size ℓ in a pairwise independent way such that each of the $\binom{s}{\ell}$ subsets has about the same probability of being selected.

More precisely, we will do the following. We choose an integer $a \geqslant 0$ such that $2^a \leqslant k^3 \cdot \binom{s}{\ell} < 2^{a+1}$, pick k numbers $r_i \in \{0, 1, \ldots, 2^a - 1\}$ at random in a pairwise independent way, and set S_i to be the $[(r_i \bmod \binom{s}{\ell})+1]$-st subset of Ω of size ℓ (say using the lexicographical order). Known constructions of such sample spaces [45] only need $O(a)$ random bits and can generate the samples from the random bits in space $O(a)$. Moreover, checking whether a given sample $S_1, \ldots, S_k$ forms an (m, ℓ) design can be done within the same space bounds. Therefore, we can cycle through all possible random bit sequences, check the corresponding candidate design and output the first valid one. This process runs in space $O(a) = O(s)$, and succeeds provided the probability of picking a valid design this way is positive. The remainder of the proof will argue the latter.

Claim 3.5.1. Let S, S' be subsets of Ω of size ℓ chosen independently and uniformly at random. Then for some constant d_β,

$$\Pr\left[\|S \cap S'\| \geqslant 2\beta^2 s\right] \leqslant d_\beta \cdot s \cdot \exp\left(-\frac{\beta^4 s}{2}\right).$$

Proof. First consider a subset S of Ω obtained by doing the following independently for every $i \in \Omega$: Put i in S with probability β. Similarly, and independently, construct S'. Then, by Chernoff's bounds,

$$\Pr\left[\|S \cap S'\| \geqslant 2\beta^2 s\right] \leqslant \exp\left(-\frac{\beta^4 s}{2}\right).$$

Stirling's formula yields that

$$\Pr\left[\|S\| = \beta s\right] \sim \frac{1}{\sqrt{2\pi\beta(1-\beta)}} \cdot \frac{1}{\sqrt{s}}.$$

So,

$$\Pr\left[\|S \cap S'\| \geqslant 2\beta^2 s \mid \|S\| = \|S'\| = \beta s\right] \leqslant d_\beta \cdot s \cdot \exp\left(-\frac{\beta^4 s}{2}\right)$$

for some constant d_β depending on β. Since the above distribution of S and S' conditioned on $|S| = |S'| = \beta s$ coincides with the uniform distribution of the statement of the claim, this finishes the proof of Claim 3.5.1.

There is a constant $d < 2k^3$ such that for any $1 \leqslant i \leqslant k$ and any $T \subseteq \Omega$ with $\|T\| = \ell$,

$$\frac{d}{2^a} \leqslant \Pr[S_i = T] \leqslant \frac{d+1}{2^a}.$$

Because of the pairwise independence, it follows that for any $1 \leqslant i < j \leqslant k$, the distribution of (S_i, S_j) differs from uniform by at most

$$\binom{s}{\ell}^2 \cdot \left[(\frac{d+1}{2^a})^2 - (\frac{d}{2^a})^2\right] = (2d+1)\left(\frac{\binom{s}{\ell}}{2^a}\right)^2$$

$$< (2c+1)(\frac{2}{k^3})^2$$

$$< \frac{4(4k^3+1)}{k^6}$$

$$< \frac{17}{k^3}$$

in L_1-norm. Therefore, by Claim 3.5.1,

$$\Pr\left[\,\|S_i \cap S_j\| \geqslant 2\beta^2 s\,\right] \leqslant \frac{17}{k^3} + d_\beta \cdot s \cdot \exp\left(-\frac{\beta^4 s}{2}\right).$$

Recall that $m \doteq \alpha s$, $\ell \doteq \beta s$, and $\beta \doteq c\alpha$. Hence, for $\alpha \leqslant 1/(2c^2)$,

$$\Pr[S_1, S_2, \ldots, S_k \text{ is not an } (m, \ell) \text{ design}]$$
$$\leqslant \binom{k}{2} \cdot \left(\frac{17}{k^3} + d_\beta \cdot s \cdot \exp\left(-\frac{\beta^4 s}{2}\right)\right). \tag{3.16}$$

The right-hand side of (3.16) approaches 0 for $k = 2^{\gamma s}$ provided $0 < \gamma < \frac{\beta^4 \ln e}{4} = \frac{c^4 \alpha^4 \ln e}{4}$. This finishes the proof of Lemma 3.5.4.

3.6 Conclusion and Open Questions

In this chapter, we have demonstrated the power of relativization in the area of derandomization. We gave several examples, most notably Arthur-Merlin games, and are convinced that more will follow. Critical to our argument is the idea that the analyses of the Nisan-Wigderson generator and other constructions work for a large class of predicates and statistical tests – whenever the generator fails a statistical test, the computation of the predicate on which the generator is based reduces to the computation of the test. This idea lies at the heart of the recent extractor constructions by Trevisan [135]. In fact, Miltersen [98] explicitly delineates the role of relativization in these constructions.

The derandomization framework we presented is quite general. Finding other interesting applications merits some effort.

All our derandomization results use some complexity theoretic assumption. The weakest of our assumptions, e.g., that the polynomial-time hierarchy does not collapse, are widely accepted. The strongest ones, e.g., the existence of a Boolean function in E with circuit complexity $2^{\Omega(n)}$, are more contrived, especially when we allow the circuits access to an oracle for SAT. The validity of these assumptions requires further research. Because of Corollary 2.2.1, disproving them would separate P from NP.

4. Sparseness of Complete Languages

This chapter is the first one on our quest for structural properties that can distinguish between complexity classes: the existence of hard languages with low density. Our main result establishes the logical completeness of this approach for separating polynomial time from logarithmic space using reductions with a bounded number of queries. Similar techniques apply to various other complexity classes, in the deterministic as well as in the randomized setting.

4.1 Introduction

A language L is *sparse* if it contains at most a polynomial number of the exponentially many possible strings of each length. Formally, L is sparse if there exists a polynomial p such that the *census function* $c_L : \mathbb{N} \to \mathbb{N} : n \to \|L \cap \Sigma^{\leqslant n}\|$ satisfies $c_L(n) \leqslant p(n)$ for every integer $n \geqslant 0$.

Recently, complexity theorists made much progress on the sparse hard language problem for P, i.e., the question whether there are sparse hard languages for P under various logspace reducibilities. Ogihara [105] showed that the existence of a sparse hard language for P under logspace many-one reductions implies that $P \subseteq DSPACE[\log^2 n]$, and Cai and Sivakumar [42] subsequently proved that this hypothesis actually yields $P = L$. Cai, Naik and Sivakumar [41] next considered truth-table reductions. They argued that the existence of a sparse hard language for P under logspace bounded truth-table reductions implies $P = NC^2$ [40], but left the implication $P = L$ open. We establish here as our main result that this final collapse does follow:

Theorem 4.1.1 (Main Theorem). *There is no sparse hard language for* P *under logspace bounded truth-table reductions unless* $P = L$.

In order to situate the sparse hard language problem for P, let us first look at the analogous problem for NP.

4.1.1 The Sparse Hard Language Problem for NP

Researchers have spent considerable effort investigating whether there are sparse hard languages for NP under various polynomial-time reducibilities. Two major issues motivate them in doing so:

D. van Melkebeek: Randomness and Completeness in Computational Complexity, LNCS 1950, pp. 77–112, 2000.
© Springer-Verlag Berlin Heidelberg 2000

- A fundamental result by Meyer [25] states that the languages polynomial-time *Turing reducible* to sparse languages are precisely those that have polynomial-size (non-uniform) circuits. The same holds for truth-table reductions, i.e., Turing reductions with non-adaptive queries. Consequently, a sparse hard language for NP under polynomial-time Turing reductions exists iff a sparse hard language for NP under polynomial-time truth-table reductions exists iff every language in NP has polynomial-size circuits.
- Berman and Hartmanis [25] observed that all known languages complete for NP under polynomial-time *many-one reductions*, are polynomial-time isomorphic, i.e., there exist bijective polynomial-time-computable and polynomial-time-invertible many-one reductions between them. They conjectured that this property holds for all NP-complete languages. Since polynomial-time isomorphic languages have polynomially related densities, and the NP-complete language SAT has exponential density, the Berman-Hartmanis conjecture implies that there are no sparse complete languages for NP under polynomial-time many-one reductions.

Intermediate types of reductions, such as bounded truth-table reductions, also play an important role.

Note that if P = NP, sparse complete languages for NP obviously exist under any reasonable polynomial-time reducibility. In this respect, Mahaney [92] settled the problem for many-one reductions: There is no sparse hard language for NP under polynomial-time many-one reductions unless P = NP. It appears very difficult to prove that the same holds for Turing reductions, but Karp and Lipton [74] showed that the existence of a sparse hard language for NP under polynomial-time Turing reductions collapses the polynomial-time hierarchy to the second level. In bridging the gap between many-one reductions and Turing reductions, Ogiwara and Watanabe [107] obtained a breakthrough by extending Mahaney's theorem to bounded truth-table reductions: There is no sparse hard language for NP under polynomial-time bounded truth-table reductions unless P = NP.

Given this state of affairs, complexity theorists wondered whether randomization might help: They started investigating the existence of sparse hard languages for NP under randomized polynomial-time reductions.

Cai, Naik and Sivakumar [41] showed that there is no sparse hard language for NP under polynomial-time randomized two-sided error many-one reductions with confidence as small as inversely polynomial unless NP = RP. We prove as one of our results that the same holds for bounded truth-table reductions.

4.1.2 The Sparse Hard Language Problem for P

This chapter mainly deals with the sparse hard language problem for P: Are there sparse hard languages for P under logspace reducibilities? Similar considerations as for the sparse hard language problem for NP motivate this question:

– The languages that reduce to sparse languages under *Turing reductions* computable by logspace-uniform log-depth circuits are exactly those that have (non-uniform) polynomial-size log-depth circuits, and the same holds for truth-table reductions instead of Turing reductions.

– Based on the observation that all known languages complete for P under logspace *many-one reductions*, are in fact logspace isomorphic, Hartmanis [60] conjectured that all P-complete languages are logspace isomorphic. By the same token as above, since a P-complete language of exponential density exists, this implies that languages complete for P under logspace many-one reductions cannot be sparse.

As before, note that if P = L, sparse complete languages for P clearly exist under any reasonable logspace reducibility. Recently, Ogihara [105] made significant progress in showing this condition also necessary in the case of many-one reductions, and Cai and Sivakumar [42] actually proved it: There is no sparse hard language for P under logspace many-one reductions unless P = L. Cai, Naik and Sivakumar [41] then tried to extend this result to bounded truth-table reductions, and we establish this extension here: There is no sparse hard language for P under logspace bounded truth-table reductions unless P = L. We generalize this theorem and obtain new results for various sparseness conditions, space bounds and bounds on the number of queries of the truth-table reduction. However, the problem remains open for general logspace truth-table reductions, which are equivalent to logspace Turing reductions [79].

Regarding randomized reductions, Cai, Naik and Sivakumar [41] showed that there is no sparse hard language for P under logspace randomized two-sided error many-one reductions with confidence at least inversely polynomial unless all of P has randomized logspace algorithms with zero error, provided two-way read access to the random bit tape used. We establish that this theorem carries through for bounded truth-table reductions.

4.1.3 Overview of this Chapter

Section 4.2 deals with deterministic reductions. We first describe previous work and indicate how our results relate to it. Next we prove our Main Theorem that there is no sparse hard language for P under logspace bounded truth-table reductions unless P collapses to L. As in previous papers [105, 42, 41, 40], the proof structure parallels the one used by Ogiwara and Watanabe [107] for NP. We construct a space-efficient algorithm for the P-complete circuit value problem, based on the reduction of a well-chosen auxiliary language in P to a sparse language. We use the auxiliary language defined by Cai and Sivakumar [42], which encapsulates Reed-Solomon encodings [91] of the gate values of the circuits. The main ingredients of the algorithm are an NC^1 Vandermonde system solver [50] to recover the encoded gate values, and a novel combinatorial argument for exploiting sparseness. Similar to Cai and Sivakumar's construction, in case of reductions computable in NC^1, our algorithm for the circuit value problem is actually NC^1. We single out the crucial new way of exploiting the sparseness in a separate Combinatorial Lemma, and also consider some consequences of the Main Theorem for complexity classes above P.

Then we generalize our Main Theorem and obtain an analogue for P of Homer and Longpré's result [65] for NP. The generalization parameterizes the sparseness condition, the space bound and the bound on the number of queries of the truth-table reduction. Another instantiation of this Generic Theorem yields that that there is no quasipolynomially dense hard language for P under polylog-space truth-table reductions using polylogarithmically many queries unless P is in polylog-space.

Finally, we apply the proof technique to NL and L, as Cai and Sivakumar [43] did for their results. This shows that there is no sparse hard language for NL under logspace bounded truth-table reductions unless NL = L, and that there is no sparse hard language for L under NC^1-computable bounded truth-table reductions unless $L = NC^1$.

Section 4.3 presents our results on randomized reductions with two-sided error. We start off again with a description of earlier work. Then we establish an analogue of our Main Theorem for such randomized reductions with confidence at least inversely polynomial: There is no sparse hard language for P under randomized two-sided error bounded truth-table reductions computable in logspace and with confidence at least inversely polynomial unless P is in randomized logspace, provided two-way read access to the random tape. This extends a result by Cai, Naik and Sivakumar [41] for many-one reductions. As in that paper, the proof uses the Hadamard encoding [91] of gate assignments of circuits defined by Ogihara [105] to construct an auxiliary language. Instead of the Vandermonde system solver in the deterministic case, we apply Goldreich and Levin's algorithm [56] to recover the encoded gate values, and combine it with a modified version of our Combinatorial Lemma.

Next we parameterize the Randomized Main Theorem in the same vein as the deterministic Main Theorem. The resulting Randomized Generic Theorem also yields that there is no quasipolynomially dense hard language for P under randomized two-sided error polylog-space truth-table reductions with confidence at least inversely quasipolynomial and making polylogarithmically many queries unless P is in randomized polylog-space, again using two-way read access to the random tape.

Finally, we apply the same technique to complexity classes other than P. As in the deterministic case, we obtain results for NL and L. Moreover, in the randomized case we can also apply our construction to NP by virtue of Valiant and Vazirani's reduction [137], as Cai, Naik and Sivakumar [41] showed for many-one reductions: There is no sparse hard language for NP under randomized two-sided error polynomial-time bounded truth-table reductions with confidence at least inversely polynomial unless NP = RP.

We conclude this chapter by mentioning possible directions for further research in Section 4.4.

4.2 Deterministic Reductions

We start off with an overview of previous work, and describe how our results evolve from it. The reader can skip this subsection without loss of continuity. Then we prove our Main Theorem, which we next parameterize to a Generic Theorem for P. Finally, we apply the same technique to the sparse hard language problem for NL and L.

Throughout this section, we will make frequent use of finite fields. For any integer $b \geqslant 1$, $GF(2^b)$ denotes the finite field with 2^b elements. It can be defined as the set of equivalence classes of polynomials over $GF(2)$ modulo an irreducible polynomial $f(x)$ of degree b over $GF(2)$. Consequently, its elements can be represented as polynomials of degree less than b over $GF(2)$. For $b \in \{2 \cdot 3^t \mid t \in \mathbb{N}\}$, $f(x) = x^b + x^{b/2} + 1$ is irreducible over $GF(2)$ [82], and we will use this polynomial to construct $GF(2^b)$ for such b's.

4.2.1 Previous Work

The proofs of results on the sparse hard language problem for NP usually go by constructing in polynomial-time a language of assignments to the variables of a given formula that contains at least one satisfying assignment in case of a satisfiable formula. Since we can check the validity of an assignment in polynomial-time, this yields a polynomial-time algorithm for the NP-complete problem SAT, which shows that P = NP. For the sparse hard language problem for P, we can use a similar approach based on the P-completeness of CVP. In this case we use gate assignments as membership witnesses which we can check for validity in logspace. So, using the reduction of some language(s) A in P to a sparse language S, we have to construct within the given resource bounds a set of gate assignments which contains the correct one for the given input. We will call such a set a witness set.

Much of the progress on this kind of problems relies on an appropriate choice of A. Ogihara [105] considered the language

$$A_1 = \{\langle C, x, y, a \rangle \mid C \text{ circuit with } |x| \text{ inputs}, x \in \Sigma^*, y \in \Sigma^m, a \in \Sigma$$
$$\text{and } \oplus_{y_j=1} g_j = a\}, \tag{4.1}$$

where m is the number of gates of C, $g_1, \ldots, g_m$ denote the gate values of C on input x, and $\oplus$ symbols exclusive or. This language is in P and has the following simple, but interesting properties: Let f be a many-one reduction of A_1 to a language S.

Property 4.2.1. If $f(\langle C, x, y, a \rangle) \in S$, then

$$\oplus_{y_j=1} g_j = a. \tag{4.2}$$

Property 4.2.2. For any syntactically correct $\langle C, x, y \rangle$, one of $f(\langle C, x, y, 0 \rangle)$ and $f(\langle C, x, y, 1 \rangle)$ is in S.

If S is sparse, for any fixed instance $\langle C, x \rangle$ of CVP, Property 4.2.2 guarantees the existence of a string $w = f(\langle C, x, y^*, a^* \rangle) \in S$ to which many $(y, a) \in \Sigma^m \times \Sigma$ are mapped by f, so that according to Property 4.2.1

$$\oplus_{y_j = 1} g_j = \oplus_{y_j^* = 1} g_j \oplus a^* \oplus a. \tag{4.3}$$

This equation actually also holds if $w \notin S$. In any case, if $y \neq y^*$, it allows to express one of the gate values as the parity of some other gate values.

Based on this observation, Ogihara managed to transform using $O \log^2 n)$ space each of the gates of the given circuit C into parity gates with the same values for the given input x, except for an $O(\log n)$ sized subset G of the gates. Since the circuit value problem for parity circuits is in DSPACE$[\log^2 n]$, it suffices to cycle through all possible assignments to the $O(\log n)$ gates in G to construct a DSPACE$[\log^2 n]$ enumerable witness set for CVP. A DSPACE$[\log^2 n]$ algorithm for CVP follows.

Cai and Sivakumar [42] also used the language A_1, but viewed (4.2) as the linear equation

$$\sum_{j=1}^{m} y_j g_j = a \tag{4.4}$$

over GF(2) in the gate values $g_1, \ldots, g_m$. Their algorithm tried to set up a system of such equations of rank $m - O(\log m)$, which allowed them to obtain a witness set for CVP in NC^2 based on the following facts:

Fact 4.2.1. The rank of a matrix can be determined in arithmetic NC^2 [99].

Fact 4.2.2. A square system of linear equations of full rank can be solved in arithmetic NC^2 [29].

Note that when working over GF(2), arithmetic NC^2 is equivalent to its Boolean counterpart.

Using Fact 4.2.1, given a system of equations of rank $m - O(\log m)$ over GF(2) in the gate values, Cai and Sivakumar construct in NC^2 a subset of these equations and an $O(\log m)$ sized subset G of the gates, such that the resulting system in the other gate values is square and of full rank. The application of Fact 4.2.2 to these systems for all possible assignments to the $O(\log m)$ gates in G in parallel, results in an NC^2 witness set for CVP. They show that the system consisting of all equations over GF(2) corresponding to (4.3) for $(y, a), (y^*, a^*) \in Y \subseteq \Sigma^m \times \Sigma$ for which $f(\langle C, x, y, a \rangle) = f(\langle C, x, y^*, a^* \rangle)$, has rank $m - O(\log m)$ with high probability, if Y is a polynomial sized uniform sample from $\Sigma^m \times \Sigma$. This yields an ZPNC^2 algorithm for CVP.

Next they prove that the rank of this system is always $m - O(\log m)$, if $Y = D \times \Sigma$ with D the following "small-bias sample space" [100, 6]:

$$D = \{(\prec u^i, v \succ)_{i=0}^{m-1} \mid u, v \in \mathrm{GF}(2^b)\}, \tag{4.5}$$

where $b \in \{2 \cdot 3^t \mid t \in \mathbb{N}\}$ with $b \in O(\log m)$, and $\prec \cdot, \cdot \succ$ represents the standard inner product of the vector space $\mathrm{GF}(2^b)$ over $\mathrm{GF}(2)$. This way, they effectively derandomize their ZPNC^2 algorithm to obtain an NC^2 procedure for CVP.

Finally, probably inspired by the construction of the sample space D used in the derandomization, Cai and Sivakumar considered the language

$$A_2 = \{\langle C, x, u, v \rangle \mid C \text{ circuit with } |x| \text{ inputs, } x \in \Sigma^*, u, v \in \mathrm{GF}(2^b)$$

$$\text{for some } b \in \{2 \cdot 3^t \mid t \in \mathbb{N}\} \text{ and } \sum_{j=1}^{m} u^{j-1} g_j = v\}, \tag{4.6}$$

where m again denotes the number of gates of C, and $g_1, \ldots, g_m$ the gate values of C on input x. This language also is in P and has the following properties similar to A_1: Let f be a many-one reduction of A_2 to a language S.

Property 4.2.3. If $f(\langle C, x, u, v \rangle) \in S$, then

$$\sum_{j=1}^{m} u^{j-1} g_j = v. \tag{4.7}$$

Property 4.2.4. For any syntactically correct $\langle C, x, u \rangle$ where $u \in \mathrm{GF}(2^b)$, there is (exactly) one $v \in \mathrm{GF}(2^b)$ such that $f(\langle C, x, u, v \rangle) \in S$.

For fixed $\langle C, x \rangle$, we say that $\langle u, v \rangle$ generates equation (4.7). The equations that result from Property 4.2.3 form a Vandermonde system, which is particularly interesting because we can determine the rank of and solve Vandermonde systems in NC^1 [50]. If b is sufficiently large, Property 4.2.4 guarantees that for at least one pair $(u^*, v^*) \in \mathrm{GF}(2^b) \times \mathrm{GF}(2^b)$ the set

$$E(u^*, v^*) \doteq \{(u, v) \in \mathrm{GF}(2^b) \times \mathrm{GF}(2^b) \mid f(\langle C, x, u, v \rangle) = w\}$$

contains at least m pairs, where $w \doteq f(\langle C, x, u^*, v^* \rangle) \in S$. Hence, it contains only generators of correct equations, and these equations form a Vandermonde system of full column rank m. If S is sparse, $b \in \Omega(\log m)$ suffices. So, the solutions to an $m \times m$ system generated by $E(u^*, v^*)$ for all possible pairs $(u^*, v^*) \in \mathrm{GF}(2^b) \times \mathrm{GF}(2^b)$ form a witness set for CVP with complexity NC^1 modulo the complexity of the reduction, and complexity L if we take the logspace complexity of the reduction into account. The corresponding circuit for CVP is sketched in Figure 4.1, where E_j denotes the set $E(u^*, v^*)$ for the j-th pair (u^*, v^*). This way, Cai and Sivakumar proved that the existence of a sparse hard language for P under logspace many-one reductions implies that CVP $\in$ L. We will use the same scheme to prove that proposition for logspace bounded truth-table reductions, that is: Construct a logspace algorithm for CVP with the structure outlined in Figure 4.1 using a logspace bounded truth-table reduction of A_2 to a sparse language S.

When assuming the existence of a k-truth-table reduction of A_1 or A_2 to a language S, there is no analogue of Properties 2 and 4, i.e., we cannot guarantee that many of the queries belong to S, and hence, if S is sparse, many map to the same query (in S). However, for the case of a reduction from A_1, Cai, Naik and Sivakumar [41] made (a slightly weaker version of) the following observation: Let Y be any subset of $\Sigma^m \times \Sigma$.

- Either there is a popular query, i.e., a string w that the reduction queries for many inputs $\langle C, x, y, a \rangle$ where (y, a) ranges over Y. In that case, we can reduce the problem to one involving a $(k-1)$-truth-table reduction by restricting the inputs to the ones for which the reduction queries w, and assuming both $w \in S$ and $w \notin S$ in parallel. Since many pairs (y, a) in Y map to w, this restriction does not decrease the number of pairs (y, a) by too much, and in one of the parallel executions, the assumption we make is correct.
- Either there are no popular queries, i.e., for any string w there are no more than say p pairs $(y, a) \in Y$ for which the reduction queries w on input $\langle C, x, y, a \rangle$. If s is a bound on the length of the queries, this implies that there are at most $c_S(s) \cdot p$ pairs (y, a) in Y for which some queries belong to S. Hence, if we partition Y into $c_S(s) \cdot p + 1$ classes of equal size (± 1), then for at least one class the assumption that all queries made are outside of S is correct, and that class contains at least $\lfloor \frac{\|Y\|}{c_S(s) \cdot p + 1} \rfloor$ pairs. All classes can be processed in parallel, and provided $c_S(s) \cdot p$ is not too large compared to $\|Y\|$, once again, we end up with large subclasses Y' of Y for at least one of which we make correct assumptions.

Cai, Naik and Sivakumar then showed that for a sufficiently large uniform sample Y of $\Sigma^m \times \Sigma$, with high probability, for every large subset Y' of Y the system of equations

$$\sum_{j=1}^{m} y_j g_j = a + \chi_{A_1}(\langle C, x, y, a \rangle) + 1, \tag{4.8}$$

where (y, a) ranges over Y', has high rank. Note that equation (4.8) is always correct, even if $\langle C, x, y, a \rangle \notin A_1$, because we are working over GF(2). We can compute the right-hand side of (4.8) using our assumptions about the membership to S of the queries, provided these assumptions are correct. By the above procedure we can construct in NC^1 a class of large subsets Y' for at least one of which all our assumptions about the membership queries are right. Cai, Naik and Sivakumar proved that a polynomial sized sample Y suffices to obtain rank $m - O(\log m)$ with high probability, so the same strategy as discussed above for many-one reductions allowed them to solve CVP in ZPNC^2.

If we want to apply this idea using a bounded truth-table reduction from A_2 instead of from A_1, there is an additional difficulty related to the fact that we are no longer computing over GF(2). In the case of A_1, for every (y, a)

for which the memberships to S of the truth-table queries are known, we can construct a correct equation (4.8), even if the reduction rejects. For A_2 on the other hand, this is only the case for generators (u, v) of *correct* equations, i.e., when the reduction accepts, and this only happens for a small fraction of the generators. The reduction rejecting tells us that our guess for the right-hand side is wrong, but unlike when working over GF(2), that knowledge does not suffice to deduce the correct value of the right-hand side.

So, we have to restrict our attention to the set of generators (u, v) for which the reduction accepts. If there is a query that is popular among generators of correct equations, we can reduce the problem as above. However, there is a complication in the other case. In considering only the set G of generators for which the reduction accepts assuming all queries outside of S, we exclude at most $c_S(s) \cdot p$ of the generators of correct equations, so that should not be a problem. But there can be a lot of generators of incorrect equations in G for which not all queries are outside of S, because the bound p only holds for generators of correct equations. Therefore, we cannot tightly bound the number of generators in G for which we erroneously assume the reduction only queries strings outside of S. So, we cannot use the idea of partitioning G into subsets of equal size, at least one of which only contains generators all of whose queries are outside of S, since the resulting subsets would have to be too small. We will solve this problem by using variable sized subsets of a particular kind obtained by considering *intervals* of allowable queries.

For the sake of completeness of the overview, we mention the result by Cai, Naik and Sivakumar [41, 40] that the existence of a sparse hard language for P under logspace bounded truth-table reductions implies that $P \subseteq NC^2$. They use a reduction from A_1 for all elements of the set D defined by equation (4.5) and certain error-correcting capabilities of this small-bias sample space. This allows them to distill out of the equations (4.4) for all $(y, a) \in D \times \Sigma$ for which the reduction accepts assuming all queries outside of S, a correct full rank Vandermonde system over GF(2^b) in the gate values, provided the assumption does not introduce too many false equations of the form (4.4). They show that if it does, the NC^2 approach of Cai and Sivakumar [42] works. However, our work does not build upon this construction.

4.2.2 Main Result

In this subsection, we establish our Main Theorem. The proof will rely on a Combinatorial Lemma indicating how in general a space efficient reduction to a sparse language can be exploited, and on a known algorithm to solve Vandermonde systems of equations [50]. We will first prove the Main Theorem, and then the Combinatorial Lemma. We will also sketch the Vandermonde system solver. Finally, we will mention some consequences of the Main Theorem for complexity classes above P.

Proof of the Main Theorem. Assuming the existence of a sparse hard language for P under logspace bounded truth-table reductions, we will show how to decide in logspace the P-complete language CVP.

A useful aspect of CVP in this context is that it has natural logspace verifiable membership proofs: Gate assignments can be checked for validity in logspace. One way of solving CVP consists of cycling through all possible gate assignments and checking each of them for validity. In general this approach does not yield a logspace algorithm, because generating all gate assignments requires linear space, but the bounded truth-table reducibility of P to a sparse language will allow us to reduce the search space to a subset we can generate in logspace.

In order to do so, we consider the auxiliary language A_2 defined by Cai and Sivakumar [42]:

$$A_2 = \{\langle C, x, u, v\rangle \,|\, C \text{ circuit with } |x| \text{ inputs}, x \in \Sigma^*, u, v \in \mathrm{GF}(2^b)$$

$$\text{for some } b \in \{2 \cdot 3^t \,|\, t \in \mathbb{N}\} \text{ and } \sum_{j=1}^{m} u^{j-1} g_j = v\}, \tag{4.9}$$

where $g_1, \ldots, g_m$ denote the gate values of C on input x. For any instance $y \doteq \langle C, x\rangle$ of CVP with m gates, and any $b \in \{2 \cdot 3^t \,|\, t \in \mathbb{N}\}$, A_2 contains a Reed-Solomon encoding [91] of the gate assignment of C on input x, which has the following property: The knowledge of m pairs $(u, v) \in \mathrm{GF}(2^b) \times \mathrm{GF}(2^b)$ such that $\langle C, x, u, v\rangle \in A_2$ enables us to recover the gate assignment as the solution of the $m \times m$ Vandermonde system $\Sigma_{j=1}^{m} u^{j-1} g_j = v$. Provided m divides $2^b - 1$, we can solve such systems in space $O(b)$ using the algorithm described by Eberly [50], which we will sketch in Section 4.2.2.

Lemma 4.2.1. *Given an irreducible polynomial $f(x)$ of degree b over $\mathrm{GF}(2)$ defining $\mathrm{GF}(2^b)$, an $n \times n$ full rank Vandermonde system over $\mathrm{GF}(2^b)$ can be solved by* DSPACE$[b]$ *uniform circuits of depth $O(b)$, provided $n|(2^b - 1)$.*

Note that we use $f(x) = x^b + x^{b/2} + 1$ as the irreducible polynomial over $\mathrm{GF}(2)$ defining $\mathrm{GF}(2^b)$.

So, ignoring for a second the condition that m divides $2^b - 1$, we are done if, for a given instance y of CVP, we can generate in logspace a collection of sets at least one of which is a subset of $A_2 \cap D(y)$ of size at least m, where $D(y) \doteq \{\langle y, u, v\rangle | u, v \in \mathrm{GF}(2^{b(y)})\}$ for some function $b : \Sigma^* \to \mathbb{N}$ such that $b(y) \in O(\log |y|)$. Observe that $||A_2 \cap D(y)|| = 2^{b(y)}$.

The next Combinatorial Lemma allows us to do that. We will prove the lemma in Section 4.2.2. It uses the following terminology. We say that a set system $D : \Sigma^* \to 2^{\Sigma^*}$ can be generated in space $s(n)$ if there is a Turing machine that on input $y \in \Sigma^n$ enumerates the elements of $D(y)$ using work space $s(n)$.

Lemma 4.2.2 (Combinatorial Lemma). *Let A be logspace k-truth-table reducible to a sparse language S for some $k \in \mathbb{N}$, and let $D : \Sigma^* \to 2^{\Sigma^*}$*

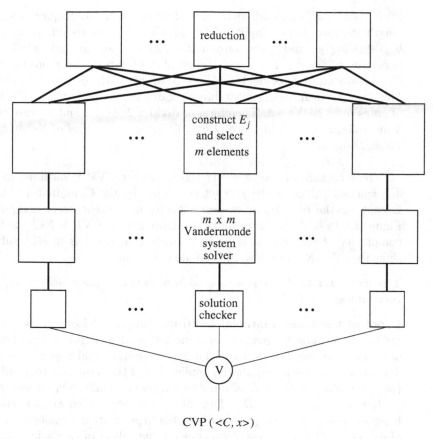

Fig. 4.1. Structure of an algorithm for the circuit value problem

be a set system that can be generated in logspace. Suppose that the reduction queries strings of length at most $s(n)$ on inputs of $D(y)$ for $y \in \Sigma^n$. Then there is a logspace algorithm that on input $y \in \Sigma^n$ generates a collection of subsets of $D(y)$ at least one of which is a subset of A of size at least

$$\frac{\|A \cap D(y)\|}{e \cdot (c_S(s(n)) + 1)^k},\tag{4.10}$$

where e denotes the base of the natural logarithm.

We can apply this lemma to the language A_2 defined by (4.9), since A_2 belongs to P, whence by hypothesis logspace k-truth-table reduces to a sparse language S for some $k \in \mathbb{N}$. To prove A_2 in P, we use the fact that we constructed $\mathrm{GF}(2^b)$ based on the explicit irreducible polynomial $f(x) = x^b + x^{b/2} + 1$, which allows us to perform all arithmetic in polynomial-time. There are functions $b : \Sigma^* \to \{2 \cdot 3^t \mid t \in \mathbb{N}\}$ and $s : \mathbb{N} \to \mathbb{N}$ such that $\|A_2 \cap D(y)\| = 2^{b(y)} \geqslant (2^{b(y)/2} - 1) \cdot e \cdot (c_S(s(n)) + 1)^k$, and

$2^{b(y)/2} - 1 \geqslant n$, and such that the reduction of A_2 to S queries strings of length at most $s(n)$ on inputs of $D(y)$ for $y \in \Sigma^n$. Moreover, we can choose $b(y) \in O(\log|y|)$ and space constructible, so that we can generate D in logspace. Since $2^{b(y)/2} - 1 \geqslant n$ and the number of gates is no more than n, the Combinatorial Lemma yields a collection of sets with the properties we need. Moreover, by introducing extra dummy gates we can assume that the number of gates $m = 2^{b(y)/2} - 1$. Therefore, m divides $2^{b(y)} - 1$ and we can solve the Vandermonde system in space $O(b) \subseteq O(\log|y|)$.   (End of the proof of the Main Theorem.)

The structure of the resulting algorithm for CVP is outlined in Figure 4.1, where E_j denotes the j-th set generated by the Combinatorial Lemma. Except for the reductions, we can actually implement every component of Figure 4.1 in NC^1, implying that our algorithm for CVP is NC^1 modulo the complexity of the reduction. Since proving that CVP is in NC^1 suffices to show that $\mathsf{P} = \mathsf{NC}^1$, we obtain the following result.

Theorem 4.2.1. *There is no sparse hard language for* P *under* $\leqslant_{\mathrm{btt}}^{\mathsf{NC}^1}$*-reductions unless* $\mathsf{P} = \mathsf{NC}^1$*.*

Proof of the Combinatorial Lemma. Suppose A logspace k-truth-table reduces to a sparse language S for some $k \in \mathbb{N}$. Drawing meaningful conclusions about membership to A based only on a polynomial upper bound on the density of S, seems to require the application of the reduction to a sufficiently (polynomially) large set D of inputs with polynomially related lengths.

If we do that for a set $D \doteq D(y)$ of a set system which we can generate in logspace, and $A \cap D$ is large, we will be able to generate in logspace a collection of subsets of D at least one of which is a large subset of A. Basically, in order to obtain that subset, we will cycle through elements of D and try to use the logspace reduction to determine membership of these elements to A. The only problem is that we do not know the membership to S of the queries the reduction makes. Therefore, we will try to find a large subset of $A \cap D$ for which we can guess the membership to S of the queries the reduction makes on its elements. More specifically, we will consider a set of RA-pairs, i.e., pairs of restrictions of D and corresponding assumptions about membership to S of the queries the reduction makes on inputs from D satisfying the restriction, such that the following conditions hold:

1. Given an RA-pair, we can check in logspace whether a given element of D satisfies the restriction, and determine the membership bits of the queries made by the reduction on that element, as implied by the assumption.
2. We can generate in logspace the set of all RA-pairs.
3. For at least one RA-pair, the membership bits implied by the assumption are correct for all inputs from D satisfying the restriction, and many inputs from $A \cap D$ satisfy the restriction.

Clearly, we reach our goal if we manage to meet these conditions: Cycle through the set of RA-pairs, and for each of them, output the corresponding subset of D by cycling through the elements of D and checking whether it satisfies the restriction and whether the reduction accepts it using the membership bits implied by the assumption.

In order to obtain such a collection of RA-pairs, consider the set $Q(D)$ of all queries the reduction makes on inputs belonging to D. The set S partitions $Q(D) \setminus S$ into a polynomial number of intervals. See Figure 4.2.

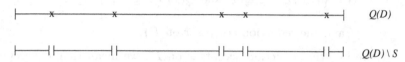

Fig. 4.2. How S partitions $Q(D) \setminus S$

If none of the strings in S is queried for many inputs in $A \cap D$, then, S being sparse and $A \cap D$ large, a lot of inputs in $A \cap D$ must have all of their queries outside of S. Since each of these inputs maps to at most k intervals of $Q(D) \setminus S$ and the number of k-subsets of intervals is polynomial, at least one subset of k intervals must contain in its union all queries of a polynomial fraction of those inputs in $A \cap D$ that have all their queries outside of S. So, the restriction of D to inputs for which the reduction only queries strings in the union of these k intervals, together with the assumption that all queries are outside of S, forms an RA-pair satisfying condition 3 (using an appropriate interpretation of "many" in this condition). The set of RA-pairs of this type, ranging over all k-subsets of intervals of $Q(D)$, clearly meets condition 1, and also condition 2, because we can generate the intervals of $Q(D)$ in logspace by cycling through all pairs of points of $Q(D)$.

In case there are popular queries in S, i.e., some strings in S are queried for many inputs in $A \cap D$, we can first restrict our attention to the inputs in D for which the reduction queries all strings in a maximal set P of jointly popular queries in S. The queries in P being jointly popular, this restriction does not reduce the size of $A \cap D$ by too much (second part of condition 3). Then we are left with a $(k - \|P\|)$-truth-table reduction to S without popular queries, so we can apply the procedure described in the previous paragraph. Since a set P of jointly popular queries necessarily is a subset of the queries made on some input of D, we can generate all possible P's in logspace by cycling through all points in D and, for each of them, through all (nonempty) subsets of the queries the reduction makes. So, with the associated assumption that all queries in P are in S, condition 2 is met. Conditions 1 and 3 are clearly also satisfied.

The resulting combined RA-pairs we consider are parameterized by a (possibly empty) subset P of queries the reduction makes on some input of D, and a subset of $k - ||P||$ intervals $I_1, \ldots, I_{k-||P||}$ of $Q(D)$. The corresponding restriction G' of D is

$$G' = \{x \in D \mid P \subseteq Q(x) \text{ and } Q(x) \setminus P \subseteq \bigcup_{i=1}^{k-||P||} I_i\}, \tag{4.11}$$

and the associated assumption is that $Q(x) \cap S = P$ for $x \in G'$. The subset G of D generated by this RA-pair is

$$G = \{x \in D \mid P \subseteq Q(x) \text{ and } Q(x) \setminus P \subseteq \bigcup_{i=1}^{k-||P||} I_i$$

and the reduction accepts x on $P\}$,

where by "the reduction accepts x on P" we mean that it accepts x when using P instead of S to answer membership queries about S. It follows from the foregoing discussion that these RA-pairs satisfy all 3 conditions we needed.

We now quantify the above argument.

Proof (of the Combinatorial Lemma). For any $n \in \mathbb{N}$ and $y \in \Sigma^n$, we will establish the existence of a set G' of type (4.11) with $P \subseteq S$ and the intervals I_i disjoint from S, for which $||A \cap G'||$ has the required size (4.10). We already argued that this suffices to prove the lemma.

Let $Q(x)$ denote the set of queries that the reduction makes on input x, D denote $D(y)$, $Q(D)$ the set of all queries on inputs $x \in D$, and d the bound (4.10).

Given any function $p : \{0, \ldots, k+1\} \to [0, \infty)$, it is obvious that there is a set $P \subseteq S$ such that:

$$||\{x \in A \cap D \mid P \subseteq Q(x)\}|| \geqslant p(||P||) \tag{4.12a}$$

$$(\forall w \in S \setminus P) \, ||\{x \in A \cap D \mid P \cup \{w\} \subseteq Q(x)\}|| \leqslant p(||P|| + 1), \tag{4.12b}$$

provided that $p(0) \leqslant ||A \cap D||$ and we set $p(k+1) = 0$. The function p describes a popularity criterion, and the set P represents a maximal subset of jointly popular queries in S with respect to p. We will determine p later on, once we know all properties we need of it, and it will become clear then why we allow p to have real non-integral values (because d is non-integral). Note that the range of $||P||$ is $\{0, \ldots, k\}$.

Consider the set of inputs $G'' = \{x \in A \cap D \mid Q(x) \cap S = P\}$.

Claim 4.2.1. $||G''|| \geqslant p(||P||) - c_S(s(n)) \cdot p(||P|| + 1)$.

Indeed, the set G'' contains all elements of the set on the left-hand side of (4.12a), except for those that have at least one query in $S \setminus P$. Because of (4.12b) the number of exceptions is bounded by $c_S(s(n)) \cdot p(||P|| + 1)$.

Claim 4.2.2. There are intervals $I_1, \ldots, I_{k-||P||}$ of $Q(D) \setminus S$ such that:

$$||\{x \in G'' | Q(x) \setminus P \subseteq \bigcup_{i=1}^{k-||P||} I_i\}|| \geq \frac{||G''||}{\max(1, \binom{c_S(s(n))+1}{k-||P||})}.$$

This is because S partitions $Q(D) \setminus S$ in at most $c_S(s(n)) + 1$ intervals (see Figure 4.2), and for each $x \in G''$, $Q(x) \setminus P$ is in the union of at most $k - ||P||$ of these intervals.

The combination of Claims 4.2.1 and 4.2.2 yields that the set G' defined by (4.11) satisfies

$$||A \cap G'|| \geq \frac{p(||P||) - c_S(s(n)) \cdot p(||P|| + 1)}{\max(1, \binom{c_S(s(n))+1}{k-||P||})},$$

which is at least d, provided that for $i \in \{0, \ldots, k\}$

$$\frac{p(i) - c_S(s(n)) \cdot p(i+1)}{\max(1, \binom{c_S(s(n))+1}{k-i})} \geq d.$$

It is straightforward to check that the function

$$p(i) = d \cdot \sum_{j=0}^{k-i} (c_S(s(n)) + 1)^{k-i-j} \binom{c_S(s(n)) + 1}{j}$$

satisfies these conditions. The upper bound for $p(0)$ is also met, since $p(0) \leq d \cdot (c_S(s(n)) + 1)^k \cdot \sum_{j=0}^{k} \frac{1}{j!} \leq ||A \cap D||$. The existence of p concludes the proof of the lemma.

Solving Vandermonde systems in NC^1. The fact that we can solve Vandermonde systems over finite fields in NC^1 forms a cornerstone of our deterministic constructions. We sketch a proof here and refer to the paper by Eberly [50] for the details. We do the analysis only for finite fields of characteristic 2, because that is what we need in the proof of our Main Theorem, but the extension to other characteristics is straightforward.

Proof (of Lemma 4.2.1). Solving the Vandermonde system $\sum_{j=1}^{n} c_j x_i^{j-1} = y_i$ for $i = 1, \ldots, n$ in $c_1, \ldots, c_n$ over $GF(2^b)$ amounts to finding the coefficients of the polynomial $p(x) = \sum_{j=1}^{n} c_j x^{j-1} \in GF(2^b)[x]$ interpolating the points (x_i, y_i), $i = 1, \ldots, n$. Lagrange's formula states that

$$p(x) = \sum_{i=1}^{n} y_i \cdot \prod_{k \neq i} \frac{x - x_k}{x_i - x_k}.$$

Since n divides $2^b - 1$, $GF(2^b)$ contains a primitive n-th root ω of unity. We can determine the coefficients of p by evaluating $p(\omega^i)$ for $i = 0, \ldots, n-1$, and then applying the discrete Fourier transform with base ω^{-1}:

$$c_j = \sum_{i=0}^{n-1} \omega^{-(j-1)i} p(\omega^i). \tag{4.13}$$

Using a representation of elements of $GF(2^b)$ as b-dimensional vectors over $GF(2)$, we can add r elements with $\mathsf{DSPACE}[\log b + \log r]$ uniform circuits of depth $O(\log r)$. Using the representation of nonzero elements of $GF(2^b)$ as powers of ω, we can multiply r elements with $\mathsf{DSPACE}[\log b + \log r]$ uniform circuits of depth $O(\log b + \log r)$. A careful analysis of the resulting circuit to evaluate equation (4.13) using Lagrange's formula to compute the values $p(\omega^i)$ for $i = 0, \ldots, n-1$, shows that we only have to perform such additions and multiplications of $r \in O(n)$ elements, and hence transitions between the two representations, a constant number of times along each path of the circuit. We can hardwire the transformations between the two representations in circuits of depth $O(b)$. The space we need to generate a primitive n-th root ω and to compute these transformation circuits is $O(b)$. Therefore, the resulting circuit for solving the $n \times n$ Vandermonde system over $GF(2^b)$ has depth $O(b)$, and we can generate it in space $O(b)$.

Consequences of the Main Theorem for classes above P. Recall that the class #P contains all functions $f : \Sigma^* \to \mathbb{N}$ for which there exists a nondeterministic polynomial-time Turing machine M such that $f(x)$ equals the number of accepting computations of M on input x. For any integer $k \geqslant 2$, $\mathsf{Mod}_k\mathsf{P}$ contains those L for which there exists an $f \in$ #P such that an input x belongs to L iff $f(x) \not\equiv 0 \bmod k$, i.e., $f(x)$ is not a multiple of k. $\mathsf{Mod}_2\mathsf{P}$ is often denoted as $\oplus\mathsf{P}$. A GapP function is the difference of two #P functions. The class PP (for "probabilistic P") contains all languages L for which there exists a GapP function f such that an input x belongs to L iff $f(x) > 0$. The class $\mathsf{C}_=\mathsf{P}$ (read "C equals P") contains those L for which there exists an $f \in$ GapP such that $x \in \mathsf{L}$ iff $f(x) = 0$. We refer to the survey by Fortnow [54] for background on these counting classes.

Ogiwara and Watanabe [107] and Ogiwara and Lozano [106] proved that for $\mathcal{C}$ equal to NP, PP, $\mathsf{C}_=\mathsf{P}$, $\mathsf{Mod}_k\mathsf{P}$ for some $k \geqslant 2$, or PSPACE, there is no sparse hard language for $\mathcal{C}$ under polynomial-time bounded truth-table reductions unless $\mathcal{C} = \mathsf{P}$. Combining this result with Theorems 4.1.1 and 4.2.1 leads to the following observations. We refer the unfamiliar reader to the survey paper by Fortnow [54] for the definition of the complexity classes involved.

Corollary 4.2.1. *Let $\mathcal{C}$ be NP, PP, $\mathsf{C}_=\mathsf{P}$ or $\mathsf{Mod}_k\mathsf{P}$ for some $k \geqslant 2$. There is no sparse hard language for $\mathcal{C}$ under $\leqslant^\mathsf{L}_{btt}$-reductions unless $\mathcal{C} = \mathsf{L}$.*

Corollary 4.2.2. *There is no sparse hard language for PSPACE under $\leqslant^\mathsf{L}_{btt}$-reductions.*

Corollary 4.2.3. *Let $\mathcal{C}$ be NP, PP, $\mathsf{C}_=\mathsf{P}$ or $\mathsf{Mod}_k\mathsf{P}$ for some $k \geqslant 2$. There is no sparse hard language for $\mathcal{C}$ under $\leqslant^{\mathsf{NC}^1}_{btt}$-reductions unless $\mathcal{C} = \mathsf{NC}^1$.*

4.2.3 Generic Theorem for P

In this subsection, we generalize our Main Theorem to a Generic Theorem by parameterizing the sparseness condition, the space bound and the bound on the number of truth-table queries of the reduction. We first state and prove the Generic Combinatorial Lemma and the Generic Theorem, and then consider some interesting instantiations other than the Main Theorem.

Statement and Proof. The Combinatorial Lemma readily parameterizes.

Lemma 4.2.3 (Generic Combinatorial Lemma). *Let A be truth-table reducible to S, and $D : \Sigma^* \to 2^{\Sigma^*}$ be a set system that can be generated in space $b(n)$. Suppose that the reduction queries at most $k(n)$ strings of length at most $s(n)$ and uses at most $a(n)$ space on inputs of $D(y)$ for $y \in \Sigma^n$. Then there is an algorithm running in space $O(k(n) \cdot (a(n) + b(n)))$ that on input $y \in \Sigma^n$ generates a collection of subsets of $D(y)$ at least one of which is a subset of A of size at least*

$$\frac{\|A \cap D(y)\|}{e \cdot (c_S(s(n)) + 1)^{k(n)}},$$

where e denotes the base of the natural logarithm.

Proof. We use the same algorithm as in the proof of the Combinatorial Lemma, i.e., for a given $y \in \Sigma^n$, we cycle through the set of RA-pairs associated with y, and for each of them, output the corresponding subset of $D(y)$ by cycling through the elements of $D(y)$ and checking whether it satisfies the restriction and whether the reduction accepts it using the membership bits implied by the assumption. The counting argument carries through and shows that the collection of subsets of $D(y)$ we generate contains at least one subset of A of the required size. So, we only have to check the space complexity of the algorithm.

Cycling through all RA-pairs amounts to:

- Cycling for all elements of $D(y)$ through all subsets of queries the reduction makes on that input. We can do this in $O(b(n) + k(n))$ space, namely $O(b(n))$ space to go through the list of elements of $D(y)$, and $k(n)$ or less bits to keep track of which queries belong to the subset.
- Cycling through $k(n)$ or less intervals of $Q(D(y))$ (see Lemma 4.2.2 for notation). For a single interval, it suffices to keep track of its endpoints, and we can represent them as the i-th query the reduction makes on some input of $D(y)$, which takes $O(b(n) + \log k(n)) \subseteq O(b(n) + a(n))$ space. So, this part has space complexity $O(k(n) \cdot (a(n) + b(n)))$.

With the given representations, we can check in $O(a(n))$ space whether an element of $D(y)$ satisfies the restriction, and whether the reduction accepts using the membership bits of the queries as implied by the assumption. It follows that the overall space complexity is $O(k(n) \cdot (a(n) + b(n)))$.

(End of the proof of the Generic Combinatorial Lemma.)

Using this lemma, we can generalize the Main Theorem.

Theorem 4.2.2 (Generic Theorem). *There is no hard language for* P *of census at most* $c(n)$ *under truth-table reductions that query at most* $O(k(n))$ *strings of length at most* $O(s(n))$ *and run in space* $O(a(n))$ *on inputs of length* n *unless* $\mathsf{P} \subseteq \mathsf{DSPACE}[t(n^{O(1)})]$, *where*

$$t(n) = k(n) \cdot (a(n) + b(n))$$
$$b(n) = \log n + k(n) \cdot \log c(s(n)),$$

provided $b(n) \in o(n)$ *and the following conditions hold:* $b(n)$ *is space constructible,* $a(O(n)) \subseteq O(a(n))$, $\log c(O(s(O(n)))) \subseteq O(\log c(s(n)))$, *and* $k(O(n)) \subseteq O(k(n))$.

Proof. Since CVP is complete for P under logspace many-one reductions, it suffices to show that we can solve it in $\mathsf{DSPACE}[t(n)]$ assuming the existence of a language S of census at most $c(n)$ that is hard for P under truth-table reductions that query at most $O(k(n))$ strings of length at most $O(s(n))$ and run in space $O(a(n))$ on inputs of length n.

As in the proof of the Main Theorem, we will construct an algorithm for CVP with the structure of Figure 4.1: Using the Generic Combinatorial Lemma, we produce a collection of Vandermonde systems, at least one of which has the gate values as its unique solution. Solving these systems and checking the resulting gate assignments for validity then completes the algorithm.

We apply the Generic Combinatorial Lemma to the language A_2 defined by (4.9) and the set system $D(y) \doteq \{\langle y, u, v \rangle \,|\, u, v \in \mathrm{GF}(2^{b^*(y)})\}$, where $b^* : \Sigma^* \to \{2 \cdot 3^t \,|\, t \in \mathbb{N}\}$ is such that $b^*(y) \approx \alpha \cdot b(|y|)$ for a sufficiently large constant α. It is clear that we can generate D in space $O(b(n))$. Let $y \in \Sigma^n$. Note that since $b^*(y) \in o(n)$, there is a constant β independent of α such that the the size of elements of $D(y)$ is asymptotically bounded by βn, and such that the reduction of A_2 to S queries at most $k^*(n) \leqslant \beta \cdot k(\beta n)$ strings of length at most $s^*(n) \leqslant \beta \cdot s(\beta n)$, and runs in space $a^*(n) \leqslant \beta \cdot a(\beta n)$ on inputs of $D(y)$. Under the given technical conditions, this implies that there is a constant γ independent of α such that asymptotically $k^*(n) \cdot \log(c(s^*(n)) + 1) \leqslant \gamma \cdot k(n) \cdot \log c(s(n))$. Consequently,

$$\frac{\|A_2 \cap D(y)\|}{e \cdot (c_S(s^*(n)) + 1)^{k^*(n)}} \geqslant \frac{2^{b^*(y)}}{e \cdot (c(s^*(n)) + 1)^{k^*(n)}} \geqslant 2^{b^*(y)/2} - 1,$$

provided that $\alpha \cdot b(n) \geqslant 2(\gamma \cdot k(n) \cdot \log c(s(n)) + \log e)$, which asymptotically holds for $\alpha > 2\gamma$. Since $b(n) \geqslant \log n$, the right-hand side is at least n for α sufficiently large. So, the Vandermonde system of correct equations we obtain has full column rank and dimension $2^{b^*(y)/2} - 1$ dividing $2^{b^*(y)} - 1$. We can recover the gate values from it in a space efficient way by applying Lemma 4.2.1.

Under the same technical conditions, the application of the Generic Combinatorial Lemma requires $O(t(n))$ space. Since we only need $O(b(n)) \subseteq$

$O(t(n))$ space to solve the Vandermonde systems and check the resulting gate assignments for validity, our final algorithm for CVP has space complexity $O(t(n))$.

Instantiations. For polynomially dense hard languages we obtain the following instantiation of the Generic Theorem, of which our Main Theorem is a special case.

Theorem 4.2.3. *Let $e \geqslant 1$ and $f \geqslant 0$. There is no sparse hard language for* P *under truth-table reductions computable in space $O(\log^e n)$ that make at most $O(\log^f n)$ queries unless* P $\subseteq$ DSPACE$[\log^{e+2f} n]$.

Proof. Observing that $s(n) \in 2^{O(\log^e n)}$ in the Generic Theorem, immediately yields that $t(n) \in O(\log^{e+2f} n)$.

For quasipolynomially dense hard languages we get:

Theorem 4.2.4. *Let $d > 0$, $e \geqslant 1$ and $f \geqslant 0$. There is no hard language for* P *with density bounded by $2^{O(\log^d n)}$ under truth-table reductions computable in space $O(\log^e n)$ that make at most $O(\log^f n)$ queries unless* P $\subseteq$ DSPACE$[\log^a n]$, *where $a = \max(de + 2f, e + f)$.*

Proof. Observing that $s(n) \in 2^{O(\log^e n)}$ in the Generic Theorem yields that $b(n) \in O(\log n + \log^{de+f} n)$, and $t(n) \in O(\log^a n)$.

In particular the following holds.

Corollary 4.2.4. *There is no quasipolynomially dense hard language for* P *under polylog-space truth-table reductions using no more than polylogarithmically many queries unless* P *is in polylog-space.*

4.2.4 Extension to Classes Other Than P

In this subsection, we show how we can apply the idea of the Main Theorem to collapse a complexity class $\mathcal{C}_1$ other than P to a class $\mathcal{C}_2$ that contains NC^1, assuming the existence of a sparse hard language for $\mathcal{C}_1$ under bounded truth-table reductions computable with the power of $\mathcal{C}_2$. In order for the technique to be applicable, languages in $\mathcal{C}_1$ must have unique membership proofs that can be constructed in $\mathcal{C}_1$ and checked in $\mathcal{C}_2$. We can encode the membership proofs as solutions of Vandermonde systems and use the Combinatorial Lemma to recover them in a space efficient way using a space efficient bounded truth-table reduction of the encoding auxiliary language to a sparse language. This approach works for NL and L, as we will see now.

Theorem 4.2.5. *There is no sparse hard language for* NL *under $\leqslant^L_{btt}$-reductions unless* NL $=$ L.

Proof. Assuming the existence of a sparse hard language for NL under $\leqslant^L_{btt}$-reductions, we will show how to solve in logspace the NL-complete problem DAG-STCON. Recall that DAG-STCON is the language containing all triples $\langle G, s, t \rangle$ where G is a DAG and s and t are two of its vertices such that there is a directed path in G from vertex s to vertex t.

In order to do so, we consider a variant A_3 of the auxiliary language defined by Cai and Sivakumar [43]:

$$A_3 = \{\langle G, s, u, u^2, u^3, \ldots, u^{m-1}, v \rangle |$$

$$G \text{ DAG with } m \text{ vertices, } s \text{ vertex of } G, u, v \in \text{GF}(2^b)$$

$$\text{for some } b \in \{2 \cdot 3^t \mid t \in \mathbb{N}\} \text{ and } \sum_{j=1}^m u^{j-1} g_j = v\},$$

where g_j is a Boolean indicating whether G contains a directed path from s to the j-th vertex of G. Provided G is acyclic, the values $g_1, \ldots, g_m$ constitute a logspace verifiable proof of membership of $\langle G, s, t \rangle$ to DAG-STCON: We only have to check for every vertex $w \neq s$ of G that its g-value is 1 only if there an incoming edge from another vertex of G with g-value 1, and that vertex t has g-value 1. We can clearly perform these checks in logspace.

A_3 contains Reed-Solomon encodings of these values, just as A_2 in the proof of the Main Theorem. To check membership to A_3, in addition to some syntactical tests which clearly can be performed in NL, we have to do the following:

- Check that G is acyclic. We can do that in coNL, whence also in NL [67, 130].
- Check the successive powers of u for correctness. This involves verifying that the component of the input corresponding to u^j equals the product of u and the component of the input corresponding to u^{j-1} for $j = 2, \ldots, m-1$. We can do this in space $O(\log m + \log b)$, because we can compute the product of two elements of $\text{GF}(2^b)$ in space $O(\log b)$ by computing the product of the corresponding polynomials of degree less than b over $\text{GF}(2)$ and then reducing this product modulo $f(x) = x^b + x^{b/2} + 1$. To calculate the residue of a polynomial of degree less than $2b - 1$ modulo $f(x)$ in space $O(\log b)$, we use the fact that
$$x^j \bmod f(x) \quad = \quad x^{j-b/2} + x^{j-b} \quad \text{for } b \leqslant j < \tfrac{3}{2}b$$
$$x^{j-\frac{3}{2}b} \quad \text{for } \tfrac{3}{2}b \leqslant j < 2b.$$
- Check that the equation $\sum_{j=1}^m u^{j-1} g_j = v$ holds. We can do this in L^{NL}, whence in NL, since the g_j's can be computed within that complexity class, and once we have the successive powers of u, computing the left-hand side sum is easily performed in $O(\log m + \log b)$ space.

So, $A_3 \in \text{NL}$, whence by hypothesis logspace k-truth-table reduces to the sparse language S for some $k \in \mathbb{N}$. Therefore, we can apply the same combination of the Combinatorial Lemma and the logspace Vandermonde system solver as in the proof of the Main Theorem to obtain a collection of values for $(g_j)_{j=1}^m$ which we can generate in logspace and such that at least one of them is correct. This yields a logspace algorithm for DAG-STCON with the structure of Figure 4.1.   *(End of the proof of Theorem 4.2.5.)*

Once again, we can easily verify that the algorithm we construct in the above proof is actually NC^1 modulo the complexity of the reduction. Therefore, as DAG-STCON is complete for NL under $\leqslant_m^{\mathsf{NC}^1}$-reductions, we also obtain:

Theorem 4.2.6. *There is no sparse hard language for* NL *under* $\leqslant_{\mathrm{btt}}^{\mathsf{NC}^1}$-*reductions unless* NL $=\mathsf{NC}^1$.

Regarding the sparse hard language problem for L, we can prove the following.

Theorem 4.2.7. *There is no sparse hard language for* L *under* $\leqslant_{\mathrm{btt}}^{\mathsf{NC}^1}$-*reductions unless* L $=\mathsf{NC}^1$.

Proof. Assuming the existence of a sparse hard language for L under $\leqslant_{\mathrm{btt}}^{\mathsf{NC}^1}$-reductions, we will show how to solve in NC^1 the L-complete problem F-STCON. Recall that F-STCON is the language consisting of all triples $\langle G, s, t \rangle$ where G is a forest and s and t are two of its vertices such that s and t are connected in G.

Consider the auxiliary language

$$A_4 = \{\langle G, s, t, u, u^2, \dots, u^{m-1}, v \rangle \mid$$
$$G \text{ forest with } m \text{ edges}, s, t \text{ vertices of } G, u, v \in \mathrm{GF}(2^b)$$
$$\text{for some } b \in \{2 \cdot 3^t \mid t \in \mathbb{N}\} \text{ and } \sum_{j=1}^m u^{j-1} e_j = v\},$$

where e_j is a Boolean indicating whether s and t belong to the same component of G and the j-th edge of G is on the unique path connecting s and t in G. Provided G is acyclic, the values $e_1, \dots, e_m$ constitute an NC^1-verifiable proof of membership of $\langle G, s, t \rangle$ to F-STCON: It suffices to check that either $s = t$ or else in the subgraph of G defined by the e_j's with value 1, s and t have degree 1 and all other vertices have degree 0 or 2. We can clearly test this in NC^1.

A_4 contains Reed-Solomon encodings of the values $e_1, \dots, e_m$ like A_3 in the proof of the Theorem 4.2.5. Similar to that proof, to check membership to A_4, we basically have to do the following:

– Check that G is acyclic. Since this is equivalent to the membership of $\langle G, t, t \rangle$ to F-STCON, and F-STCON $\in$ L, we can perform this check in logspace. The underlying key is the concept of a lexicographic walk in a graph. A lexicographic walk starting at a vertex w moves in the first step to the lexicographically first neighbor of w (if any), and then proceeds in the following steps to the neighbor which is lexicographically next after the one we just left, or the lexicographically first neighbor if we just left the lexicographically last one. The walk ends when we return to w from its lexicographically last neighbor. To check whether the graph G is acyclic, it suffices to perform from every vertex of G a lexicographic walk for no more than $2m$ steps, and check whether during that walk for every vertex w' visited, we go from w' to every one of its neighbors exactly once and in cyclic lexicographic order [66]. All of this can be done in logspace.

– Check the successive powers of u for correctness. This can be done in logspace as argued in the proof of Theorem 4.2.5.

– Check that the equation $\sum_{j=1}^{m} u^{j-1} e_j = v$ holds. Since $e_j = 1$ iff $\langle G, s, t \rangle \in$ F-STCON and $\langle G - e_j, s, t \rangle \notin$ F-STCON, and F-STCON $\in L$, we can compute the e_j's in logspace. Using the powers of u given in the input, we can then compute the sum involved in space $O(\log m + \log b)$.

Therefore, $A_4 \in L$, whence by hypothesis k-truth-table reduces to the sparse language S for some $k \in \mathbb{N}$ through a reduction computable in NC^1. So, once more, we can apply a combination of the Combinatorial Lemma and the NC^1 Vandermonde system solver as in the proof of the Main Theorem to obtain a collection of values for $(e_j)_{j=1}^{m}$ which we can generate in NC^1 and such that at least one of them is correct. This yields an NC^1 algorithm for F-STCON with the structure of Figure 4.1. $\qed$

4.3 Randomized Reductions

In this section, we describe our results on the existence of sparse hard languages under randomized bounded truth-table reductions with two-sided error, using the multiple access model of randomness, in which the Turing machine has two-way read access to a random bit tape. We start with a description of earlier work, which the reader can skip without loss of continuity. Then we prove an analogue of the Main Theorem for randomized two-sided error bounded truth-table reductions with confidence at least inversely polynomial. As in the deterministic case, we next parameterize it to a Randomized Generic Theorem for P. Finally, we prove similar results on the sparse hard language problem for NL, L, and also for NP.

We will often use the term "inversely polynomial" to refer to a function in $\Omega(n^{-a})$ for some $a > 0$.

4.3.1 Previous Work

Cai, Naik and Sivakumar [41] proved that there is no sparse hard language for P under randomized two-sided error many-one reductions computable in logspace and with confidence at least inversely polynomial unless $P \subseteq ZP^*L$. They used Hadamard encodings [91] in the form of the auxiliary language A_1 defined by Ogihara [105], and a randomized algorithm by Goldreich and Levin [56] to recover the code word. The same approach will allow us to extend their result to bounded truth-table reductions.

Cai, Naik and Sivakumar applied the same technique to the sparse hard language problem for NL and L. Using the randomized reduction from satisfiability to unique satisfiability by Valiant and Vazirani [137], they were also able to obtain the first known result on the existence of sparse hard languages for NP under randomized many-one reductions with *two-sided* error: There is no sparse hard language for NP under polynomial-time randomized two-sided error many-one reductions with confidence at least inversely polynomial unless NP ⊆ RP. Earlier, Ranjan and Rohatgi [113] had shown this theorem for reductions with one-sided error on the non-membership side. Arvind, Köbler and Mundhenk [15] improved upon that, but the question whether the statement was true of reductions with one-sided error on the membership side, and of reductions with two-sided error remained open. Cai, Naik and Sivakumar answered that question positively, and we will show that the same holds for bounded truth-table reductions with two-sided error.

4.3.2 Main Result

In this section, we establish the analogue of our Main Theorem in the randomized setting.

Theorem 4.3.1 (Randomized Main Theorem). *There is no sparse hard language for* P *under* $\leqslant_{btt}^{BPL^*}$*-reductions with confidence at least inversely polynomial unless* P ⊆ ZPL**.*

The proof uses Hadamard encodings [91] instead of Reed-Solomon encodings as in the deterministic case. It is based on the randomized algorithm by Goldreich and Levin [56] to decode Hadamard codes, and on a randomized version of the Combinatorial Lemma. We first prove the Randomized Main Theorem, then the Randomized Combinatorial Lemma, and finally we sketch the algorithm by Goldreich and Levin.

Proof of the Randomized Main Theorem. Assuming the existence of a sparse hard language for P under randomized two-sided error bounded truth-table reductions computable in logspace and with confidence at least inversely polynomial, we will show that the P-complete language CVP is in ZPL*.

As in the deterministic case, we will make use of gate assignments as logspace verifiable membership proofs for CVP. Using the randomized bounded truth-table reducibility of P to a sparse language, we will generate in randomized logspace a list of gate assignments that with high probability contains at least one valid assignment. We can then check each of them for validity in logspace, yielding a ZPL* algorithm.

To create that list, we consider the auxiliary language A_5 defined by Ogihara [105]:

$$A_5 = \{\langle C, x, w\rangle \mid C \text{ circuit with } |x| \text{ inputs and } m \text{ gates}, x \in \Sigma^*,$$

$$w \in (GF(2))^m \text{ and } \sum_{j=1}^{m} w_j g_j = 1\}, \tag{4.14}$$

where g_j denotes the value of the j-th gate of C on input x, and the arithmetic is over GF(2). For any instance $y \doteq \langle C, x \rangle$ of CVP with m gates, $(\chi_A(\langle y, w \rangle))_{w \in (\mathrm{GF}(2))^m}$ is the Hadamard encoding of the gate values of C on input x. An interesting property of this encoding is that a randomized oracle with confidence at least inversely polynomial suffices to recover the code word in randomized NC^1. Goldreich and Levin [56] showed a way to do this, and we will sketch it in Section 4.3.2.

Lemma 4.3.1 (Goldreich-Levin [56]). *Let $\epsilon : \mathbb{N} \to (0, \frac{1}{2}]$, and suppose that $\ell(m) \doteq \log(\frac{2m}{\epsilon^2})$ is space constructible. Then there exists a $\mathsf{DSPACE}[\ell(m)]$ uniform family of randomized oracle circuits $(C_m)_m$ of depth $O(\ell(m))$ making $(2^{\ell(m)} - 1)m$ parallel oracle queries of length m, such that C_m on input 1^m outputs a list of $2^{\ell(m)}$ elements of Σ^m and the following holds: For any randomized Boolean oracle B on $\Sigma^* \times \Sigma^*$, for any $y \in \Sigma^*$, $m \in \mathbb{N}$, and $g \in \Sigma^m$, if*

$$\Pr[B(y, w) = g \cdot w] \geqslant \frac{1}{2} + \epsilon(m) \tag{4.15}$$

then

$$\Pr[\textit{output of } C_m(1^m) \textit{ with oracle } B(y, \cdot) \textit{ contains } g] \geqslant \frac{1}{2},$$

where the former probability is with respect to the uniform distribution of w over Σ^m and the underlying distribution of $B(y, \cdot)$, the latter with respect to the uniform distribution over the random bits fed to C_m and the underlying distribution of $B(y, \cdot)$, and $g \cdot w$ denotes the inner product of g and w as vectors over GF(2).

So, we have to construct a randomized oracle B that can be computed by a logspace randomized Turing machine with two-way read access to its random tape, such that B approximates χ_A well in the following sense: For any instance y of CVP of length n with m gates

$$\Pr[B(y, w) = \chi_A(\langle y, w \rangle)] \geqslant \frac{1}{2} + \epsilon(m),$$

where $\epsilon(m)$ is at least inversely polynomial (so that $\ell(m)$ is logarithmic in m). The probability is with respect to the uniform distribution over Σ^m and the underlying probability measure of $B(y, \cdot)$. We cannot just use the reduction to construct B, because we do not know how to determine the membership to S of the queries in randomized logspace. However, it suffices to approximate χ_A well on a subset of instances of high probability. Indeed, suppose σ is a randomized predicate such that $\Pr[\sigma]$ is at least inversely polynomial in m, and π is a randomized predicate such that $\Pr[\pi = \chi_{A_S} \mid \sigma] - \frac{1}{2}$ is also at least inversely polynomial in m. Let B act as follows: If σ holds, then output π, otherwise output a random bit. Then

$$\Pr[B = \chi_{A_5}] = \Pr[\sigma] \cdot \Pr[\pi = \chi_{A_5} \mid \sigma] + (1 - \Pr[\sigma]) \cdot \frac{1}{2}$$

$$= \frac{1}{2} + \Pr[\sigma] \cdot (\Pr[\pi = \chi_{A_5} \mid \sigma] - \frac{1}{2}),$$

which exceeds $\frac{1}{2}$ by at least the inverse of a polynomial in m. So, provided we can compute σ and π in randomized logspace, we are done.

The following Randomized Combinatorial Lemma yields the randomized predicates σ and π we will use. We will prove the Lemma in Section 4.3.2.

Lemma 4.3.2 (Randomized Combinatorial Lemma). *Let A be logspace k-truth-table reducible to a language S by a randomized two-sided error reduction for some $k \in \mathbb{N}$, and let $D : \Sigma^* \to 2^{\Sigma^*}$ be a set system. Suppose that the reduction queries strings of length at most $s(n)$, uses $r(n)$ random bits, and has confidence at least $\delta(n)$ on inputs of $D(y)$ for $y \in \Sigma^n$. Then there are Boolean functions σ and π of 2 variables such that for any $y \in \Sigma^n$,*

$$\Pr_{z \in_u D(y), |\rho| = r(n)} [\sigma(z, \rho)] \geq \frac{\delta(n)^2}{2(c_S(s(n)) + 1)^{2k}} \quad (4.16\text{a})$$

$$\Pr_{z \in_u D(y), |\rho| = r(n)} [\pi(z, \rho) = \chi_A(z) \mid \sigma(z, \rho)] \geq \frac{1}{2} + \frac{\delta(n)}{4}. \quad (4.16\text{b})$$

Moreover, if we can uniformly sample $D(y)$ in randomized space $O(\log n)$, and $E : \Sigma^* \to 2^{\Sigma^* \times \Sigma^*}$ is a set system such that $E(y) \subseteq D(y) \times \Sigma^{r(|y|)}$ and E can be generated in randomized logspace (given two-way read access to a random bit tape), then for any polynomial $p(n)$, on input $y \in \Sigma^n$ we can generate a collection of lists at least one of which equals $((\sigma(z, \rho), \pi(z, \rho))_{(z,\rho) \in E(y)}$ with confidence at least $1 - \exp(\frac{-\delta(n)^2 p(n)}{(c_S(s(n))+1)^{2k}})$, using logarithmic work space and two-way read access to a random bit tape.

We can apply this lemma to the language A_5, since A_5 belongs to P, whence by hypothesis logspace k-truth-table reduces to a sparse language S for some $k \in \mathbb{N}$. We choose $D(y) \doteq \{\langle y, w \rangle \mid w \in (\mathrm{GF}(2))^m\}$, where $y \doteq \langle C, x \rangle$ and m is the number of gates of C. Since the reduction is computable in randomized logspace, and inputs of $D(y)$ have length $O(n)$ for $y \in \Sigma^n$, the reduction queries strings of length at most a polynomial $s(n)$, uses a polynomial $r(n)$ number of random bits, and has confidence $\delta(n)$ at least inversely polynomial on inputs from $D(y)$ for $y \in \Sigma^n$. Therefore, (4.16a) and (4.16b) guarantee that $\Pr[\sigma]$ and $\Pr[\pi = \chi_{A_5} \mid \sigma] - \frac{1}{2}$ are at least inversely polynomial in n, and hence also in m. By picking w of length m from the random bit tape, we can uniformly sample $D(y)$ in logspace.

The set $E(y)$ consists of $(2^{\ell(m)} - 1)m$ pairs of the form $(\langle y, w \rangle, \rho_{\langle y, w \rangle})$, where w ranges over the oracle queries the circuit C_m on input 1^m makes, and $\rho_{\langle y, w \rangle}$ is chosen uniformly at random from $\Sigma^{r(n)}$. Since all queries of C_m are made in parallel, the set $E(y) \subseteq D(y) \times \Sigma^{r(n)}$ is well-defined, and it is clear that we can generate the set system E in logspace, given two-way read access to a random bit tape. We can choose the polynomial $p(n)$ to be at least $(c_S(s(n)) + 1)^{2k} \cdot \delta^{-2}(n)$, so by Lemma 4.3.2 we can generate a collection of lists at least one of which equals $((\sigma(z, \rho), \pi(z, \rho))_{(z,\rho) \in E(y)}$ with probability at least $1 - e^{-1}$, using logarithmic work space and two-way read access to a random bit tape.

For each of these lists, we will simulate the circuit C_m on input 1^m using σ and π as given by the list to answer the oracle queries to $B(y, \cdot)$. With probability no less than $\frac{1}{2} - e^{-1}$, at least one of these simulations will produce a list of vectors that contains g. The same gate assignment checker as in the Main Theorem allows to weed out all other vectors.

It is straightforward to check that the resulting algorithm for CVP is in ZPL*.   *(End of the proof of the Randomized Main Theorem.)*

Except for the reduction, we can actually implement every component of our algorithm for CVP in ZPNC^1. Since all queries to the reduction are asked in parallel, and CVP is complete for P under NC^1-computable many-one reductions, we also obtain the following.

Theorem 4.3.2. *There is no sparse hard language for* P *under* $\leqslant_{\mathrm{btt}}^{\mathsf{BPNC}^1}$*- reductions with confidence at least inversely polynomial unless* $\mathsf{P} \subseteq \mathsf{ZPNC}^1$.

Proof of the Randomized Combinatorial Lemma. Suppose A logspace k-truth-table reduces to a language S for some $k \in \mathbb{N}$ under a randomized two-sided error reduction, and $D : \Sigma^* \to 2^{\Sigma^*}$ is a set system such that the reduction queries strings of length at most $s(n)$, uses $r(n)$ random bits, and has confidence at least $\delta(n)$ on inputs of $D(y)$ for $y \in \Sigma^n$. For a given $y \in \Sigma^n$, we would like to find a subset of $D(y) \times \Sigma^{r(n)}$ of high measure on which the success probability of the randomized reduction is almost as good as the overall success probability, and such that we can guess efficiently which instances of a given list belong to the subset (predicate σ), and for these determine the outcome of the reduction (predicate π). As in the Combinatorial Lemma, we will guarantee the latter condition by making sure that for the subset constructed we know the membership to S of the queries the reduction makes. This will again involve finding a set P of jointly popular queries in S, and a collection of intervals disjoint from S, and the subset will consist of those instances for which the reduction queries all of P and the other queries are in the union of the intervals (and hit each of the intervals). The counting is a bit different from the deterministic case, and goes as follows.

Proof (of the Randomized Combinatorial Lemma). Let $y \in \Sigma^n$. For $z \in D(y)$ and $\rho \in \Sigma^{r(n)}$, let $Q(z, \rho)$ denote the queries the reduction makes on input z and random seed ρ. D will be short for $D(y)$, and $Q(D)$ will denote the set of all queries the reduction makes on inputs from D and random seeds of length $r(n)$. We will write $e^P(z, \rho)$ for the Boolean indicating whether the reduction accepts the input z on random seed ρ using P instead of S to determine the membership of the queries to S.

We first construct the Boolean functions σ and π using the following claims.

Claim 4.3.1. There exists a set $P \subseteq S$ such that

$$\Pr_{z \in_u D, |\rho|=r(n)}[Q(z,\rho) \cap S = P] \geqslant \frac{\delta(n)}{(c_S(s(n))+1)^k}$$

$$\Pr_{z \in_u D, |\rho|=r(n)}[e^P(z,\rho) = \chi_A(z) \mid Q(z,\rho) \cap S = P] \geqslant \frac{1}{2} + \frac{\delta(n)}{2}.$$

This is because if there were no such set P, then

$$\Pr[e^S(z,\rho) = \chi_A(z)] - \frac{1}{2}$$

$$= \sum_{P \subseteq S \cap \Sigma^{\leqslant s(n)}} \Pr[P] \cdot \left(\Pr[e^S(z,\rho) = \chi_A(z) \mid P] - \frac{1}{2}\right)$$

$$= \sum_{\substack{P \subseteq S \cap \Sigma^{\leqslant s(n)} \\ \Pr[P] \geqslant \frac{\delta(n)}{(c_S(s(n))+1)^k}}} \Pr[P] \cdot \left(\Pr[e^S(z,\rho) = \chi_A(z) \mid P] - \frac{1}{2}\right) +$$

$$\sum_{\substack{P \subseteq S \cap \Sigma^{\leqslant s(n)} \\ \Pr[P] < \frac{\delta(n)}{(c_S(s(n))+1)^k}}} \Pr[P] \cdot \left(\Pr[e^S(z,\rho) = \chi_A(z) \mid P] - \frac{1}{2}\right)$$

$$< \frac{\delta(n)}{2} + \sum_{i=0}^{k} \binom{c_S(s(n))}{i} \cdot \frac{\delta(n)}{(c_S(s(n))+1)^k} \cdot \frac{1}{2}$$

$$\leqslant \delta(n),$$

where we use P as a shortcut for the event that $Q(z,\rho) \cap S = P$, and all probabilities are with respect to the uniform distribution of (z,ρ) over $D \times \Sigma^{r(n)}$. In the last step, we are using the inequality $\sum_{i=0}^{k} \binom{c}{i} \leqslant (c+1)^k$. We obtain a contradiction to the fact that the reduction has confidence $\delta(n)$, and therefore prove Claim 4.3.1.

Claim 4.3.2. There exists a collection of at most $k - \|P\|$ intervals I_i, $i \in \mathcal{I}$, of $Q(D) \setminus S$ such that

$$\Pr_{z \in_u D, |\rho|=r(n)}[Q(z,\rho) \setminus P \subseteq \cup_{i \in \mathcal{I}} I_i \text{ and } Q(z,\rho) \text{ hits every } I_i \mid$$

$$P \subseteq Q(z,\rho)] \geqslant \frac{\delta(n)}{2(c_S(s(n))+1)^{k-\|P\|}}$$

$$\Pr_{z \in_u D, |\rho|=r(n)}[e^S(z,\rho) = \chi_A(z) \mid P \subseteq Q(z,\rho) \text{ and } Q(z,\rho) \setminus P \subseteq \cup_{i \in \mathcal{I}} I_i$$

$$\text{and } Q(z,\rho) \text{ hits every } I_i] \geqslant \frac{1}{2} + \frac{\delta(n)}{4}.$$

This follows from Claim 4.3.1 by essentially the same argument. Without loss of generality, we can assume that the reduction always makes exactly k queries. In case $||P|| = k$ or $c_S(s(n)) = 0$, Claim 4.3.1 immediately implies 4.3.2. Assume $||P|| < k$ and $c_S(s(n)) > 0$. The set S divides $Q(D) \setminus S$ into the union of m intervals $I_1, \ldots, I_m$ ($1 \leqslant m \leqslant c_S(s(n))$), and the reduction maps each instance to a collection of 1 up to $k - ||P||$ of these intervals. Suppose there were no subset $\mathcal{I}$ of $\{1, \ldots, m\}$ such that $\Pr[\mathcal{I} \mid P] \geqslant \frac{\delta(n)}{2(c_S(s(n))+1)^{k-||P||}}$ and $\Pr[e^S(z, \rho) = \chi_A(z) \mid \mathcal{I}$ and $P] \geqslant \frac{1}{2} + \frac{\delta(n)}{4}$, where we use P as a shortcut for the event that $Q(z, \rho) \cap S = P$, $\mathcal{I}$ for the event that $Q(z, \rho) \setminus P \subseteq \cup_{i \in \mathcal{I}} I_i$ and $Q(z, \rho)$ hits every I_i for $i \in \mathcal{I}$, and again all probabilities are with respect to the uniform distribution of (z, ρ) over $D \times \Sigma^{r(n)}$. Then

$$\Pr[e^S(z, \rho) = \chi_A(z) \mid Q(z, \rho) \cap S = P] - \frac{1}{2}$$

$$= \sum_{\varnothing \neq \mathcal{I} \subseteq \{1, \ldots, m\}} \Pr[\mathcal{I} \mid P] \cdot (\Pr[e^S(z, \rho) = \chi_A(z) \mid \mathcal{I} \text{ and } P] - \frac{1}{2})$$

$$= \sum_{\substack{\varnothing \neq \mathcal{I} \subseteq \{1, \ldots, m\} \\ Q(\mathcal{I})}} \Pr[\mathcal{I} \mid P] \cdot (\Pr[e^S(z, \rho) = \chi_A(z) \mid \mathcal{I} \text{ and } P] - \frac{1}{2}) +$$

$$\sum_{\substack{\varnothing \neq \mathcal{I} \subseteq \{1, \ldots, m\} \\ \neg Q(\mathcal{I})}} \Pr[\mathcal{I} \mid P] \cdot (\Pr[e^S(z, \rho) = \chi_A(z) \mid \mathcal{I} \text{ and } P] - \frac{1}{2})$$

$$< \frac{\delta(n)}{4} + \sum_{i=1}^{k-||P||} \binom{m}{i} \cdot \frac{\delta(n)}{2(c_S(s(n))+1)^{k-||P||}} \cdot \frac{1}{2}$$

$$\leqslant \frac{\delta(n)}{2},$$

where $Q(\mathcal{I})$ denotes the condition $\Pr[\mathcal{I} \mid P] \geqslant \frac{\delta(n)}{2(c_S(s(n))+1)^{k-||P||}}$. In the last step, we used the inequality $\sum_{i=0}^{\ell} \binom{m}{i} \leqslant (m+1)^{\ell}$ again. The final inequality contradicts Claim 4.3.1, and that way proves Claim 4.3.2.

We define $\sigma(z, \rho)$ to be the Boolean indicating whether $P \subseteq Q(z, \rho)$ and $Q(z, \rho) \setminus P \subseteq \cup_{i \in \mathcal{I}} I_i$ and $Q(z, \rho)$ hits every I_i for $i \in \mathcal{I}$, and $\pi(z, \rho)$ to be $e^P(z, \rho)$. Claims 4.3.1 and 4.3.2 combined show that σ and π satisfy conditions (4.16a) and (4.16b).

Now, we will see how we can randomly generate a collection of lists such that, with confidence at least $1 - \exp(\frac{-\delta(n)^2 p(n)}{(c_S(s(n))+1)^{2k}})$, at least one of which equals $((\sigma(z, \rho), \pi(z, \rho))_{(z, \rho) \in E(y)}$. We will only need logarithmic work space in order to do so, provided two-way read access to the random bit tape.

We generate a multiset F of $2p(n)$ instances chosen uniformly at random from $D \times \Sigma^{r(n)}$. F contains an instance satisfying σ with probability at least $1 - (1 - \frac{\delta(n)^2}{2(c_S(s(n))+1)^{2k}})^{2p(n)} \geqslant 1 - \exp(\frac{-\delta(n)^2 p(n)}{(c_S(s(n))+1)^{2k}})$. Then, as in the Combinatorial Lemma, we will consider, for every instance of F, every subset of the queries the reduction makes on that instance as a candidate P' for P, and consider every collection of k or fewer intervals of the set of all queries on inputs from $E(y)$ as candidates for the intervals I_i, $i \in \mathcal{I}$. For each of these candidates, we output the list consisting of a pair for each instance of $E(y)$, where the pair corresponding to (z, ρ) consists of

- a Boolean indicating whether $P' \subseteq Q(z, \rho)$, $Q(z, \rho) \setminus P$ is in the union of the candidate intervals, and each of the candidate intervals is hit by $Q(z, \rho)$, and
- the Boolean $e^{P'}(z, \rho)$, indicating whether the reduction accepts z on random seed ρ using P' to decide membership to S of the queries.

If F contains at least one instance satisfying σ, $((\sigma(z, \rho), \pi(z, \rho))_{(z, \rho) \in E(y)}$ will be among the lists produced. Moreover, by the argument given in the proof of the Combinatorial Lemma, it is clear that we can generate these lists in randomized logspace, provided two-way read access to the random bit tape. We need the two-way read access to regenerate the instances of $E(y)$ and F when needed. *(End of the proof of the Randomized Combinatorial Lemma.)*

Note that applying the Randomized Combinatorial Lemma to deterministic reductions yields a result similar to the Combinatorial Lemma, but the lower bound corresponding to equation (4.10) is weaker: the fraction of $A \cap D(y)$ we obtain here is essentially the square of the fraction the Combinatorial Lemma guarantees.

Recovering linear functions in randomized NC^1. Our randomized constructions heavily depend on the ability to recover in randomized NC^1 the coefficients of a linear Boolean function over $(GF(2))^m$ using a randomized oracle for the function. Therefore, we give an outline of the description and analysis of the algorithm that Goldreich and Levin proposed for this problem [56].

Proof (of Lemma 4.3.1). Fix $y \in \Sigma^*$, $m \in \mathbb{N}$, and a string $g \in \Sigma^m$ for which (4.15) holds. We will omit the argument m for ℓ and ϵ.

We pick ℓ elements $w_1, \ldots, w_\ell \in \Sigma^m$ uniformly at random, and guess the values γ_i of $g \cdot w_i$ for $i = 1, \ldots, \ell$. For each of the 2^ℓ possible values of $\gamma_1 \gamma_2 \ldots \gamma_\ell$, we will output an element of Σ^m. The j-th bit of this element is the majority over all $a = a_1 a_2 \ldots a_\ell \in \Sigma^\ell$ different from 0^ℓ of the bit

$$B(y, e_j + \sum_{i=1}^{\ell} a_i w_i) + \sum_{i=1}^{\ell} a_i \gamma_i,$$

where e_j denotes $0^{j-1}10^{m-j}$ and the arithmetic is over the field $GF(2)$.

Consider the vector g' we output for the choice $\gamma_i = g \cdot w_i$, $i = 1, \ldots, \ell$. For $a \neq 0^\ell$, $e_j + \sum_{i=1}^{\ell} a_i w_i$ is uniformly distributed over Σ^m, and these random variables for different a's are pairwise independent. Therefore, for any $j \in \{1, \ldots, m\}$, Chebyshev's inequality yields that

$$\Pr[g'_j \neq g_j]$$

$$= \Pr[\sum_{0^\ell \neq a \in \Sigma^\ell} \chi[B(y, e_j + \sum_{i=1}^{\ell} a_i w_i) + g \cdot \sum_{i=1}^{\ell} a_i w_i \neq g_j] \geqslant 2^{\ell-1}]$$

$$= \Pr[\sum_{0^\ell \neq a \in \Sigma^\ell} \chi[B(y, e_j + \sum_{i=1}^{\ell} a_i w_i) \neq g \cdot (e_j + \sum_{i=1}^{\ell} a_i w_i)] \geqslant 2^{\ell-1}]$$

$$\leqslant \Pr[\sum_{0^\ell \neq a \in \Sigma^\ell} \chi[B(y, e_j + \sum_{i=1}^{\ell} a_i w_i) \neq g \cdot (e_j + \sum_{i=1}^{\ell} a_i w_i)]$$

$$- E\left[\sum_{0^\ell \neq a \in \Sigma^\ell} \chi[B(y, e_j + \sum_{i=1}^{\ell} a_i w_i) \neq g \cdot (e_j + \sum_{i=1}^{\ell} a_i w_i)]\right]$$

$$\leqslant 2^{\ell-1} - (2^\ell - 1)(\frac{1}{2} - \epsilon)]$$

$$\leqslant \sigma^2\left(\sum_{0^\ell \neq a \in \Sigma^\ell} \chi\left[B(y, e_j + \sum_{i=1}^{\ell} a_i w_i) \neq g \cdot (e_j + \sum_{i=1}^{\ell} a_i w_i)\right]\right) /$$

$$((2^\ell - 1)\epsilon + \frac{1}{2})^2$$

$$< \frac{1}{2^\ell \epsilon^2},$$

where the probabilities are with respect to the uniform distribution of the w_i's and the underlying distribution of B. So, $\Pr[g' \neq g] < m/(2^\ell \epsilon^2) \leqslant \frac{1}{2}$, i.e., with probability at least $\frac{1}{2}$, g is among the elements of Σ^m we output.

It is straightforward to check that this procedure can be implemented as a randomized oracle circuit C_m of depth $O(\ell(m))$ making $(2^\ell - 1)m$ parallel queries of length m to $B(y, \cdot)$, and that we can generate these circuits in space $O(\ell(m))$.

4.3.3 Randomized Generic Theorem for P

In this section, we generalize the Randomized Main Theorem to a Randomized Generic Theorem for P by parameterizing the sparseness condition, and the space bound, the bound on the number of truth-table queries and the confidence of the randomized reduction. We also consider some instantiations of the Randomized Generic Theorem other than the Randomized Main Theorem, analogous to the ones made in the deterministic case.

Statement. The Randomized Combinatorial Lemma parameterizes as follows.

Lemma 4.3.3 (Randomized Generic Combinatorial Lemma). *Let A be truth-table reducible to a language S by a randomized two-sided error reduction, and let $D : \Sigma^* \to 2^{\Sigma^*}$ be a set system. Suppose that the reduction queries at most $k(n)$ strings of length at most $s(n)$, uses $r(n)$ random bits and work space at most $a(n)$ (given two-way read access to a random bit tape), and has confidence at least $\delta(n)$ on inputs of $D(y)$ for $y \in \Sigma^n$. Then there are Boolean functions σ and π of 2 variables such that for any $y \in \Sigma^n$,*

$$\Pr_{z \in_u D(y), |\rho| = r(n)} [\sigma(z, \rho)] \geqslant \frac{\delta(n)^2}{2(c_S(s(n)) + 1)^{2k}}$$

$$\Pr_{z \in_u D(y), |\rho| = r(n)} [\pi(z, \rho) = \chi_A(z) \mid \sigma(z, \rho)] \geqslant \frac{1}{2} + \frac{\delta(n)}{4}.$$

Moreover, suppose we can uniformly sample $D(y)$ in randomized space $b(n)$, and $E : \Sigma^* \to 2^{\Sigma^* \times \Sigma^*}$ is a set system such that $E(y) \subseteq D(y) \times \Sigma^{r(|y|)}$ and we can generate E using at most $b(n)$ work space (given two-way read access to a random bit tape). Then for any function $p : \mathbb{N} \to \mathbb{N}$ such that $\log p(n)$ is space constructible, on input $y \in \Sigma^n$, we can generate a collection of lists at least one of which equals $((\sigma(z, \rho), \pi(z, \rho))_{(z, \rho) \in E(y)}$ with confidence at least $1 - \exp(\frac{-\delta(n)^2 p(n)}{(c_S(s(n)) + 1)^{2k}})$, using work space $O(k(n) \cdot (a(n) + b(n)) + \log p(n) + \log r(n))$ and two-way read access to a random bit tape, provided $\log r(n)$ is space constructible.

Proof. The proof is a straightforward combination of the one for the Randomized Combinatorial Lemma and the space bound analysis given in the proof of the Generic Combinatorial Lemma.

Plugging in this lemma in the proof of the Randomized Main Theorem yields:

Theorem 4.3.3 (Randomized Generic Theorem). *There is no hard language for P of census at most $c(n)$ under randomized two-sided error truth-table reductions that query at most $O(k(n))$ strings of length at most $O(s(n))$, run in space $O(a(n))$ (given two-way read access to a random bit tape) and have confidence at least $\Omega(\delta(n))$ on inputs of length n unless $\mathsf{P} \subseteq \mathsf{ZPSPACE}^*[t(n^{O(1)})]$, where*

$$t(n) = k(n) \cdot (a(n) + b(n))$$
$$b(n) = \log n + k(n) \cdot \log c(s(n)) + \log \delta^{-1}(n),$$

provided the following technical conditions hold: $b(n)$ is space constructible, $a(O(n)) \subseteq O(a(n))$, $\log c(O(s(O(n)))) \subseteq O(\log c(s(n)))$, $k(O(n)) \subseteq O(k(n))$, and $\log \delta^{-1}(O(n)) \subseteq O(\log \delta^{-1}(n))$.

Proof. Since CVP is complete for P under logspace many-one reductions and P is closed under complement, it suffices to show that we can solve CVP in $\mathsf{ZPSPACE}^*[t(n)]$ assuming the existence of a language S of census at most $c(n)$ that is hard for P under randomized two-sided error truth-table reductions that query at most $O(k(n))$ strings of length at most $O(s(n))$, run in space $O(a(n))$ (provided two-way read access to a random bit tape) and have confidence at least $\Omega(\delta(n))$ on inputs of length n.

The algorithm is the same as in the proof of the Randomized Main Theorem. We only have to analyze its space complexity under the parameterizations considered.

Let y be an instance of CVP of length n with m gates. Under the given technical conditions, the space needed for the simulations of the randomized circuit C_m of Lemma 4.3.1 using an oracle is $O(\ell(m)) \subseteq O(b(n))$. Consequently, the space complexity of the set system E is $O(b(n) + \log r(n)) \subseteq O(b(n) + a(n))$. In order for the success probability to be bounded from below by a constant, we choose $\log p(n) \in \theta(b(n))$ in the application of the Randomized Generic Combinatorial Lemma. The space needed to construct the lists with oracle answers is then $O(t(n))$. Since the simulations themselves only require $O(b(n))$ space as argued above, and the solution checker runs in logspace, the overall space complexity of the algorithm is $O(t(n))$.

Instantiations. By the same simple observations as in the deterministic case, we obtain the following instantiations of the Randomized Generic Theorem for polynomially dense hard languages. The Randomized Main Theorem is a special case of the first one.

Theorem 4.3.4. *Let $e \geqslant 1$ and $f \geqslant 0$. There is no sparse hard language for P under randomized two-sided error truth-table reductions computable in space $O(log^e n)$ (given two-way read access to a random bit tape) with confidence at least inversely polynomial that make at most $O(\log^f n)$ queries unless $P \subseteq ZPSPACE^*[\log^{e+2f} n]$.*

Theorem 4.3.5. *Let $e \geqslant 1$, $f \geqslant 0$ and $g > 0$. There is no sparse hard language for P under randomized two-sided error truth-table reductions computable in space $O(log^e n)$ (given two-way read access to a random bit tape) with confidence at least $2^{-O(\log^g n)}$ that make at most $O(\log^f n)$ queries unless $P \subseteq ZPSPACE^*[\log^a n]$, where $a = \max(e + 2f, f + g)$.*

For quasipolynomially dense hard languages we get:

Theorem 4.3.6. *Let $d > 0$, $e \geqslant 1$ and $f, g \geqslant 0$. There is no hard language for P with density bounded by $2^{O(\log^d n)}$ under randomized two-sided error truth-table reductions computable in space $O(\log^e n)$ (given two-way read access to a random bit tape) with confidence at least $2^{-O(\log^g n)}$ that make at most $O(\log^f n)$ queries unless $P \subseteq ZPSPACE^*[\log^a n]$, where $a = \max(de + 2f, e + f, f + g)$.*

In particular the following holds.

Corollary 4.3.1. *There is no quasipolynomially dense hard language for P under randomized two-sided error truth-table reductions computable in* *polylog-space (given two-way read access to a random bit tape) with confidence at least inversely quasipolynomial and using no more than polylogarithmically many queries unless* P $\subseteq$ ZPSPACE*[polylog$n$].

4.3.4 Extension to Classes Other Than P

In this subsection, we apply the idea of the Randomized Main Theorem to prove theorems of the form: There is no sparse hard language for C_1 under randomized two-sided error bounded truth-table reductions with confidence at least inversely polynomial and computable within the randomized class C_2 unless $C_1 \subseteq C_2$. For the technique to work, languages in C_1 must have unique membership proofs that can be constructed in C_1 and checked in C_2, and C_2 has to contain randomized NC^1. We can then Hadamard encode the membership proofs and use the Randomized Combinatorial Lemma and Lemma 4.3.1 to recover them with high probability in C_2. As in the deterministic case, this approach works for NL and L. In the randomized case, we can also apply it to NP. Languages in NP are not known to have unique membership proofs, but Valiant and Vazirani [137] showed that randomness allows us to reduce the number of proofs with high probability to one, if there is one.

Theorem 4.3.7. *There is no sparse hard language for* NL *under* $\leqslant_{btt}^{BPL^*}$*-reductions with confidence at least inversely polynomial unless* NL $\subseteq$ ZPL*.

Proof. Assuming the existence of a sparse hard language for NL under $\leqslant_{btt}^{BPL^*}$-reductions with confidence at least inversely polynomial, we will show how to solve in RL* the NL-complete problem DAG-STCON. Since NL is closed under complement [67, 130], this suffices to show that NL $\subseteq$ ZPL*.

We use the auxiliary language

$$A_6 = \{\langle G, s, t, w \rangle | \ G \text{ DAG with } m \text{ vertices}, s, t \text{ vertices of } G,$$

$$w \in (\text{GF}(2))^m \text{ and } \sum_{j=1}^{m} w_j g_j = 1\},$$

where g_j is a Boolean indicating whether G contains a directed path from the j-th vertex of G to t, and the arithmetic is over GF(2) . We argued in the proof of Theorem 4.2.5 that the values $g_1, \ldots, g_m$ constitute a logspace verifiable proof of membership of $\langle G, s, t \rangle$ to DAG-STCON.

A_6 incorporates Hadamard encodings of these values. Since the language of DAG's is in coNL = NL, and we can compute the values g_j and check the equation $\sum_{j=1}^{m} w_j g_j = 1$ in L^{NL} = NL, it is obvious that $A_6 \in$ NL, whence by hypothesis reduces to a sparse language through a $\leqslant_{btt}^{BPL^*}$-reduction with confidence at least inversely polynomial. Therefore, applying Lemma 4.3.1 and the Randomized Combinatorial Lemma as in the proof of the Randomized Main Theorem, allows to generate in randomized logspace a list of strings in

Σ^m which contains $g_1 g_2 \ldots g_m$ with probability bounded from 0. So, it suffices to submit each of these strings to the logspace proof checker to obtain our RL^* algorithm for DAG-STCON. *(End of the proof of Theorem 4.3.7.)*

The above algorithm for DAG-STCON is actually RNC^1 modulo the complexity of the reduction and has only parallel queries to the reduction. DAG-STCON being complete for NL under $\leqslant_m^{\mathsf{NC}^1}$-reductions, the next theorem follows.

Theorem 4.3.8. *There is no sparse hard language for* NL *under* $\leqslant_{btt}^{\mathsf{BPNC}^1}$- *reductions with confidence at least inversely polynomial unless* $\mathsf{NL} \subseteq \mathsf{ZPNC}^1$.

For L we obtain:

Theorem 4.3.9. *There is no sparse hard language for* L *under* $\leqslant_{btt}^{\mathsf{BPNC}^1}$- *reductions with confidence at least inversely polynomial unless* $\mathsf{L} \subseteq \mathsf{ZPNC}^1$.

Proof. Assuming the existence of a sparse hard language for L under $\leqslant_{btt}^{\mathsf{BPNC}^1}$- reductions with confidence at least inversely polynomial, we will show how to solve in RNC^1 the L-complete problem F-STCON. Since L is closed under complementation, the latter implies that $\mathsf{L} \subseteq \mathsf{ZPNC}^1$.

Consider the auxiliary language

$$A_7 = \{\langle G, s, t, w \rangle \mid G \text{ forest with } m \text{ edges, } s, t \text{ vertices of } G,$$

$$w \in (\mathrm{GF}(2))^m \text{ and } \sum_{j=1}^{m} w_j e_j = 1\},$$

where e_j is a Boolean indicating whether s and t belong to the same component of G and the j-th edge of G is on the unique path connecting s and t in G. The arithmetic is over $\mathrm{GF}(2)$. We showed in the proof of Theorem 4.2.7 that the values $e_1, \ldots, e_m$ constitute an NC^1-verifiable proof of membership of $\langle G, s, t \rangle$ to F-STCON. It is also obvious from the arguments in that proof that $A_7 \in \mathsf{L}$.

A_7 contains Hadamard encodings of the values $e_1, \ldots, e_m$, and by hypothesis, it reduces to a sparse language through a $\leqslant_{btt}^{\mathsf{BPNC}^1}$-reduction with confidence at least inversely polynomial. Therefore, another application of Lemma 4.3.1 and the Randomized Combinatorial Lemma and as in the proof of the Randomized Main Theorem, yields an RNC^1 algorithm that with probability bounded from 0, outputs a list containing the string $e_1 e_2 \ldots e_m$. We can then use the NC^1 solution checker to weed out the incorrect ones. The resulting algorithm for F-STCON is in RNC^1.

(End of the proof of Theorem 4.3.9.)

Valiant and Vazirani [137] constructed a $\leqslant_m^{\mathsf{RNC}^1}$-reduction of satisfiability to unique satisfiability that has confidence $\Omega(n^{-1})$. It allows us to apply the strategy behind the Randomized Main Theorem to NP.

Theorem 4.3.10. *There is no sparse hard language for* NP *under* $\leqslant^{\mathsf{BPL}^*}_{\mathrm{btt}}$ *reductions with confidence at least inversely polynomial unless* NP = RL*.

Proof. Assuming the existence of a sparse hard language for NP under $\leqslant^{\mathsf{BPL}^*}_{\mathrm{btt}}$ reductions with confidence randomized two-sided error bounded truth-table reductions computable in logspace (given two-way read access to a random bit tape) and with confidence at least inversely polynomial, we will show how to check in RL* the satisfiability of Boolean formulae with at most one satisfying assignment (USAT). This suffices to show that NP $\subseteq$ RL*, because SAT is NP-complete under $\leqslant^{\mathsf{L}}$ m-reductions, and Valiant and Vazirani proved that we can self-reduce SAT using an $\leqslant^{\mathsf{RL}^*}_{\mathrm{m}}$-reduction such that with confidence $\Omega(n^{-1})$, a satisfiable formula is reduced to one with exactly one satisfying assignment.

Consider the language

$$A_8 = \{\langle \varphi, w \rangle \mid \varphi \text{ Boolean formula on } m \text{ variables}, w \in \Sigma^m \text{ and}$$
$$(\exists b \in \Sigma^m)\,[\varphi(b) \text{ and } w \cdot b = 1]\},$$

where $w \cdot b$ represents the inner product of w and b as vectors in $(\mathrm{GF}(2))^m$. It is clear that $A_8 \in$ NP, so by hypothesis A_8 reduces to a sparse language under a $\leqslant^{\mathsf{BPL}^*}_{\mathrm{btt}}$-reduction with confidence at least inversely polynomial.

In case φ has exactly one satisfying assignment b^*, $(\chi_{A_8}(\langle \varphi, w \rangle))_{w \in (\mathrm{GF}(2))^m}$ is the Hadamard encoding of this unique satisfying assignment. Using Lemma 4.3.1 and the Randomized Combinatorial Lemma as in the proof of the Randomized Main Theorem, we can recover b^* in RL* in the sense of generating a list of assignments that contains b^* with bounded positive probability. Since we can check whether a given assignment satisfies φ in logspace, doing that for all assignments of the above list yields an RL* algorithm for the promise problem USAT. *(End of the proof of Theorem 4.3.10.)*

Again, the algorithm we constructed for SAT is actually RNC^1 modulo the complexity of the reduction, and only has parallel queries to the reduction. Since SAT is complete for NP under $\leqslant^{\mathsf{NC}^1}_{\mathrm{m}}$-reductions, we obtain:

Theorem 4.3.11. *There is no sparse hard language for* NP *under* $\leqslant^{\mathsf{BPNC}^1}_{\mathrm{btt}}$ *reduction with confidence at least inversely polynomial unless* NP = RNC^1.

Finally, we can also prove an analogue result for (presumably) stronger reductions, namely polynomial-time-computable ones.

Theorem 4.3.12. *There is no sparse hard language for* NP *under* $\leqslant^{\mathsf{BPP}}_{\mathrm{btt}}$ *reduction with confidence at least inversely polynomial unless* NP = RP.

Proof. The proof follows the lines of the one for Theorem 4.3.10. It suffices to observe that the Randomized Combinatorial Lemma also holds when the language A is *polynomial-time* bounded truth-table reducible to the sparse language S by a randomized two-sided error reduction, and that the algorithm it provides then also runs in polynomial-time, as does the algorithm for SAT obtained by combination with Lemma 4.3.1 like in Theorem 4.3.10.

4.4 Conclusion and Open Questions

For various complexity classes $\mathcal{C}$ and $\mathcal{D}$ such that $\mathcal{C} \subseteq \mathcal{D}$, we established that $\mathcal{C}$ equals $\mathcal{D}$ iff $\mathcal{D}$ has a sparse $\leqslant^{\mathcal{C}}_{btt}$-hard language. Therefore, proving that there are no sparse $\leqslant^{\mathcal{C}}_{btt}$-hard languages for $\mathcal{D}$ is a good approach for separating $\mathcal{C}$ from $\mathcal{D}$.

In case of the P versus L problem, it is easy to see that our Generic Theorem, based on the hypothesis that $P \neq L$, only rules out the existence of sparse hard languages for P under logspace truth-table reductions with a *bounded* number of queries, even if we relax the sparseness condition. If we allow the number of queries to increase modestly with the input size, e.g., polylogarithmically, we get other unlikely inclusions of P in space-bounded complexity classes. However, without any explicit bound on the number of queries, we do not get a collapse at all. Can we do better using another approach?

A more technical problem is the following. Regarding randomized reductions with two-sided error, it is an open question whether our results also hold for the more natural read-once concept for randomized space-bounded computation. In this model, the Turing machine only has one-way read access to its random tape, as opposed to the multiple access randomness model, in which the machine has two-way read access to its random tape. The randomized algorithms we construct use the latter model, because they basically simulate randomized circuits, and randomized circuits inherently have the ability to reuse their random seeds. Nisan [102] gives strong evidence that in general the multiple access model is more powerful than the read-once model, but in this specific context that may not be the case.

5. Autoreducibility of Complete Languages

This chapter looks at another property of complete languages that allows us to separate complexity classes, namely their redundancy. We will investigate a very general notion of redundancy, known as autoreducibility.

5.1 Introduction

A language A is autoreducible if we can decide whether an input x belongs to A in polynomial-time by making queries about membership of strings different from x to A.

Trakhtenbrot [133] first looked at autoreducibility in both the unbounded and space-bounded models. Ladner [76] showed that there exist Turing-complete computably enumerable languages that are not autoreducible. Ambos-Spies [8] first transferred the notion of autoreducibility to the polynomial-time setting. More recently, Yao [139] and Beigel and Feigenbaum [23] have studied a randomized variant of autoreducibility known as "coherence."

In this chapter, we ask for what complexity classes do all the complete languages have the autoreducibility property. In particular we show:

- All Turing-complete languages for $\Delta_k^{\exp}$ are autoreducible for any constant k, where $\Delta_{k+1}^{\exp}$ denotes the languages that are exponential-time Turing-reducible to Σ_k^p.
- There exists a Turing-complete language for doubly exponential space that is not autoreducible.

Since the union of all classes $\Delta_k^{\exp}$ coincides with the exponential-time hierarchy, we obtain a separation of the exponential-time hierarchy from doubly exponential space and thus of the polynomial-time hierarchy from exponential space. Although these results also follow from the space hierarchy theorems [61] which we have known for a long time, our proof does not directly use diagonalization, rather separates the classes by showing that they have different structural properties.

Issues of relativization do not apply to this work because of oracle access (see [53]): A polynomial-time autoreduction cannot view as much of the oracle as an exponential or doubly exponential computation. To illustrate this point

D. van Mehlkebeek: Randomness and Completeness in Computational Complexity, LNCS 1950, pp. 113–140, 2000.

we show that there exists an oracle relative to which some complete language for exponential time is not autoreducible.

Note that if we can settle whether the Turing-complete languages for doubly exponential time are all autoreducible one way or the other, we will have a major separation result. If there exists a Turing-complete language for doubly exponential time that is not autoreducible, then we get that the exponential-time hierarchy is strictly contained in doubly exponential time thus that the polynomial-time hierarchy is strictly contained in exponential time. If all of the Turing-complete languages for doubly exponential time are autoreducible, we get that doubly exponential time is strictly contained in doubly exponential space, and thus polynomial time strictly in polynomial space. We will also show that this assumption implies a separation of nondeterministic logarithmic space from nondeterministic polynomial time. Similar implications hold for space-bounded classes (see Section 5.5). Autoreducibility questions about doubly exponential time and exponential space thus remain an exciting line of research.

We also study the nonadaptive variant of the problem. Our main results scale down one exponential as follows.

- All truth-table-complete languages for Δ_k^p are truth-table-autoreducible for any constant k, where Δ_{k+1}^p denotes those languages polynomial-time Turing-reducible to Σ_k^p.
- There exists a truth-table-complete language for exponential space that is not truth-table-autoreducible.

Again, finding out whether all truth-table-complete languages for intermediate classes, namely polynomial space and exponential time, are truth-table-autoreducible, would have major implications.

In contrast to the above results we exhibit the limitations of our approach: For the restricted reducibility where we are only allowed to ask two nonadaptive queries, all complete languages for EXP, EXPSPACE, EEXP, EEXPSPACE, etc., are autoreducible.

We also argue that uniformity is crucial for our technique of separating complexity classes, because our nonautoreducibility results fail in the nonuniform setting. Razborov and Rudich [115] show that if strong pseudo-random generators exist, "natural proofs" cannot separate certain nonuniform complexity classes. Since this paper relies on uniformity in an essential way, their result does not apply.

Regarding the randomized variant of autoreducibility mentioned above, we can strengthen our results and construct a Turing-complete language for doubly exponential space that is not even randomly autoreducible. We leave the analogue of this theorem in the nonadaptive setting open: Does there exist a truth-table-complete language for exponential space that is not randomly truth-table autoreducible? We do show that every truth-table-complete language for exponential time is randomly truth-table autoreducible. So, a positive answer to the open question would establish that exponential time is strictly contained in exponential space. A negative answer, on the other hand, would imply a separation of nondeterministic logarithmic space from nondeterministic polynomial time.

Here is the outline of this chapter. First, we formally define autoreducibility and its variants in Section 5.2. Next, in Section 5.3 we establish our negative autoreducibility results, for the adaptive as well as the nonadaptive case. Then we prove the positive results in Section 5.4, where we also briefly look at the randomized and nonuniform settings. Section 5.5 discusses the separations that follow from our results and would follow from improvements on them. Finally, we conclude in Section 5.6 and mention some possible directions for further research.

5.2 Definitions

Given a Turing reduction M, we denote the set of queries of M on input x with oracle B by $Q_{M^B}(x)$; in case of nonadaptive reductions, we omit the oracle B in the notation.

A language A is *autoreducible* if there is a reduction M of A to itself that never queries its own input, i.e., for any input x and any oracle B, $x \notin Q_{M^B}(x)$. We call such M an *autoreduction* of A.

We will also discuss randomized and nonuniform variants. A language is *randomly autoreducible* if it has a randomized autoreduction with bounded two-sided error. Yao [139] first studied this concept under the name "coherence". A language is *nonuniformly autoreducible* if it has an autoreduction that uses polynomial advice. For all these notions, we can consider both the adaptive and the nonadaptive case. For randomized autoreducibility, nonadaptiveness means that the queries only depend on the input and the random seed.

For any integer $k \geqslant 1$, a QBF$_k$-formula is a fully quantified Boolean formula with no more than $k - 1$ quantifier alternations. A QBF$_0$-formula is a quantified Boolean formula without quantifiers, i.e., a Boolean formula. The language TQBF$_k$ of all true QBF$_k$-formulae is $\leqslant_m^P$-complete for Σ_k^P. For $k = 1$, this reduces to the fact that the language SAT of satisfiable Boolean formulae is $\leqslant_m^P$-complete for NP.

5.3 Nonautoreducibility Results

In this section, we show that large complexity classes have complete languages that are not autoreducible.

Theorem 5.3.1. *There is a $\leqslant_{2-T}^P$-complete language for EEXPSPACE that is not autoreducible.*

Most natural classes containing EEXPSPACE also have this property, e.g., EEEXPTIME and EEEXPSPACE.

We can even construct the complete language in Theorem 5.3.1 to defeat every randomized autoreduction.

Theorem 5.3.2. *There is a $\leqslant_{2-T}^{P}$-complete language for* EEXPSPACE *that is not $\leqslant_{T}^{BPP}$-autoreducible.*

In the nonadaptive setting, we obtain:

Theorem 5.3.3. *There is a $\leqslant_{3-tt}^{P}$-complete language for* EXPSPACE *that is not nonadaptively autoreducible.*

Unlike the case of Theorem 5.3.1, our construction does not seem to yield a truth-table-complete language that is not randomly nonadaptively autoreducible. In fact, as we shall show in Section 5.4.3, such a result would separate EXP from EXPSPACE. See also Section 5.5.

We will detail in Section 5.4.3 that our nonautoreducibility results do not hold in the nonuniform setting.

5.3.1 Adaptive Autoreductions

Suppose we want to construct a nonautoreducible Turing-complete language for a complexity class $\mathcal{C}$, i.e., a language A such that:

1. A is not autoreducible.
2. A is Turing-hard for $\mathcal{C}$.
3. A belongs to $\mathcal{C}$.

If $\mathcal{C}$ has a $\leqslant_{m}^{P}$-complete language K, realizing goals 1 and 2 is not too hard: We can encode K in A, and at the same time diagonalize against all auto-reductions. A straightforward implementation would be to encode $K(y)$ as $A(\langle 0, y \rangle)$, and stage-wise diagonalize against all $\leqslant_{T}^{P}$-reductions M by picking for each M an input x not of the form $\langle 0, y \rangle$ that is not queried during previous stages, and setting $A(x) = 1 - M^{A}(x)$. However, this construction does not seem to achieve the third goal. In particular, deciding the membership of a diagonalization string x to A might require computing $A(\langle 0, y \rangle) = K(y)$ on inputs y of length $|x|^{c}$, assuming M runs in time n^{c}. Since we have to do this for all potential autoreductions M, we can only bound the resources (time, space) needed to decide A by a function in $t(n^{\omega(1)})$, where $t(n)$ denotes the amount of resources some deterministic Turing machine accepting K uses. That does not suffice to keep A inside $\mathcal{C}$.

To remedy this problem, we will avoid the need to compute $K(y)$ on large inputs y, say of length at least $|x|$. Instead, we will make sure we can encode the membership of such strings to *any* language, not just K, and at the same time diagonalize against M on input x. We will argue that we can do this by considering two possible coding regions at every stage as opposed to a fixed one: the left region L, containing strings of the form $\langle 0, y \rangle$, and the right region R, similarly containing strings of the form $\langle 1, y \rangle$. The following states that we can use one of the regions to encode an arbitrary sequence, and set the other region such that the output of M on input x is fixed and indicates the region used for encoding.

Statement 5.3.1. Either it is the case that for any setting of L there is a setting of R such that $M^A(x)$ accepts, or for any setting of R there is a setting of L such that $M^A(x)$ rejects.

This allows us to achieve goals 1 and 2 from above as follows. In the former case, we will set $A(x) = 0$ and encode K in L (at that stage); otherwise we will set $A(x) = 1$ and encode K in R. Since the value of $A(x)$ does not affect the behavior of M^A on input x, we diagonalize against M in both cases. Also, in any case

$$K(y) = A(\langle A(x), y \rangle),$$

so deciding K is still easy when given A. Moreover — and crucially — in order to compute $A(x)$, we no longer have to decide $K(y)$ on large inputs y, of length $|x|$ or more. Instead, we have to check whether the former case in Statement 5.3.1 holds or not. Although quite complex a task, it only depends on M and on the part of A constructed so far, not on the value of $K(y)$ for any input of length $|x|$ or more: We verify whether we can encode *any* sequence, not just the characteristic sequence of K for lengths at least $|x|$, and at the same time diagonalize against M on input x. Provided the complexity class $\mathcal{C}$ is sufficiently powerful, we can perform this task in $\mathcal{C}$.

There is still a catch, though. Suppose we have found out that the former case in Statement 5.3.1 holds. Then we will use the left region L to encode K (at that stage), and we know we can diagonalize against M on input x by setting the bits of the right region R appropriately. However, deciding exactly how to set these bits of the noncoding region requires, in addition to determining which region we should use for coding, the knowledge of $K(y)$ for all y such that $|x| \leqslant |y| \leqslant |x|^c$. In order to also circumvent the need to decide K for too large inputs here, we will use a slightly stronger version of Statement 5.3.1 obtained by grouping quantifiers into blocks and rearranging them. We will partition the coding and noncoding regions into intervals. We will make sure that for any given interval, the length of a string in that interval (or any of the previous intervals) is no more than the square of the length of any string in that interval. Then we will block-wise alternately set the bits in the coding region according to K, and the corresponding ones in the noncoding region so as to maintain the diagonalization against M on input x as in Statement 5.3.1. This way, in order to compute the bit $A(\langle 1, z \rangle)$ of the noncoding region, we will only have to query K on inputs y with $|y| \leqslant |z|^2$, as opposed to $|y| \leqslant |z|^c$ for an arbitrarily large c depending on M as was the case before.

This is what happens in the next lemma, which we prove in a more general form, because we will need the generalization later on in Section 5.5.

Lemma 5.3.1. *Fix a language K, and suppose we can decide it simultaneously in time $t(n)$ and space $s(n)$. Let $\alpha : \mathbb{N} \to (0, \infty)$ be a constructible monotone unbounded function, and suppose there is a deterministic Turing machine accepting* TQBF *that takes time $t'(n)$ and space $s'(n)$ on QBF-formulae of size $2^{n^{\alpha(n)}}$ with at most $\log \alpha(n)$ alternations. Then there is a language A such that:*

1. *A is not autoreducible.*
2. *$K \leqslant_{2\text{-T}}^{\text{P}} A$.*
3. *We can decide A simultaneously in time $O(2^{n^2} \cdot t(n^2) + 2^n \cdot t'(n))$ and space $O(2^{n^2} + s(n^2) + s'(n))$.*

Proof. Fix a function α satisfying the hypotheses of the lemma, and let $\beta = \sqrt{\alpha}$. Let $M_1, M_2, \ldots$ be a standard enumeration of autoreductions clocked such that M_i runs in time $n^{\beta(i)}$ on inputs of length n. Our construction starts out with A being the empty language, and then adds strings to A in subsequent stages $i = 1, 2, 3, \ldots$ defined by the following sequence:

$$\begin{cases} n_0 = 0 \\ n_{i+1} = n_i^{\beta(n_i)} + 1. \end{cases}$$

Note that since M_i runs in time $n^{\beta(i)}$, M_i cannot query strings of length n_{i+1} or more on input 0^{n_i}.

Fix an integer $i \geqslant 1$ and let $m = n_i$. For any integer j, $0 \leqslant j \leqslant \log \beta(m)$, let I_j denote the set of all strings with lengths in the interval $[m^{2^j}, \min(m^{2^{j+1}}, m^{\beta(m)} + 1))$. Note that $\{I_j\}_{j=0}^{\log \beta(m)}$ forms a partition of the set I of strings with lengths in $[m, m^{\beta(m)} + 1) = [n_i, n_{i+1})$ with the property that for any $0 \leqslant k \leqslant \log \beta(m)$, the length of any string in $\cup_{j=0}^{k} I_j$ is no more than the square of the length of any string in I_k.

During the i-th stage of the construction, we will encode the restriction $K|_I$ of K to I into $\{\langle b, y \rangle \mid b \in \{0, 1\}$ and $y \in I\}$, and use the string 0^m for diagonalizing against M_i, applying the next strengthening of Statement 5.3.1 to do so:

Claim 5.3.1. For any language A, at least one of the following holds:

$$(\forall \ell_y)_{y \in I_0} (\exists r_y)_{y \in I_0} (\forall \ell_y)_{y \in I_1} (\exists r_y)_{y \in I_1}$$
$$\ldots (\forall \ell_y)_{y \in I_{\log \beta(m)}} (\exists r_y)_{y \in I_{\log \beta(m)}} M_i^{A'}(0^m) \text{ accepts} \tag{5.1}$$

or

$$(\forall r_y)_{y \in I_0} (\exists \ell_y)_{y \in I_0} (\forall r_y)_{y \in I_1} (\exists \ell_y)_{y \in I_1}$$
$$\ldots (\forall r_y)_{y \in I_{\log \beta(m)}} (\exists \ell_y)_{y \in I_{\log \beta(m)}} M_i^{A'}(0^m) \text{ rejects}, \tag{5.2}$$

where A' denotes $A \cup \{\langle 0, y \rangle \mid y \in I$ and $\ell_y = 1\} \cup \{\langle 1, y \rangle \mid y \in I$ and $r_y = 1\}$.

Here we use $(Q\, z_y)_{y \in Y}$ as a shorthand for $(Q\, z_{y_1})\, (Q\, z_{y_2}) \ldots (Q\, z_{y_{\|Y\|}})$, where Y denotes the set $\{y_1, y_2, \ldots, y_{\|Y\|}\}$ and all variables are quantified over $\{0, 1\}$. Without loss of generality we assume that the range of the pairing function $\langle \cdot, \cdot \rangle$ is disjoint from 0^*.

Proof (of Claim 5.3.1). Fix A. If (5.1) does not hold, then its negation holds, i.e,

$$(\exists \ell_y)_{y \in I_0}\, (\forall r_y)_{y \in I_0}\, (\exists \ell_y)_{y \in I_1}\, (\forall r_y)_{y \in I_1}$$

$$\ldots (\exists \ell_y)_{y \in I_{\log \beta(m)}}\, (\forall r_y)_{y \in I_{\log \beta(m)}}\, M_i^{A'}(0^m) \text{ rejects.} \tag{5.3}$$

Switching the quantifiers $(\exists \ell_y)_{y \in I_j}$ and $(\forall r_y)_{y \in I_j}$ pairwise for every $0 \leqslant j \leqslant \log \beta(m)$ in (5.3) yields the weaker statement (5.2). This finishes the proof of Claim 5.3.1.

---

if formula (5.1) holds
    then for $j = 0, \ldots, \log \beta(m)$
        $(\ell_y)_{y \in I_j} \leftarrow (K(y))_{y \in I_j}$
        $(r_y)_{y \in I_j} \leftarrow$ the lexicographically first value satisfying
            $(\forall \ell_y)_{y \in I_{j+1}}\, (\exists r_y)_{y \in I_{j+1}}\, (\forall \ell_y)_{y \in I_{j+2}}\, (\exists r_y)_{y \in I_{j+2}}$
              $\ldots (\forall \ell_y)_{y \in I_{\log \beta(m)}}\, (\exists r_y)_{y \in I_{\log \beta(m)}}\, M_i^{A'}(0^m)$ accepts,
          where $A' = A \cup \{\langle 0, y \rangle \mid y \in I \text{ and } \ell_y = 1\}$
                    $\cup \{\langle 1, y \rangle \mid y \in I \text{ and } r_y = 1\}$
    endfor
    $A \leftarrow A \cup \{\langle 0, y \rangle \mid y \in I \text{ and } \ell_y = 1\} \cup \{\langle 1, y \rangle \mid y \in I \text{ and } r_y = 1\}$
    else { formula (5.2) holds }
    for $j = 0, \ldots, \log \beta(m)$
        $(r_y)_{y \in I_j} \leftarrow (K(y))_{y \in I_j}$
        $(\ell_y)_{y \in I_j} \leftarrow$ the lexicographically first value satisfying
            $(\forall r_y)_{y \in I_{j+1}}\, (\exists \ell_y)_{y \in I_{j+1}}\, (\forall r_y)_{y \in I_{j+2}}\, (\exists \ell_y)_{y \in I_{j+2}}$
              $\ldots (\forall r_y)_{y \in I_{\log \beta(m)}}\, (\exists \ell_y)_{y \in I_{\log \beta(m)}}\, M_i^{A'}(0^m)$ accepts,
          where $A' = A \cup \{\langle 0, y \rangle \mid y \in I \text{ and } \ell_y = 1\}$
                    $\cup \{\langle 1, y \rangle \mid y \in I \text{ and } r_y = 1\}$
    endfor
    $A \leftarrow A \cup \{0^m\} \cup \{\langle 0, y \rangle \mid y \in I \text{ and } \ell_y = 1\} \cup \{\langle 1, y \rangle \mid y \in I \text{ and } r_y = 1\}$
endif

Fig. 5.1. Stage i of the construction of the language A in Lemma 5.3.1

Figure 5.1 describes the i-th stage in the construction of the language A. Note that the lexicographically first values in this algorithm always exist, so the construction works fine. We now argue that the resulting language A satisfies the properties of Lemma 5.3.1.

1. The construction guarantees that by the end of stage i, $A(0^m) = 1 - M_i^{A \setminus \{0^m\}}(0^m)$ holds. Since M_i on input 0^m cannot query 0^m (because M_i is an autoreduction) nor any of the strings added during subsequent stages (because M_i does not even have the time to write down any of these strings), $A(0^m) = 1 - M_i^A(0^m)$ holds for the final language A. So, M_i is not an autoreduction of A. Since this is true of any autoreduction M_i, the language A is not autoreducible.

2. During stage i, we encode $K|_I$ in the left region iff we do not put 0^m into A; otherwise we encode $K|_I$ in the right region. So, for any $y \in I$, $K(y) = A(\langle A(0^m), y \rangle)$. Therefore, $K \leqslant_{2-T}^P A$.

3. First note that A only contains strings of the form 0^m with $m = n_i$ for some integer $i \geqslant 1$, and strings of the form $\langle b, y \rangle$ with $b \in \{0, 1\}$ and $y \in \Sigma^*$.

   Assume we have executed the construction of A up to but not including stage i and stored the result in memory. The additional work to decide the membership to A of a string belonging to the i-th stage, is as follows.

   Case 0^m

   Since $0^m \in A$ iff (5.1) does not hold and (5.1) is a $\text{QBF}_{2 \log \beta(m)}$-formula of size $2^{O(m^{\beta(m)})} \leqslant 2^{m^{\alpha(m)}}$, we can decide whether $0^m \in A$ in time $O(t'(m))$ and space $O(s'(m))$.

   Case $\langle b, z \rangle$ where $b = A(0^m)$ and $z \in I$

   Then $\langle b, z \rangle \in A$ iff $z \in K$, which we can decide in time $t(|z|)$ and space $s(|z|)$.

   Case $\langle b, z \rangle$ where $b = 1 - A(0^m)$ and $z \in I$

   Say $z \in I_k, 0 \leqslant k \leqslant \log \beta(m)$. In order to compute whether $\langle b, z \rangle \in A$, we run the part of stage i corresponding to the values of j in Figure 5.1 up to and including k, and store the results in memory. This involves computing K on $\cup_{j=0}^k I_j$ and deciding $O(2^{|z|})$ $\text{QBF}_{2 \log \beta(m)}$-formulae of size $2^{O(m^{\beta(m)})} \leqslant 2^{m^{\alpha(m)}}$, namely one formula for each $y \in \cup_{j=0}^k I_j$ which precedes or equals z in lexicographic order. The latter takes $O(2^{|z|} \cdot t'(m))$ time and $O(2^{|z|} + s'(m))$ space. Since every string in $\cup_{j=0}^k I_j$ is of size no more than $|z|^2$, we can do the former in time $O(2^{|z|^2} \cdot t(|z|^2))$ and space $O(2^{|z|^2} + s(|z|^2))$. So, the requirements for this stage are $O(2^{|z|^2} \cdot t(|z|^2) + 2^{|z|} \cdot t'(|z|))$ time and $O(2^{|z|^2} + s(|z|^2) + s'(|z|))$ space.

   A similar analysis also shows that we can perform the stages up to but not including i in time $O(2^m \cdot (t(m) + t'(m)))$ and space $O(2^m + s(m) + s'(m))$. All together, this yields the time and space bounds claimed for A.

   (End of the proof of Lemma 5.3.1.)

Using the upper bound $2^{n^{\alpha(n)}}$ for $s'(n)$, the smallest standard complexity class to which Lemma 5.3.1 applies, seems to be **EEXPSPACE**. This results in Theorem 5.3.1.

Proof (of Theorem 5.3.1). In Lemma 5.3.1, set K a $\leqslant_{m}^{P}$-complete language for EEXPSPACE, and $\alpha(n) = n$.

In Section 5.4.2, we will see that $\leqslant_{2-T}^{P}$ in the statement of Theorem 5.3.1 is optimal: Theorem 5.4.5 shows that Theorem 5.3.1 fails for $\leqslant_{2-tt}^{P}$.

We note that the proof of Theorem 5.3.1 carries through for $\leqslant_{T}^{EXPSPACE}$-reductions with polynomially bounded query lengths. This yields the strengthening given by Theorem 5.3.2.

5.3.2 Nonadaptive Autoreductions

Diagonalizing against nonadaptive autoreductions M is easier. If M runs in time $\tau(n)$, there can be no more than $\tau(n)$ coding strings that interfere with the diagonalization, as opposed to $2^{\tau(n)}$ in the adaptive case. This allows us to reduce the complexity of the language constructed in Lemma 5.3.1 as follows.

Lemma 5.3.2. *Fix a language K, and suppose we can decide it simultaneously in time $t(n)$ and space $s(n)$. Let $\alpha : \mathbb{N} \to (0, \infty)$ be a constructible monotone unbounded function, and suppose there is a deterministic Turing machine accepting TQBF that takes time $t'(n)$ and space $s'(n)$ on QBF-formulae of size $n^{\alpha(n)}$ with at most $\log \alpha(n)$ alternations. Then there is a language A such that:*

1. *A is not nonadaptively autoreducible.*
2. *$K \leqslant_{3-tt}^{P} A$.*
3. *We can decide A simultaneously in time $O((2^{n} + n^{\alpha(n)}) \cdot (t(n^2) + t'(n)))$ and space $O(2^{n} + n^{\alpha(n)} + s(n^2) + s'(n))$.*

Proof. The construction of the language A is the same as in Lemma 5.3.1 (see Figure 5.1) apart from the following differences:

- $M_1, M_2, \ldots$ now is a standard enumeration of nonadaptive autoreductions clocked such that M_i runs in time $n^{\beta(i)}$ on inputs of length n. Note that the set $Q_M(x)$ of possible queries M makes on input x contains no more than $|x|^{\beta(i)}$ elements.
- During stage $i \geqslant 1$ of the construction, I denotes the set of all strings y with lengths in $[m, m^{\beta(m)} + 1) = [n_i, n_{i+1})$ such that $\langle 0, y \rangle \in Q_{M_i}(0^m)$ or $\langle 1, y \rangle \in Q_{M_i}(0^m)$, and I_j for $0 \leqslant j \leqslant \log \beta(m)$ denotes the set of strings in I with lengths in $[m^{2^j}, \min(m^{2^{j+1}}, m^{\beta(m)} + 1))$. Note that the only ℓ_y's and r_y's that affect the validity of the predicate "$M_i^{A'}(0^m)$ accepts" in formula (5.1) and the corresponding formulae in Figure 5.1, are those for which $y \in I$.
- At the end of stage i in Figure 5.1, we add the following line:

$$A \leftarrow A \cup \{\langle b, y \rangle \mid b \in \{0, 1\}, y \in \Sigma^*$$
$$\text{with } m \leqslant |y| < m^{\beta(m)} + 1, y \notin I \text{ and } K(y) = 1\}.$$

This ensures coding $K(y)$ for strings y with lengths in $[n_i, n_{i+1})$ such that neither $\langle 0, y \rangle$ nor $\langle 1, y \rangle$ are queried by M_i on input 0^m. Although not essential, we choose to encode them in both the left and the right region.

The proof that A satisfies the 3 properties claimed, carries over. Only the time and space analysis in the third point needs modification. The crucial simplification over the adaptive case lies in the fact that (5.1) and the similar formulae in Figure 5.1 now become $\mathrm{QBF}_{2\log\beta(n)}$-formulae of size $n^{O(\beta(m))}$ as opposed to of size $2^{O(m^{\beta(m)})}$ in Lemma 5.3.1. More specifically, referring to the proof of Lemma 5.3.1, we have the following cases regarding the work at stage i of the construction.

Case 0^m
   The above mentioned simplification takes care of this case.
Case $\langle b, z \rangle$ where $b = A(0^m)$ and $z \in I$
   The argument of Lemma 5.3.1 carries over as such.
Case $\langle b, z \rangle$ where $b = 1 - A(0^m)$ and $z \in I$
   Computing K on $\cup_{j=0}^{k} I_j$ and storing the result can be done in time $O(m^{\beta(m)} \cdot t(|z|^2))$ and space $O(m^{\beta(m)} + s(|z|^2))$. Deciding the $O(m^{\beta(m)})$ $\mathrm{QBF}_{2\log\beta(m)}$-formulae of size $m^{O(\beta(m))} \leqslant m^{\alpha(m)}$ involved requires no more than $O(m^{\beta(m)} \cdot t'(m))$ time and $O(m^{\beta(m)} + s'(m))$ space.
Case $\langle b, z \rangle$ where $b \in \{0, 1\}$, $m \leqslant |z| \leqslant m^{\beta(m)} + 1$, and $z \notin I$
   This is an additional case. By construction, $\langle b, z \rangle \in A$ iff $z \in K$, which we can decide in time $t(|z|)$ and space $s(|z|)$.

By similar analysis, a rough estimate of the resources required for the previous stages of the construction is $O(2^m \cdot (t(m) + t'(m)))$ time and $O(2^m + s(m) + s'(m))$ space, resulting in a total as stated in the lemma. *(End of the proof of Lemma 5.3.2.)*

As a consequence, we can lower the space complexity in the equivalent of Theorem 5.3.1 from doubly exponential to singly exponential, yielding Theorem 5.3.3. In section 5.4.2, we will show we cannot reduce the number of queries from 3 to 2 in Theorem 5.3.3.

If we restrict the number of queries the nonadaptive autoreduction is allowed to make to some fixed polynomial, the proof technique of Theorem 5.3.3 also applies to EXP. In particular, we obtain:

Theorem 5.3.4. *There is a $\leqslant_{3-tt}^{P}$-complete language for* EXP *that is not $\leqslant_{btt}^{P}$-autoreducible.*

5.4 Autoreducibility Results

For small complexity classes, all complete languages turn out to be autoreducible. Beigel and Feigenbaum [23] established this property of all levels of the polynomial-time hierarchy as well as of PSPACE, the largest class for which it was known to hold before our work. In this section, we will prove it for the Δ-levels of the exponential-time hierarchy.

As to nonadaptive reductions, the question was even open for all levels of the polynomial-time hierarchy. We will show here that the $\leqslant_{tt}^P$-complete languages for the Δ-levels of the polynomial-time hierarchy are nonadaptively autoreducible. For any complexity class containing EXP, we will prove that the $\leqslant_{2-tt}^P$-complete languages are $\leqslant_{2-tt}$-autoreducible.

Finally, we will also consider nonuniform and randomized autoreductions.

Throughout this section, we will assume without loss of generality an encoding γ of a computation of a given oracle Turing machine M on a given input x with the following properties. γ will be a marked concatenation of successive instantaneous descriptions of M, starting with the initial instantaneous description of M on input x, such that:

- Given a pointer to a bit in γ, we can find out whether that bit represents the answer to an oracle query by probing a constant number of bits of γ.
- If it is the answer to an oracle query, the corresponding query is a substring of the prefix of γ up to that point, and we can easily compute a pointer to the beginning of that substring without probing γ any further.
- If it is not the answer to an oracle query, we can perform a local consistency check for that bit which only depends on a constant number of previous bit positions of γ and the input x. Formally, there exist a function g_M and a predicate e_M, both polynomial-time computable, and a constant c_M such that the following holds: For any input x, any index i to a bit position in γ, and any j, $1 \leqslant j \leqslant c_M$, $g_M(x; i, j)$ is an index no larger than i, and

$$e_M(x; i, \gamma_{g_M(x;i,1)}, \gamma_{g_M(x;i,2)}, \ldots, \gamma_{g_M(x;i;c_M)}) \tag{5.4}$$

indicates whether γ passes the local consistency test for its i-th bit γ_i. Provided the prefix of γ up to but not including position i is correct, the local consistency test is passed iff γ_i is correct.

We call such an encoding a *valid computation* of M on input x iff the local consistency tests (5.4) for all the bit positions i that do not correspond to oracle answers, are passed, and the other bits equal the oracle's answer to the corresponding query. Any other string we will call a *computation*.

5.4.1 Adaptive Autoreductions

We will first show that every $\leqslant_T^P$-complete language for EXP is autoreducible, and then generalize to all Δ-levels of the exponential-time hierarchy.

Theorem 5.4.1. *Every $\leqslant_T^P$-complete language for EXP is autoreducible.*

Here is the proof idea: For any of the standard deterministic complexity classes $\mathcal{C}$, we can decide each bit of the computation on a given input x within $\mathcal{C}$. So, if A is a $\leqslant_T^P$-complete language for $\mathcal{C}$ that can be decided by a machine M within the confines of the class $\mathcal{C}$, then we can $\leqslant_{\mathrm{T}}^{\mathrm{P}}$-reduce deciding the i-th bit of the computation of M on input x to A. Now, consider the two (possibly invalid) computations we obtain by applying the above reduction to every bit position, answering all queries except for x according to A, and assuming $x \in A$ for one computation, and $x \notin A$ for the other.

Note that the computation corresponding to the right assumption about $A(x)$, is certainly correct. So, if both computations yield the same answer (which we can efficiently check using A without querying x), that answer is correct. If not, the other computation contains a mistake. We cannot check both computations entirely to see which one is right, but given a pointer to the first incorrect bit of the wrong computation, we can efficiently verify that it is mistaken by checking only a constant number of bits of that computation. The pointer is again computable within $\mathcal{C}$.

In case $\mathcal{C} \subseteq \mathsf{EXP}$, using a $\leqslant_{\mathrm{T}}^{\mathrm{P}}$-reduction to A and assuming $x \in A$ or $x \notin A$ as above, we can determine the pointer with oracle A (but without querying x) in polynomial time, since the pointer's length is polynomially bounded.

We now fill out the details.

Proof (of Theorem 5.4.1). Fix a $\leqslant_{\mathrm{T}}^{\mathrm{P}}$-complete language A for EXP. Say A is accepted by a Turing machine M such that the computation of M on an input of size n has length $2^{p(n)}$ for some fixed polynomial p. Without loss of generality the last bit of the computation gives the final answer. Let g_M, e_M, and c_M be the formalization of the local consistency test for M as described by (5.4).

Let $\mu(\langle x, i \rangle)$ denote the i-th bit of the computation of M on input x. We can compute μ in EXP, so there is an oracle Turing machine R_μ $\leqslant_{\mathrm{T}}^{\mathrm{P}}$-reducing μ to A.

Provided it exists, let $\sigma(x)$ be the first index i, $1 \leqslant i \leqslant 2^{p(|x|)}$, such that $R_\mu^{A \setminus \{x\}}(\langle x, i \rangle) \neq R_\mu^{A \cup \{x\}}(\langle x, i \rangle)$ Again, we can compute σ in EXP, so there is a $\leqslant_{\mathrm{T}}^{\mathrm{P}}$-reduction R_σ from σ to A.

Consider the algorithm in Figure 5.2 for deciding A on input x. The

---

if $R_\mu^{A \setminus \{x\}}(\langle x, 2^{p(|x|)} \rangle) = R_\mu^{A \cup \{x\}}(\langle x, 2^{p(|x|)} \rangle)$
    then accept iff $R_\mu^{A \cup \{x\}}(\langle x, 2^{p(|x|)} \rangle) = 1$
    else $i \leftarrow R_\sigma^{A \cup \{x\}}(x)$
        accept iff $e_M(x; i, R_\mu^{A \setminus \{x\}}(\langle x, g_M(x; i; 1) \rangle), R_\mu^{A \setminus \{x\}}(\langle x, g_M(x; i, 2) \rangle),$
                $\ldots, R_\mu^{A \setminus \{x\}}(\langle x, g_M(x; i, c_M) \rangle)) = 0$
endif

Fig. 5.2. Autoreduction for the language A of Theorem 5.4.1 on input x

algorithm is a polynomial-time oracle Turing machine with oracle A that does not query its own input x. We now argue that it correctly decides A on input x. We distinguish between two cases:

Case $R_\mu^{A\setminus\{x\}}((x, 2^{p(|x|)})) = R_\mu^{A\cup\{x\}}((x, 2^{p(|x|)}))$

Since at least one of the computations $R_\mu^{A\setminus\{x\}}((x, \cdot))$ or $R_\mu^{A\cup\{x\}}((x, \cdot))$ coincides with the actual computation of M on input x, and the last bit of the computation equals the final decision, correctness follows.

Case $R_\mu^{A\setminus\{x\}}((x, 2^{p(|x|)})) \neq R_\mu^{A\cup\{x\}}((x, 2^{p(|x|)}))$

If $x \in A$, then $R_\mu^{A\setminus\{x\}}((x, 2^{p(|x|)})) = 0$, so $R_\mu^{A\setminus\{x\}}((x, \cdot))$ contains a mistake. Variable i gets the correct value of the index of the first incorrect bit in this computation, so the local consistency test for $R_\mu^{A\setminus\{x\}}((x, \cdot))$ being the computation of M on input x fails on the i-th bit, and we accept x.

If $x \notin A$, $R_\mu^{A\setminus\{x\}}((x, \cdot))$ is a valid computation, so no local consistency test fails, and we reject x.

(End of the proof of Theorem 5.4.1.)

The local checkability property of computations used in the proof of Theorem 5.4.1 does not relativize, because the oracle computation steps depend on the entire query, i.e., on a number of bits that is only limited by the resource bounds of the base machine, in this case exponentially many. We next show that Theorem 5.4.1 itself also does not relativize.

Theorem 5.4.2. *Relative to some oracle, EXP has a $\leqslant_{2-T}^P$-complete language that is not autoreducible.*

Proof. Note that EXP has the following property.

Property 5.4.1. There is an oracle Turing machine N running in EXP such that for any oracle B, the language accepted by N^B is $\leqslant_m^P$-complete for EXP^B.

Without loss of generality, we assume that N runs in time 2^n. Let K^B denote the language accepted by N^B.

We will construct an oracle B and a language A such that A is $\leqslant_{2-T}^P$-complete for EXP^B and is not $\leqslant_T^{P^B}$-autoreducible.

The construction of A is the same as in Lemma 5.3.1 (see Figure 5.1) with $\beta(n) = \log n$ and $K = K^B$, except for that the reductions M_i now also have access to the oracle B.

We will encode in B information about the construction of A that reduces the complexity of A relative to B, but do it high enough so as not to destroy the $\leqslant_{2-T}^P$-completeness of A for EXP^B nor the diagonalizations against $\leqslant_T^{P^B}$-autoreductions.

We construct B in stages along with A. We start with B empty. Using the notation of Lemma 5.3.1, at the beginning of stage i, we add 0^{2^m} to B iff property (5.1) does not hold, and at the end of sub-stage j, we union B with

$$\{\langle 0^{2^{m^{2^{j+1}}}}, y\rangle \mid y \in I_j \text{ and } r(y) = 1\} \text{ if (5.1) holds at stage } i,$$

$$\{\langle 0^{2^{m^{2^{j+1}}}}, y\rangle \mid y \in I_j \text{ and } \ell(y) = 1\} \text{ otherwise.}$$

Note that this does not affect the value of $K^B(y)$ for $|y| < m^{2^{j+1}}$, nor the computations of M_i on inputs of size at most m (for sufficiently large i such that $m^{\log m} < 2^m$). It follows from the analysis in the proof of Lemma 5.3.1 that the language A is $\leqslant^P_{2-T}$-hard for EXP^B and not $\leqslant^{P^B}_T$-autoreducible.

Regarding the complexity of deciding A relative to B, note that the encoding in the oracle B allows us to eliminate the need for evaluating $\mathrm{QBF}_{\log \beta(n)}$-formulae of size $2^{n^{\beta(n)}}$. Instead, we just query B on easily constructed inputs of size $O(2^{n^2})$. Therefore, we can drop the terms corresponding to the $\mathrm{QBF}_{\log \beta(n)}$-formulae of size $2^{n^{\beta(n)}}$ in the complexity of A. Consequently, $A \in \mathsf{EXP}^B$.   (End of the proof of Theorem 5.4.2.)

Theorem 5.4.2 applies to any complexity class containing EXP that has Property 5.4.1, e.g., $\mathsf{EXPSPACE}$, EEXP, $\mathsf{EEXPSPACE}$, etc.

Sometimes, the structure of the oracle allows us to get around the lack of local checkability of oracle queries. This is the case for oracles from the polynomial-time hierarchy, and leads to the following extension of Theorem 5.4.1:

Theorem 5.4.3. *For any integer $k \geqslant 0$, every $\leqslant^P_T$-complete language for $\Delta^{\exp}_{k+1}$ is autoreducible.*

The proof idea is as follows. Let A be a $\leqslant^P_T$-complete language accepted by the deterministic oracle Turing machine M with oracle TQBF_k. First note that there is a polynomial-time Turing machine N such that a query q belongs to the oracle TQBF_k iff

$$(\exists y_1)\,(\forall y_2) \ldots (Q_k\, y_k)\, N(q, y_1, y_2, \ldots, y_k) \text{ accepts},\tag{5.5}$$

where the y_ℓ's are of size polynomial in $|q|$.

We consider the two purported computations of M on input x constructed in the proof of Theorem 5.4.1. One of them belongs to a party assuming $x \in A$, the other one to a party assuming $x \notin A$. The computation corresponding to the right assumption is correct; the other one might not be.

Now, suppose the computations differ, and we are given a pointer to the first bit position where they disagree, which turns out to be the answer to an oracle query q. Then we can have the two parties play the k-round game underlying (5.5): The party claiming $q \in \mathrm{TQBF}_k$ plays the existentially quantified y_ℓ's, the other one the universally quantified y_ℓ's. The players' strategies will consist of computing the game history so far, determining their optimal next move, $\leqslant^P_T$-reducing this computation to A, and finally producing the result of this reduction under their respective assumption about $A(x)$. This will guarantee that the party with the correct assumption plays optimally. Since this is also the one claiming the correct answer to the oracle query q, he will win the game, i.e., $N(q, y_1, y_2, \ldots, y_k)$ will equal his answer bit.

The only thing the autoreduction for A has to do, is determine the value of $N(q, y_1, y_2, \ldots, y_k)$ in polynomial time using A as an oracle but without querying x. It can do that along the lines of the base case algorithm given in Figure 5.2. If during this process, the local consistency test for N's computation requires the knowledge of bits from the y_ℓ's, we compute these via the reduction defining the strategy of the corresponding player. The bits from q we need, we can retrieve from the M-computations, since both computations are correct up to the point where they finished generating q. Once we know $N(q, y_1, y_2, \ldots, y_k)$, we can easily decide the correct assumption about $A(x)$.

The construction hinges on the hypothesis that we can $\leqslant_T^P$-reduce determining the player's moves to A. Computing these moves can become quite complex, though, because we have to recursively reconstruct the game history so far. The number of rounds k being constant, seems crucial for keeping the complexity under control. Establishing Theorem 5.4.3 for EXPSPACE, which can be thought of as alternating exponential time with an exponential number of alternations, would separate NL from NP, as we will see in Section 5.5.

Proof (of Theorem 5.4.3). Let A be a $\leqslant_T^P$-complete language for $\Delta_{k+1}^{\mathrm{exp}} = \mathrm{EXP}^{\Sigma_k^p}$ accepted by the exponential-time oracle Turing machine M with oracle TQBF_k. Let g_M, e_M, and c_M be the formalization of the local consistency test for M as described by (5.4). Without loss of generality there is a polynomial p and a polynomial-time Turing machine N such that on inputs of size n, M makes exactly $2^{p(n)}$ oracle queries, all of the form

$$(\exists y_1)\,(\forall y_2)\ldots(Q_k\, y_k)\, N(q, y_1, y_2, \ldots, y_k) \text{ accepts},\tag{5.6}$$

where q has length $2^{p^2(n)}$ and all variables y_i range over $\Sigma^{2^{p(n)}}$. Moreover, the computations of N in (5.6) each have length $2^{p^3(n)}$, and their last bit represents the answer; the same holds for the computations of M on inputs of length n. Let g_N, e_N, and c_N be the formalization of the local consistency test for N.

We first define a bunch of functions computable in $\Delta_{k+1}^{\mathrm{exp}}$. For each of them, say ξ, we fix an oracle Turing machine R_ξ that $\leqslant_T^P$-reduces ξ to A, and which the final autoreduction for A will use. The proofs that we can compute these functions in $\Delta_{k+1}^{\mathrm{exp}}$ are straightforward.

Let $\mu(\langle x, i \rangle)$ denote the i-th bit of the computation of M^{TQBF_k} on input x, and $\sigma(x)$ the first i (if any) such that $R_\mu^{A \setminus \{x\}}(\langle x, i \rangle) \neq R_\mu^{A \cup \{x\}}(\langle x, i \rangle)$. The roles of μ and σ are the same as in the proof of Theorem 5.4.1: We will use R_μ to figure out whether both possible answers for the oracle query "$x \in A$?" lead to the same final answer, and if not, use R_σ to find a pointer i to the first incorrect bit (in any) of the simulated computation getting the negative oracle answer $x \notin A$. If i turns out not to point to an oracle query, we can proceed as in the proof of Theorem 5.4.1. Otherwise, we will make use of the following functions and associated reductions to A.

We define the functions η_ℓ and y_ℓ inductively for $\ell = 1, \ldots, k$. At each level ℓ we first define η_ℓ, which induces a reduction R_{η_ℓ}, and then define y_ℓ

based on R_{η_ℓ}. All of these functions take an input x such that the i-th bit of $R_\mu^{A\setminus\{x\}}(\langle x,\cdot\rangle)$ is the answer to an oracle query (5.6), where $i = R_\sigma^{A\cup\{x\}}(x)$. We define $\eta_\ell(x)$ as the lexicographically least $y_\ell \in \Sigma^{2^{p(|x|)}}$ such that

$$\chi[(Q_{\ell+1}\,y_{\ell+1})\dots(Q_k\,y_k)\,N(q,y_1(x),y_2(x),\dots$$
$$\dots,y_{\ell-1}(x),y_\ell,y_{\ell+1},\dots,y_k)\text{ accepts }] \equiv \ell \bmod 2; \tag{5.7}$$

if this value does not exist, we set $\eta_\ell(x) = 0^{2^{p(|x|)}}$. Note that the right-hand side of (5.7) is 1 iff y_ℓ is existentially quantified in (5.6).

$$y_\ell(x) = \begin{cases} R_{\eta_\ell}^{A\cup\{x\}}(x) & \text{if } \ell \equiv R_\mu^{A\cup\{x\}}(\langle x,i\rangle) \bmod 2 \\ R_{\eta_\ell}^{A\setminus\{x\}}(x) & \text{otherwise.} \end{cases} \tag{5.8}$$

The condition on the right-hand side of (5.8) means that we use the hypothesis $x \in A$ to compute $y_\ell(x)$ from R_{η_ℓ} in case:

— either y_ℓ is existentially quantified in (5.6) and the player assuming $x \in A$ claims (5.6) holds,
— or else y_ℓ is universally quantified and the player assuming $x \in A$ claims (5.6) fails.

Otherwise we use the hypothesis $x \notin A$.

In case i points to the answer to an oracle query (5.6), the functions η_ℓ and the reductions R_{η_ℓ} incorporate the moves during the successive rounds of the game underlying (5.6). The reduction R_{η_ℓ} together with the player's assumption about membership of x to A, determines the actual move $y_\ell(x)$ during the ℓ-th round, namely $R_{\eta_\ell}^{A\cup\{x\}}(x)$ if the ℓ-th round is played by the opponent assuming $x \in A$, and $R_{\eta_\ell}^{A\setminus\{x\}}(x)$ otherwise. The condition on the right-hand side of (5.8) guarantees that the existentially quantified variables are determined by the opponent claiming the query (5.6) is a true formula, and the universally quantified ones by the other opponent. In particular, (5.8) ensures that the opponent with the correct claim about (5.6) has a wining strategy. Provided it exists, the function η_ℓ defines a winning move during the ℓ-th round of the game for the opponent playing that round, given the way the previous rounds were actually played (as described by the $y(x)$'s). For odd ℓ, i.e., y_ℓ is existentially quantified, it tries to set y_ℓ such that the remainder of (5.6) holds; otherwise it tries to set y_ℓ such that the remainder of (5.6) fails. The actual move may differ from the one given by η_ℓ in case the player's assumption about $x \in A$ is incorrect. The opponent with the correct assumption plays according to η_ℓ. Since that opponent also makes the correct claim about (5.6), he will win the game. In any case, $N(q,y_1,y_2,\dots,y_k)$ will hold iff (5.6) holds.

Finally, we define the functions ν and τ, which have a similar job as the functions μ respectively σ, but for the computation of $N(q,y_1,y_2,\dots,y_k)$ instead of the computation of $M^{\mathrm{TQBF}_k}(x)$. More precisely, $\nu(\langle x,r\rangle)$ equals the r-th bit of the computation of $N(q,y_1(x),y_2(x),\dots,y_k(x))$, where the

$y_\ell(x)$'s are defined by (5.8), and the bit with index $i = R_\sigma^{A\cup\{x\}}(x)$ in the computation $R_\mu^{A\setminus\{x\}}(\langle x,\cdot\rangle)$ is the answer to the oracle query (5.6). We define $\tau(x)$ to be the first r (if any) for which $R_\nu^{A\setminus\{x\}}(\langle x,r\rangle) \neq R_\nu^{A\cup\{x\}}(\langle x,r\rangle)$, provided the bit with index $i = R_\sigma^{A\cup\{x\}}(x)$ in the computation $R_\mu^{A\setminus\{x\}}(\langle x,\cdot\rangle)$ is the answer to an oracle query.

Now we have these functions and corresponding reductions, we can describe an autoreduction for A. On input x, it works as described in Figure 5.3. We next argue that the algorithm correctly decides A on input x. Checking

---

if $R_\mu^{A\setminus\{x\}}(\langle x, 2^{p^3(|x|)}\rangle) = R_\mu^{A\cup\{x\}}(\langle x, 2^{p^3(|x|)}\rangle)$
  then accept iff $R_\mu^{A\cup\{x\}}(\langle x, 2^{p^3(|x|)}\rangle) = 1$
  else $i \leftarrow R_\sigma^{A\cup\{x\}}(x)$
    if the i-th bit of $R_\mu^{A\setminus\{x\}}(\langle x,\cdot\rangle)$ is not the answer to an oracle query
      then accept iff $e_M(x; i, R_\mu^{A\setminus\{x\}}(\langle x, g_M(x; i, 1)\rangle)), \ldots,$
                        $R_\mu^{A\setminus\{x\}}(\langle x, g_M(x; i, c_M)\rangle)) = 0$
      else if $R_\nu^{A\setminus\{x\}}(\langle x, 2^{p^3(|x|)}\rangle) = R_\nu^{A\cup\{x\}}(\langle x, 2^{p^3(|x|)}\rangle)$
        then accept iff $R_\mu^{A\setminus\{x\}}(\langle x,i\rangle) \neq R_\mu^{A\setminus\{x\}}(\langle x, 2^{p^3(|x|)}\rangle)$
        else $r \leftarrow R_\tau^{A\cup\{x\}}(x)$
          accept iff $e_N(q, y_1, y_2, \ldots, y_k; r,$
                      $R_\nu^{A\setminus\{x\}}(\langle x, g_N(q, y_1, y_2, \ldots, y_k; r, 1)\rangle)), \ldots,$
                      $R_\nu^{A\setminus\{x\}}(\langle x, g_N(q, y_1, y_2, \ldots, y_k; r, c_N)\rangle))) = 0$
          where q denotes the query described in $R_\mu^{A\setminus\{x\}}(\langle x,\cdot\rangle)$
             to which $R_\mu^{A\setminus\{x\}}(\langle x,i\rangle)$ is the answer
          and
$$y_\ell = \begin{cases} R_{\eta_\ell}^{A\cup\{x\}}(x) & \text{if } \ell \equiv R_\mu^{A\cup\{x\}}(\langle x,i\rangle) \bmod 2 \\ R_{\eta_\ell}^{A\setminus\{x\}}(x) & \text{otherwise} \end{cases}$$
        endif
      endif
endif

Fig. 5.3. Autoreduction for the language A of Theorem 5.4.3 on input x

the other properties required of an autoreduction for A is straightforward.

We only consider the cases where $R_\mu^{A\setminus\{x\}}(\langle x, 2^{p^3(|x|)}\rangle)$ is different from $R_\mu^{A\cup\{x\}}(\langle x, 2^{p^3(|x|)}\rangle)$ and the index i points to the answer to an oracle query in $R_\mu^{A\setminus\{x\}}(\langle x,\cdot\rangle)$. We refer to the analysis in the proof of Theorem 5.4.1 for the remaining cases.

Case $R_\nu^{A\setminus\{x\}}(\langle x, 2^{p^3(|x|)}\rangle) = R_\nu^{A\cup\{x\}}(\langle x, 2^{p^3(|x|)}\rangle)$

If $x \in A$, variable i points to the first incorrect bit of $R_\mu^{A\setminus\{x\}}(\langle x,\cdot\rangle)$, which turns out to be the answer to an oracle query, say (5.6). Since

$R_\nu^{A \cup \{x\}}(\langle x, 2^{p^3(|x|)} \rangle)$ yields the correct oracle answer to (5.6),

$$R_\mu^{A \setminus \{x\}}(\langle x, i \rangle) \neq R_\nu^{A \cup \{x\}}(\langle x, 2^{p^3(|x|)} \rangle) = R_\nu^{A \setminus \{x\}}(\langle x, 2^{p^3(|x|)} \rangle),$$

and we accept x.

If $x \notin A$, both $R_\mu^{A \setminus \{x\}}(\langle x, i \rangle)$ and $R_\nu^{A \setminus \{x\}}(\langle x, 2^{p^3(|x|)} \rangle)$ give the correct answer to the oracle query i points to in the computation $R_\mu^{A \setminus \{x\}}(\langle x, \cdot \rangle)$. So, they are equal, and we reject x.

$Case$ $R_\nu^{A \setminus \{x\}}(\langle x, 2^{p^3(|x|)} \rangle) \neq R_\nu^{A \cup \{x\}}(\langle x, 2^{p^3(|x|)} \rangle)$

Then, as described in Figure 5.3, we will use the local consistency test for $R_\nu^{A \setminus \{x\}}(\langle x, \cdot \rangle)$ being the computation of $N(q, y_1(x), y_2(x), \cdots, y_k(x))$. Apart from bits in the purported computation $R_\nu^{A \setminus \{x\}}(\langle x, \cdot \rangle)$, this test may also need bits from q and from the $y_\ell(x)$'s. The $y_\ell(x)$'s can be computed straightforwardly using their definition (5.8). The bits from q we might need, can be retrieved from $R_\nu^{A \setminus \{x\}}(\langle x, \cdot \rangle)$. This is because our encoding scheme for computations has the property that the query q is a substring of the prefix of the computation up to the position indexed by i. Since either $R_\nu^{A \setminus \{x\}}(\langle x, \cdot \rangle)$ is correct everywhere, or else i is the first position where it is incorrect, the description of q in $R_\nu^{A \setminus \{x\}}(\langle x, \cdot \rangle)$ is correct in any case. Moreover, we can easily compute a pointer to the beginning of the substring q of $R_\nu^{A \setminus \{x\}}(\langle x, \cdot \rangle)$ from i.

If $x \in A$, $R_\nu^{A \setminus \{x\}}(\langle x, 2^{p^3(|x|)} \rangle)$ is incorrect, so $R_\nu^{A \setminus \{x\}}(\langle x, \cdot \rangle)$ has an error as a computation of $N(q, y_1(x), y_2(x), \ldots, y_k(x))$. Variable r gets assigned the index of the first incorrect bit in this computation, so the local consistency check fails, and we accept x.

If $x \notin A$, then $R_\nu^{A \setminus \{x\}}(\langle x, \cdot \rangle)$ describes a completely valid computation of $N(q, y_1(x), y_2(x), \ldots, y_k(x))$, so every local consistency test is passed, and we reject x.

(End of the proof of Theorem 5.4.3.)

5.4.2 Nonadaptive Autoreductions

So far, we constructed autoreductions for $\leqslant_T^P$-complete languages A. On input x, we looked at the two candidate computations obtained by reducing to A, answering all oracle queries except for x according to A, and answering query x positively for one candidate, and negatively for the other. If the candidates disagreed, we tried to find out the right one, which always existed. We managed to get the idea to work for quite powerful languages A, e.g., EXP-complete languages, by exploiting the local checkability of computations. That allowed us to figure out the wrong computation without going through the entire computation ourselves: With help from A, we first computed a pointer to the first mistake in the wrong computation, and then verified it locally.

We cannot use this adaptive approach for constructing nonadaptive auto-reductions. It seems like figuring out the wrong computation in a nonadaptive way, requires the autoreduction to perform the computation of the base machine itself, so the base machine has to run in polynomial time. Then checking the computation essentially boils down to verifying the oracle answers. Using the game characterization of the polynomial-time hierarchy along the same lines as in Theorem 5.4.3, we can do this for oracles from the polynomial-time hierarchy.

Theorem 5.4.4. *For any integer $k \geqslant 0$, every $\leqslant_{tt}^{P}$-complete language for Δ_{k+1}^{P} is nonadaptively autoreducible.*

Parallel to the adaptive case, k being constant seems crucial. In Section 5.5, we will see that proving Theorem 5.4.4 for PSPACE would separate NL from NP.

The only additional difficulty in the proof is that in the nonadaptive setting, we do not know which player has to perform the even rounds, and which one the odd rounds in the k-round game underlying a query like (5.5). But we can just have them play both scenarios, and afterwards figure out the relevant run.

Proof (of Theorem 5.4.4). Let A be a $\leqslant_{tt}^{P}$-complete language for $\Delta_{k+1}^{P} = P^{\Sigma_k^P}$ accepted by the polynomial-time oracle Turing machine M with oracle TQBF_k. Without loss of generality there is a polynomial p and a polynomial-time Turing machine N such that on inputs of size n, M makes exactly $p(n)$ oracle queries q, all of the form

$$(\exists\, y_1)\,(\forall\, y_2)\ldots(Q_k\, y_k)\, N(q, y_1, y_2, \ldots, y_k) \text{ accepts}, \tag{5.9}$$

where q has length $p^2(n)$ and all variables y_i range over $\Sigma^{p(n)}$. Let $q(x, i)$ denote the i-th oracle query of M^{TQBF_k} on input x. Note that q is computable in $P^{\Sigma_k^P}$.

Let $Q = \{\langle x, i\rangle \mid q(x, i) \in \mathrm{TQBF}_k\}$. The language Q belongs to Δ_{k+1}^{P}, so there is a $\leqslant_{tt}^{P}$-reduction R_Q from Q to A.

If for a given input x, $R_Q^{A\cup\{x\}}$ and $R_Q^{A\setminus\{x\}}$ agree on $\langle x, j\rangle$ for every $1 \leqslant j \leqslant p(|x|)$, we are home: We can simulate the base machine M using $R_Q^{A\cup\{x\}}(\langle x, j\rangle)$ as the answer to the j-th oracle query.

Otherwise, we will make use of the following functions $\eta_1, \eta_2, \ldots, \eta_k$ computable in Δ_{k+1}^{P}, corresponding oracle Turing machines $R_{\eta_1}, R_{\eta_2}, \ldots, R_{\eta_k}$ defining $\leqslant_{tt}^{P}$-reductions to A, and functions $y_1, y_2, \ldots, y_k$ also computable in Δ_{k+1}^{P}. As in the proof of Theorem 5.4.3, we define η_ℓ and y_ℓ inductively for $\ell = 1, \ldots, k$. They are defined for inputs x such that there is a smallest $1 \leqslant i \leqslant p(|x|)$ for which $R_Q^{A\setminus\{x\}}(\langle x, i\rangle) \neq R_Q^{A\cup\{x\}}(\langle x, i\rangle)$. The value of $\eta_\ell(x)$ equals the lexicographically least $y_\ell \in \Sigma^{p(|x|)}$ such that

$$\chi[(Q_{\ell+1}\, y_{\ell+1})(Q_{\ell+2}\, y_{\ell+2})\ldots(Q_k\, y_k)\, N(q(x, i), y_1(x), y_2(x), \ldots$$
$$\ldots, y_{\ell-1}(x), y_\ell, y_{\ell+1}, \ldots, \ldots, y_k) \text{ accepts }] \equiv \ell \bmod 2; \tag{5.10}$$

we set $\eta_\ell(x) = 0^{p(|x|)}$ if such string does not exist. The right-hand side of (5.10) is 1 iff y_ℓ is existentially quantified in (5.9).

$$y_\ell = \begin{cases} R_{\eta_\ell}^{A\cup\{x\}}(x) & \text{if } \ell \equiv R_Q^{A\cup\{x\}}(\langle x,i\rangle) \bmod 2 \\ R_{\eta_\ell}^{A\setminus\{x\}}(x) & \text{otherwise.} \end{cases} \qquad (5.11)$$

The condition on the right-hand side of (5.11) means that we use the hypothesis $x \in A$ to compute $y_\ell(x)$ from R_{η_ℓ} in case:

– either y_ℓ is existentially quantified in (5.9) and the assumption $x \in A$ leads to claiming that (5.9) holds,
– or else y_ℓ is universally quantified and the assumption $x \in A$ leads to claiming that (5.9) fails.

The intuitive meaning of the functions η_ℓ and the reductions R_{η_ℓ} is similar to in the proof of Theorem 5.4.3: They capture the moves during the ℓ-th round of the game underlying (5.9) for $q = q(x,i)$. The function η_ℓ encapsulates an optimal move during round ℓ if it exists, and the reduction R_{η_ℓ} under the player's assumption regarding membership of x to A, produces the actual move in that round. The condition on the right-hand side of (5.11) guarantees the correct alternation of rounds. We refer to the proof of Theorem 5.4.3 for more intuition.

Consider the algorithm in Figure 5.4. Note that the only queries to A the

---

if $R_Q^{A\setminus\{x\}}(\langle x,j\rangle) = R_Q^{A\cup\{x\}}(\langle x,j\rangle)$ for every $1 \leqslant j \leqslant p(|x|)$
  then accept iff M accepts x when the j-th oracle query
    is answered $R_Q^{A\cup\{x\}}(\langle x,j\rangle)$
  else $i \leftarrow$ first j such that $R_Q^{A\setminus\{x\}}(\langle x,j\rangle) \neq R_Q^{A\cup\{x\}}(\langle x,j\rangle)$
    accept iff $N(q,y_1,y_2,\ldots,y_k) = R_Q^{A\cup\{x\}}(\langle x,i\rangle)$
        where q denotes the i-th query of M on input x
           when the answer to the j-th oracle query
             is given by $R_Q^{A\cup\{x\}}(\langle x,j\rangle)$
        and
$$y_\ell = \begin{cases} R_{\eta_\ell}^{A\cup\{x\}}(x) & \text{if } \ell \equiv R_Q^{A\cup\{x\}}(\langle x,i\rangle) \bmod 2 \\ R_{\eta_\ell}^{A\setminus\{x\}}(x) & \text{otherwise} \end{cases}$$
  endif

Fig. 5.4. Nonadaptive autoreduction for the language A of Theorem 5.4.4 on input x

---

algorithm in Figure 5.4 needs to make, are the queries of R_Q different from x on inputs $\langle x,j\rangle$ for $1 \leqslant j \leqslant p(|x|)$, and the queries of R_{η_ℓ} different from x on input x for $1 \leqslant \ell \leqslant k$. Since R_Q and the R_{η_ℓ}'s are nonadaptive, it follows that Figure 5.4 describes a $\leqslant_{tt}^P$-reduction to A that does not query its own input. A similar but simplified argument as in the proof of Theorem 5.4.3 shows that it accepts A. So, A is nonadaptively autoreducible.

(End of the proof of Theorem 5.4.4.)

Next, we consider more restricted reductions. Using a different technique, we show:

Theorem 5.4.5. *For any complexity class C, every $\leqslant^P_{2-tt}$-complete language for C is $\leqslant^P_{2-tt}$-autoreducible, provided C is closed under exponential-time reductions that only ask one query which is smaller in length.*

In particular, Theorem 5.4.5 applies to the classes $C = $ EXP, EXPSPACE, and EEXPSPACE. In view of Theorems 5.3.1 and 5.3.3, this implies that Theorems 5.3.1, 5.3.3, and 5.4.5 are optimal.

The proof exploits the ability of EXP to simulate all polynomial-time reductions to construct an auxiliary language D within C such that any $\leqslant^P_{2-tt}$-reductions of D to some fixed complete language A has a property that induces an autoreduction on A.

Proof (of Theorem 5.4.5). Let $M_1, M_2, \ldots$ be a standard enumeration of $\leqslant^P_{2-tt}$-reductions such that M_i runs in time n^i on inputs of size n. Let A be a $\leqslant^P_{2-tt}$-complete language for C.

Consider the language D that only contains strings of the form $\langle 0^i, x \rangle$ for $i \in \mathbb{N}$ and $x \in \Sigma^*$, and is decided by the algorithm of Figure 5.5 on such an input. Except for deciding $A(x)$, the algorithm runs in exponential

---

> **case** truth-table of M_i on input $\langle 0^i, x \rangle$ with the truth-value of query x
>   set to $A(x)$
>   constant: **accept iff** M_i^A rejects $\langle 0^i, x \rangle$
>   of the form "$y \notin A$": **accept iff** $x \notin A$
>   otherwise: **accept iff** $x \in A$
> **endcase**

Fig. 5.5. Algorithm for the language D of Theorem 5.4.5 on input $\langle 0^i, x \rangle$

---

time. Therefore, under the given conditions on C, $D \in C$, so there is a $\leqslant^P_{2-tt}$-reduction M_j from D to A.

The construction of D diagonalizes against every $\leqslant^P_{2-tt}$-reduction M_i of D to A whose truth-table on input $\langle 0^i, x \rangle$ would become constant once we filled in the membership bit for x. Therefore, for every input x, one of the following cases holds for the truth-table of M_j on input $\langle 0^j, x \rangle$.

- The reduced truth-table is of the form "$y \in A$" with $y \neq x$.
  Then $y \in A \Leftrightarrow M_j$ accepts $\langle 0^j, x \rangle \Leftrightarrow x \in A$.
- The reduced truth-table is of the form "$y \notin A$" with $y \neq x$.
  Then $y \notin A \Leftrightarrow M_j$ accepts $\langle 0^j, x \rangle \Leftrightarrow x \notin A$.

> **if** $||Q_{M_j}(\langle 0^j, x \rangle) \setminus \{x\}|| = 2$
>   **then accept iff** M_j^A accepts $\langle 0^j, x \rangle$
>   **else** { $||Q_{M_j}(\langle 0^j, x \rangle) \setminus \{x\}|| = 1$ }
> $y \leftarrow$ unique element of $Q_{M_j}(\langle 0^j, x \rangle) \setminus \{x\}$
>   **accept iff** $y \in A$
> **endif**

Fig. 5.6. Autoreduction constructed in the proof of Theorem 5.4.5

– The truth-table depends on the membership to A of 2 strings different from x.

Then M_j^A does not query x on input $\langle 0^j, x \rangle$, and accepts iff $x \in A$.

The above analysis shows that the algorithm of Figure 5.6 describes a $\leqslant_{2\text{-tt}}^P$-autoreduction of A.   *(End of the proof of Theorem 5.4.5.)*

5.4.3 Randomized and Nonuniform Autoreductions

The previous results in this section trivially imply that the $\leqslant_T^P$-complete languages for the Δ-levels of the exponential-time hierarchy are randomly autoreducible, and the $\leqslant_{tt}^P$-complete languages for the Δ-levels of the polynomial-time hierarchy are randomly nonadaptively autoreducible. Randomness allows us the prove more in the nonadaptive case.

First, we can establish Theorem 5.4.4 for EXP:

Theorem 5.4.6. *Let f be a constructible function. Every $\leqslant_{f(n)\text{-tt}}^P$-complete language for* EXP *is* $\leqslant_{O(f(n))\text{-tt}}^{ZPP}$-*autoreducible. In particular, every* $\leqslant_{tt}^P$-*complete language for* EXP *is* $\leqslant_{tt}^{ZPP}$-*autoreducible.*

Proof. Let A be a $\leqslant_{f(n)\text{-tt}}^P$-complete language for EXP. Since EXP is closed under complementation, it suffices to show that A is $\leqslant_{O(f(n))\text{-tt}}^{coRP}$-autoreducible. We will apply the PCP Theorem for EXP [13] to A.

Lemma 5.4.1 ([13]). *There is a constant k such that for any language $A \in$* EXP, *there is a polynomial-time Turing machine V and a polynomial p such that for any input x:*

– If $x \in A$, then there exists a proof oracle π such that

$$\Pr_{|r|=p(|x|)} [V^\pi(x, r) \text{ accepts}] = 1.   \tag{5.12}$$

– If $x \notin A$, then for any proof oracle π

$$\Pr_{|r|=p(|x|)} [V^\pi(x, r) \text{ accepts}] \leqslant \frac{1}{2}.$$

Moreover, V never makes more than k proof oracle queries, and there is a proof oracle $\tilde{\pi} \in$ EXP independent of x such that (5.12) holds for $\pi = \tilde{\pi}$ in case $x \in A$.

Translating Lemma 5.4.1 into our terminology, we obtain:

Lemma 5.4.2. *There is a constant k such that for any language $A \in$ EXP, there is a language $B \in$ EXP and a randomized polynomial-time oracle Turing machine N that makes at most k nonadaptive queries such that for any input x:*

- *If $x \in A$, then $N^B(x)$ always accepts.*
- *If $x \notin A$, then for any oracle C, $N^C(x)$ accepts with probability at most $\frac{1}{2}$.*

Let R be a $\leqslant^P_{f(n)-tt}$-reduction of B to A, and consider the randomized machine M^A that on input x, runs N on input x with oracle $R^{A \cup \{x\}}$. M^A is a randomized polynomial-time reduction to A that asks no more than $k \cdot f(n)$ nonadaptive oracle questions and never queries its own input. The following shows it is an $\leqslant^{coRP}_{tt}$-reduction from A:

- If $x \in A$, then $R^{A \cup \{x\}} = R^A = B$, so $M^A(x) = N^B(x)$ always accepts.
- If $x \notin A$, then for $C = R^{A \cup \{x\}}$, $M^A(x) = N^C(x)$ accepts with probability at most $\frac{1}{2}$.

(End of the proof of Theorem 5.4.6.)

Note that Theorem 5.4.6 makes it plausible why we did not manage to scale down Theorem 5.3.2 by one exponent to EXPSPACE in the nonadaptive setting, as we were able to do for our other results in Section 5.3 when going from the adaptive to the nonadaptive case: This would separate EXP from EXPSPACE.

We suggest the extension of Theorem 5.4.6 to the Δ-levels of the exponential-time hierarchy as an interesting problem for further research.

Second, Theorem 5.4.4 also holds for NP.

Theorem 5.4.7. *All $\leqslant^P_{tt}$-complete languages for NP are $\leqslant^{RP}_{tt}$-autoreducible.*

Proof. Fix a $\leqslant^P_{tt}$-complete language A for NP. Let R_A denote a length nondecreasing $\leqslant^P_m$-reduction of A to SAT.

Define the language

$$W = \{\langle \phi, 0^i \rangle \mid \phi \text{ is a Boolean formula with, say } m \text{ variables, and}$$
$$(\exists a \in \Sigma^m)\,[\phi(a) \text{ and } a_i = 1]\}.$$

Since $W \in$ NP, there is a $\leqslant^P_{tt}$-reduction R_W from W to A.

We will use the following randomized algorithm by Valiant and Vazirani [137].

Lemma 5.4.3 ([137]). *There exists a polynomial-time randomized Turing machine N that on input a Boolean formula φ with n variables, outputs another quantifier free Boolean formula $\phi = N(\varphi)$ such that:*

- *If φ is satisfiable, then with probability at least $\frac{1}{4n}$, ϕ has a unique satisfying assignment.*
- *If φ is not satisfiable, then ϕ is never satisfiable.*

Now consider the following algorithm for A: On input x, run N on input $R_A(x)$, yielding a Boolean formula ϕ with, say m variables, and it accepts iff

$$\phi(R_W^{A\cup\{x\}}(\langle\phi,0\rangle), R_W^{A\cup\{x\}}(\langle\phi,00\rangle),\ldots, R_W^{A\cup\{x\}}(\langle\phi,0^i\rangle),\ldots, R_W^{A\cup\{x\}}(\langle\phi,0^m\rangle))$$

evaluates to true. Note that this algorithm describes a randomized polynomial-time truth-table reduction to A that never queries its own input. Moreover:

- If $x \in A$, then with probability at least $\frac{1}{4|x|}$, the Valiant-Vazirani algorithm N produces a Boolean formula ϕ with a unique satisfying assignment $\tilde{a}_\phi$. In that case, $(R_W^{A\cup\{x\}}(\langle\phi,0\rangle), R_W^{A\cup\{x\}}(\langle\phi,00\rangle),\ldots, R_W^{A\cup\{x\}}(\langle\phi,0^i\rangle),\ldots$
  $\ldots, R_W^{A\cup\{x\}}(\langle\phi,0^m\rangle))$ equals $\tilde{a}_\phi$, and we accept x.
- If $x \notin A$, any Boolean formula ϕ which N produces has no satisfying assignment, so we always reject x.

Executing $\Theta(n)$ independent runs of this algorithm, and accepting iff any of them accepts, yields a $\leqslant_{tt}^{RP}$-autoreduction for A.

(End of the proof of Theorem 5.4.7.)

So, for randomized autoreductions, we get similar results as for deterministic ones: Low end complexity classes turn out to have the property that their complete languages are autoreducible, whereas high end complexity classes do not. As we will see in more detail in the next section, this structural difference yields separations.

If we allow nonuniformity, the situation changes dramatically. Since randomized autoreducibility implies nonuniform autoreducibility [23], all our positive results for small complexity classes carry over to the nonuniform setting. But, as we will see next, the negative results do not, because also the complete languages for large complexity classes become autoreducible, both in the adaptive and in the nonadaptive case. So, uniformity is crucial for separating complexity classes using autoreducibility, and the Razborov-Rudich result [115] does not apply.

Feigenbaum and Fortnow [51] define the following concept of #P-robustness, of which we also consider the nonadaptive variant.

Definition 5.4.1. *A language A is #P-robust if $\#P^A \subseteq FP^A$; A is nonadaptively #P-robust if $\#P_{tt}^A \subseteq FP_{tt}^A$.*

Nonadaptive #P-robustness implies #P-robustness. For the standard deterministic and nondeterministic complexity classes containing PSPACE, all $\leqslant_T^P$-complete languages are #P-robust. For the deterministic ones it is also true that the $\leqslant_{tt}^P$-complete languages are nonadaptively #P-robust.

The following connection with nonuniform autoreducibility holds.

Theorem 5.4.8. *All #P-robust languages are nonuniformly autoreducible. All nonadaptively #P-robust languages are nonuniformly nonadaptively autoreducible.*

Proof. Feigenbaum and Fortnow [51] show that every #P-robust language is random-self-reducible. Beigel and Feigenbaum [23] prove that every random-self-reducible language is nonuniformly autoreducible (or "weakly coherent" as they call it). Their proofs carry over to the nonadaptive setting.

It follows that the $\leqslant_{tt}^{P}$-complete languages for the usual deterministic complexity classes containing PSPACE are all nonuniformly nonadaptively autoreducible. The same holds for adaptive reductions, in which case the property is also true of nondeterministic complexity classes containing PSPACE. In particular, we get the following:

Corollary 5.4.1. *All $\leqslant_{T}^{P}$-complete languages for* NEXP, EXPSPACE, EEXP, NEEXP, EEXPSPACE, *... are nonuniformly autoreducible. All $\leqslant_{tt}^{P}$-complete languages for* PSPACE, EXP, EXPSPACE, *... are nonuniformly nonadaptively autoreducible.*

5.5 Separation Results

In this section, we will see how we can use the structural property of all complete languages being autoreducible to separate complexity classes. Based on the results of Sections 5.3 and 5.4, we only get separations that were already known: EXPH $\neq$ EEXPSPACE (by Theorems 5.4.3 and 5.3.1), EXP $\neq$ EEXPSPACE (by Theorems 5.4.6 and 5.3.2), and PH $\neq$ EXPSPACE (by Theorems 5.4.4 and 5.3.3, and also by scaling down EXPH $\neq$ EEXPSPACE). However, settling the question for certain other classes, would yield impressive new separations.

We summarize the implications in Figure 5.7.

Theorem 5.5.1. *In Figure 5.7, a positive answer to a question from the first column, implies the separation in the second column, and a negative answer, the separation in the third column.*

Most of the entries in Figure 5.7 follow directly from the results of the previous sections. In order to finish the table, we use the next lemma.

Lemma 5.5.1. *If* NP = NL, *we can decide the validity of QBF-formulae of size t and with γ alternations on a deterministic Turing machine M_1 in time $t^{O(c^{\gamma})}$ and on a nondeterministic Turing machine M_2 in space $O(c^{\gamma} \log t)$, for some constant c.*

question	yes	no
Are all $\leqslant_T^P$-complete languages for EXPSPACE autoreducible?	NL $\neq$ NP	PH $\neq$ PSPACE
Are all $\leqslant_T^P$-complete languages for EEXP autoreducible?	NL $\neq$ NP P $\neq$ PSPACE	PH $\neq$ EXP
Are all $\leqslant_{tt}^P$-complete languages for PSPACE $\leqslant_{tt}^P$-autoreducible?	NL $\neq$ NP	PH $\neq$ PSPACE
Are all $\leqslant_{tt}^P$-complete languages for EXP $\leqslant_{tt}^P$-autoreducible?	NL $\neq$ NP P $\neq$ PSPACE	PH $\neq$ EXP
Are all $\leqslant_{tt}^P$-complete languages for EXPSPACE $\leqslant_{tt}^{BPP}$-autoreducible?	NL $\neq$ NP	P $\neq$ PSPACE

Fig. 5.7. Separation results using autoreducibility

Proof. We will be using the following terminology in this proof. A Σ_1-formula is a quantified Boolean formula with only existential quantifiers. Similarly, a Π_1-formula is a quantified Boolean formula with only universal quantifiers.

Since coNP = NP, by Cook's Theorem we can transform in polynomial time a Π_1-formula with free variables into an equivalent Σ_1-formula with the same free variables, and vice versa. Since NP = P, we can decide the validity of Σ_1-formulae in polynomial-time. Say both the transformation algorithm T and the satisfiability algorithm S run in time n^c for some constant c.

Let ϕ be a QBF-formula of size t with γ alternations. Consider the following algorithm for deciding ϕ: Repeatedly apply the transformation T to the largest suffix that constitutes a Σ_1- or Π_1-formula until the whole formula becomes Σ_1, and then run S on it.

This algorithm correctly decides the truth of ϕ. Since the number of alternations decreases by one during every iteration, it makes at most γ calls to T, each time at most raising the length of the formula to the power c. It follows that the algorithm runs in time $t^{O(c^\gamma)}$.

Moreover. a padding argument shows that DTIME$[\tau] \subseteq$ NSPACE$[\log \tau]$ follows from NP = NL for any time-constructible function τ. Therefore the nondeterministic result holds.   *(End of the proof of Lemma 5.5.1.)*

This allows us to improve Theorems 5.3.2 and 5.3.3 as follows under the hypothesis NP = NL.

Theorem 5.5.2. *If* NP = NL, *then* EXPSPACE *has a* $\leqslant_{2-T}^P$-*complete language that is not* $\leqslant_T^{BPP}$-*autoreducible. The same holds for* EEXP *instead of* EXPSPACE.

Proof. Combine Lemma 5.5.1 with the randomized extension of Lemma 5.3.1 used in the proof of Theorem 5.3.2.

Theorem 5.5.3. *If* NP = NL, *then* PSPACE *has a* $\leqslant^P_{3-tt}$*-complete language that is not nonadaptively autoreducible. The same holds for* EXP *instead of* PSPACE.

Proof. Combining Lemma 5.5.1 with Lemma 5.3.2 for $\alpha(n) = n$ yields the result for EXP. The one for PSPACE follows, since NP = NL implies that EXP = PSPACE.

Now, we have all ingredients for establishing Figure 5.7.

Proof (of Theorem 5.5.1). The NL $\neq$ NP implications in the "yes"-column of Figure 5.7 immediately follow from Theorems 5.5.2 and 5.5.3 by contraposition.

By Theorem 5.3.1, a positive answer to the 2nd question in Figure 5.7 would yield EEXP $\neq$ EEXPSPACE, and by Theorem 5.3.3, a positive answer to the 4th question would imply EXP $\neq$ EXPSPACE. By padding, both translate down to P $\neq$ PSPACE.

Similarly, by Theorem 5.4.3, a negative answer to the 2nd question would imply EXPH $\neq$ EEXP, which pads down to PH $\neq$ EXP. A negative answer to the 4th question would yield PH $\neq$ EXP directly by Theorem 5.4.4. By the same token, a negative answer to the 1st question results in EXPH $\neq$ EXPSPACE and PH $\neq$ PSPACE, and a negative answer to the 3rd question in PH $\neq$ PSPACE. By Theorem 5.4.6, a negative answer to the last question implies EXP $\neq$ EXPSPACE and P $\neq$ PSPACE.

(End of the proof of Theorem 5.5.1.)

We note that we can tighten all of the separations in Figure 5.7 a bit, because we can apply Lemmata 5.3.1 and 5.3.2 to smaller classes than in Theorems 5.3.1 respectively 5.3.3. One improvement along these lines that might warrant attention is that we can replace "NL $\neq$ NP" in Figure 5.7 by "coNP $\not\subseteq$ NP$\cap$NSPACE[$\log^{O(1)} n$]." This is because that condition suffices for Theorems 5.5.2 and 5.5.3, since we can strengthen Lemma 5.5.1 as follows.

Lemma 5.5.2. *If* coNP $\subseteq$ NP$\cap$NSPACE[$\log^{O(1)} n$], *we can decide the validity of QBF-formulae of size t and with γ alternations on a deterministic Turing machine M_1 in time $t^{O(c^\gamma)}$ and on a nondeterministic Turing machine M_2 in space $O(d^\gamma \log^d t)$, for some constants c and d.*

5.6 Conclusion and Open Questions

We have studied the question whether all complete languages are autoreducible for various complexity classes and various reducibilities. We obtained a positive answer for lower complexity classes in Section 5.4, and a negative one for higher complexity classes in Section 5.3. This way, we separated these lower complexity classes from these higher ones by highlighting a structural difference. The resulting separations were not new, but we argued in Section 5.5 that settling the very same question for intermediate complexity classes, would provide major new separations.

We believe that refinements to these techniques may lead to them, and would like to end this chapter with a few words about some thoughts in that direction.

One does not have to look at complete languages only. Let $\mathcal{C}_1 \subseteq \mathcal{C}_2$. Suppose we know that all complete languages for $\mathcal{C}_2$ are autoreducible. Then it suffices to construct, e.g., along the lines of Lemma 5.3.1, a hard language for $\mathcal{C}_1$ that is not autoreducible, in order to separate $\mathcal{C}_1$ from $\mathcal{C}_2$.

As we mentioned at the end of Section 5.5, we can improve Theorem 5.3.1 a bit by applying Lemma 5.3.1 to smaller space-bounded classes than EEXPSPACE. We cannot hope to gain much, though, since the coding in the proof of Lemma 5.3.1 seems to be $\mathsf{DSPACE}[2^{n^{\beta(n)}}]$-complete because of the $\mathrm{QBF}_{2 \log \beta(n)}$-formulae of size $2^{O(n^{\beta(n)})}$ involved for inputs of size n. The same holds for Theorem 5.3.3 and Lemma 5.3.2.

Generalizations of autoreducibility may allow us to push things further. For example, one could look at $k(n)$-autoreducibility where $k(n)$ bits of the language remain unknown to the querying machine. Theorem 5.4.3 goes through for $k(n) \in O(\log n)$. Perhaps one can exploit this leeway in the coding of Lemma 5.3.1 and narrow the gap between the positive and negative results. As discussed in Section 5.5, that would yield interesting separations.

6. The Size of Randomized Polynomial Time

This is the first chapter where we will give arguments about the frequency of occurrence of certain languages in order to separate complexity classes. The particular framework we will use is that of resource-bounded measure. The formalism turns to be well-suited to study the BPP versus EXP problem. In this chapter, we will show that either randomized polynomial time coincides with exponential time or else it is a small subclass of exponential time in the sense of resource-bounded measure. We will see more applications to the BPP versus EXP problem in the next two chapters.

6.1 Introduction

The zero-one law of classical Lebesgue measure states that any reasonable class of languages that is closed under finite variation has measure zero or one. It is an open question whether the zero-one law carries over to resource-bounded measure as developed by Lutz [88]. In particular, we do not know whether every complexity class within exponential time has measure zero or one.

On one hand, Regan, Sivakumar and Cai [116] showed that if strong pseudo-random generators exist then the zero-one law fails for the class of languages with polynomial-size circuits. No unconditional counterexamples are known. On the other hand, no nontrivial positive examples were known either. We establish the first one, namely for the class BPP. It remains open whether BPP has measure zero or one within exponential time but we show that one of the two must hold.

By the measure conservation property, BPP having E-measure zero implies that BPP $\neq$ EXP. Conversely, Buhrman, Fenner and Fortnow [31] showed that if MA $\neq$ EXP, then BPP has E-measure zero. This state of affairs left open the possibility that BPP differs from EXP, but does not have E-measure zero either. We exclude that possibility.

Using Impagliazzo and Wigderson's work on pseudo-randomness secure against uniform adversaries [70], we are able to bridge the remaining gap between BPP and MA, and show that the weaker hypothesis BPP $\neq$ EXP already implies that BPP has E-measure zero. So, establishing the latter is equivalent to separating BPP from EXP.

D. van Mehlkebeek: Randomness and Completeness in Computational Complexity, LNCS 1950, pp. 141–144, 2000.
© Springer-Verlag Berlin Heidelberg 2000

Theorem 6.1.1. BPP *has* E-*measure zero iff* BPP $\neq$ EXP.

The zero-one law for BPP follows from Theorem 6.1.1.

Corollary 6.1.1. BPP *either has* E-*measure zero or else has* E-*measure one.*

Note that Corollary 6.1.1 is in fact as strong as Theorem 6.1.1, since Regan et al. [116] showed that BPP having E-measure one implies that BPP$\cap$E = E and therefore that BPP = EXP.

Allender and Strauss observed that their work [5] allows us to generalize Theorem 3.3.3 and Corollary 6.1.1 to any class (instead of BPP) contained in BPP and closed under tt-reductions, e.g., ZPP.

Theorem 6.1.2. *Let* $\mathcal{C}$ *be any class contained in* BPP *and closed under tt-reductions. Then* $\mathcal{C}$ *has* E-*measure zero iff* $\mathcal{C} \neq$ EXP.

Corollary 6.1.2. *Let* $\mathcal{C}$ *be any class contained in* BPP *and closed under tt-reductions. Then* $\mathcal{C}$ *either has* E-*measure zero or else has* E-*measure one.*

For the same reason as above, Corollary 6.1.2 is as powerful as Theorem 6.1.2.

6.2 The Zero-One Law for BPP

In this section, we give the proof of Theorem 6.1.1

The left-to-right implication follows immediately from the measure conservation property. For establishing the right-to-left implication, we will use the next result by Impagliazzo and Wigderson [70].

Theorem 6.2.1. *If* BPP $\neq$ EXP, *then for every language* $A \in$ BPP *and every* $\epsilon > 0$, *there is a language* $B \in$ DTIME$[2^{n^\epsilon}]$ *such that the following holds: For any constant* $d > 0$ *and any length-preserving randomized polynomial-time Turing machine* M,

$$\Pr[A(M(1^m)) = B(M(1^m))] > 1 - m^{-d} \tag{6.1}$$

for infinitely many lengths m, *where the probability is over the internal coin tosses of* M.

We will apply Theorem 6.2.1 with $\epsilon = 1$, d any constant, and $M(1^m)$ the uniform distribution on strings of length m. In that case, for sufficiently large m, (6.1) implies

$$\Pr_{|x|=m}[A(x) = B(x)] > \frac{2}{3}, \tag{6.2}$$

where the probability is with respect to the uniform distribution over $\{0,1\}^m$.

Fix a set $B \in$ DTIME$[2^n]$. For any integer $m > 0$, consider the strategy for the game of Section 3.2 that only bets on the membership bits of strings of length m, and for each of these strings puts $\frac{1}{3}$ of its capital on the outcome that the membership is the same as for B. The corresponding martingale $d_{B,m}(w)$, say with initial capital $d_{B,m}(\lambda) = 1$, is identically 1 for $|w| < 2^{m+1}$, and constant $d_{B,m}(\omega)$ for $w \sqsubseteq \omega$ with $|w| \geqslant 2^{m+2}$. Computing $d_{B,m}(w)$ for $2^{m+1} \leqslant |w| < 2^{m+2}$ essentially amounts to deciding whether $x \in B$ for strings x of length m in lexicographic order. Since there are 2^m strings of length m, and for each of them we can decide membership to B in time 2^m, it follows that we can compute $d_{B,m}(w)$ in time $|w|^2 \log^{O(1)} |w|$.

Note that any correct bet on the membership of a string of length m, increases the capital by a factor of $1 + \frac{1}{3} = \frac{4}{3}$, whereas an incorrect one reduces it by a factor of $1 - \frac{1}{3} = \frac{2}{3}$. If ω is the characteristic sequence of a language A for which (6.2) holds, more than $\frac{2}{3}$ of the bets on strings of length m are correct. Therefore,

$$d_{B,m}(\omega) > \left(\frac{4}{3}\right)^{\frac{2}{3}2^m} \left(\frac{2}{3}\right)^{\frac{1}{3}2^m} d_{B,m}(\lambda) = \left(\frac{2^{\frac{5}{3}}}{3}\right)^{2^m} \in 2^{\Omega(2^m)}.$$

Now consider

$$d_B(w) \doteq \sum_{m=1}^{\infty} \frac{1}{m^2} d_{B,m}(w). \tag{6.3}$$

Since $\sum_{m=1}^{\infty} \frac{1}{m^2}$ converges, d_B is a well-defined martingale. Because $d_{B,m}(w)$ equals 1 for $m \geqslant \log|w|$, computing $d_B(w)$ really only requires evaluating the first $\log|w|$ terms of the right-hand side of (6.3), which we can do in time $|w|^2 \log^{O(1)} |w|$. Moreover, the above argument shows that $d_B(\omega) = \infty$ if ω is the characteristic sequence of any language A for which (6.2) holds for infinitely many m. Let $\mathcal{C}_B$ denote the class of such languages A.

Let $B_1, B_2, \ldots$ be a standard enumeration of DTIME$[2^n]$ obtained by clocking Turing machines. Then there is a fixed Turing machine deciding $x \in B_i$ in time polynomial in $i + 2^{|x|}$. By the previous analysis, this implies that $d(i, w) \doteq d_{B_i}(w)$ is computable in time polynomial in $i + |w|$. Therefore, by Theorem 2.5.2, $\mathcal{C} \doteq \cup_i \mathcal{C}_{B_i}$ has E-measure zero. By Theorem 6.2.1, the assumption BPP $\neq$ EXP implies that $\mathcal{C}$ contains BPP. So, BPP has E-measure zero if BPP $\neq$ EXP.

6.3 Generalization

In this section, we establish Theorem 6.1.2 providing a zero-one law for more classes than just BPP, e.g., ZPP.

Assume that $\mathcal{C}$ satisfies the conditions of the theorem and that $\mathcal{C}$ does not have E-measure zero. Allender and Strauss [5] showed that the E-measure of the class of languages that are not hard for BPP is zero. Their proof also works for tt-reductions, i.e., even the class of languages that are not tt-hard for BPP has E-measure zero. It follows that $\mathcal{C}$ contains a language that is tt-hard for

BPP. Since $\mathcal{C}$ is closed under tt-reductions, this implies that BPP $\subseteq \mathcal{C}$. On the other hand, by hypothesis $\mathcal{C} \subseteq$ BPP. Therefore, $\mathcal{C} =$ BPP, and Theorem 6.1.1 yields that $\mathcal{C} =$ EXP, since $\mathcal{C}$ does not have E-measure zero. This finishes the proof of Theorem 6.1.2.

6.4 Conclusion and Open Questions

We have shown that if BPP differs from EXP, then it actually is a small subset of EXP in the sense that only few languages in EXP belong to BPP. In other words, the equivalent of the probabilistic method for showing the existence of a language in EXP \ BPP is guaranteed to work, provided there is such a language.

On a more technical note, each of the following claims is known to follow from the hypothesis EXP $\neq$ MA and to imply that BPP $\neq$ EXP:

1. BPP has E-measure zero [31].
2. The class of nonadaptively autoreducible languages has E-measure zero (see Chapter 8).
3. The class of EXP-complete languages under nonadaptive reductions has E-measure zero (see Chapter 7).

Using Impagliazzo and Wigderson's work on pseudo-random generators secure against uniform adversaries [70], we were able to bridge the remaining gap in case 1 by showing that the hypothesis BPP $\neq$ EXP already implies the claim. Can we do the same in other two cases? Note that this would show that all 3 the above claims are equivalent.

7. The Frequency of Complete Languages

In this chapter, we look at the frequency of complete languages as a tool to separate complexity classes.

7.1 Introduction

Lutz introduced resource-bounded measure [87] to formalize the notions of scarceness and abundance in complexity theory. His approach makes it possible to express statements like "only a few" or "most" languages in a complexity class $\mathcal{C}$ have property Q.

We can use resource-bounded measure as a tool for separating complexity classes. For example, if we could show that the complete languages in complexity class $\mathcal{C}$ have measure zero and the complete languages in $\mathcal{D}$ do not, we would have separated $\mathcal{C}$ from $\mathcal{D}$.

In this chapter, we follow that line of research. We investigate complete and hard languages for NP, the levels of the polynomial-time hierarchy, PSPACE and EXP, and give some evidence that they have EXP-measure zero. On the other hand, the results of Bennett and Gill [24] imply that the $\leqslant_{tt}^P$-hard languages for BPP do not have EXP-measure zero; Allender and Strauss [5] even showed they have EXP-measure 1 in EXP.

We use three different approaches to obtain our results. Two of them yield unhypothesized statements on the border of what is provable by relativizable techniques. First, we significantly improve the Small Span Theorem of Juedes and Lutz [71]. The Small Span Theorem for a reducibility $\leqslant_r^P$ states that for any language A in EXP, either the class of languages that $\leqslant_r^P$-reduce to A (called the lower span of A) or the class of languages that $A \leqslant_r^P$-reduces to (the upper span of A) or both have EXP-measure 0. Since the degree of a language is the intersection of its lower and upper span, it implies that every $\leqslant_r^P$-degree has EXP-measure zero, and in particular the $\leqslant_r^P$-complete degree of any complexity class within EXP. The strongest Small Span Theorem previous to our work was due to Ambos-Spies, Neis, and Terwijn [10], who proved it for $\leqslant_{btt}^P$-reductions. The extension to reductions with a non-constant number of queries was a notorious open problem in the area. We establish the Small Span Theorem for $\leqslant_{n^{o(1)}-tt}^P$-reductions, i.e., for non-adaptive reductions

D. van Melkebeek: Randomness and Completeness in Computational Complexity, LNCS 1950, pp. 145–159, 2000.
© Springer-Verlag Berlin Heidelberg 2000

that make a subpolynomial number of queries. Longpré [84] informed us that he obtained earlier a Small Span Theorem for $\leqslant^P_{\log^{o(1)} n\text{-tt}}$-reductions.

Lutz [89] obtained a Small Span Theorem for non-uniform reductions with respect to μESPACE. Similar to his proof, our Small Span Theorem follows from the fact that most languages in EXP have a $\leqslant^P_{n^{o(1)}\text{-tt}}$-upper span with EXP-measure zero. We actually establish this fact for $\leqslant^P_{n^\alpha\text{-tt}}$-reductions for any constant $\alpha < 1$. This way, we get stronger results on the scarceness of complete languages than the ones that follow from the Small Span Theorem: Any $\leqslant^P_{n^\alpha\text{-tt}}$-degree within EXP has EXP-measure zero. Previously, it was only known for $\leqslant^P_{btt}$-reductions that the EXP-measure of the complete languages for EXP have EXP-measure zero [10, 35]. We also obtain that the EXP-measure of the $\leqslant^P_{n^\alpha\text{-tt}}$-hard languages for E and EXP is zero.

Then we take a look at EXP in particular, and use an ad hoc technique to improve the results of the first approach for this particular case. We show that the $\leqslant^P_{n^c\text{-T}}$-complete languages for EXP have EXP-measure zero for any constant c. Our proofs relativize and are on the edge of the scope of relativizable techniques: Showing the last theorem for unbounded growing exponent c would separate BPP from EXP.

Therefore, we next look at what we can show under a non-relativizing reasonable but yet unproven complexity theoretic hypothesis, namely the assumption that MA $\neq$ EXP. Babai, Fortnow, Nisan and Wigderson [18] established the existence of a pseudo-random generator that can be used to simulate BPP in subexponential time for infinitely many input lengths unless MA = EXP. Using this pseudo-random generator, we are able to prove that the complete languages for EXP under $\leqslant^P_T$-reductions that make their queries in lexicographic order, have E-measure zero unless EXP = MA. In particular, the $\leqslant^P_{tt}$-complete languages for EXP have E-measure zero unless EXP = MA.

The organization of this chapter is as follows. We first describe our results for arbitrary subclasses of EXP in Section 7.2. Then we discuss our results particular to EXP. Section 7.3 contains those without any complexity theoretic assumption; Section 7.4 those using the hypothesis MA $\neq$ EXP. Finally, we give some comments and mention remaining open problems.

7.2 Complete Languages under Nonadaptive Reductions with n^α Queries and a Small Span Theorem

In this section, we establish our results on the measure of complete and hard languages for complexity classes within EXP. The following theorem forms the main ingredient. It states that most languages in EXP have a small upper span under $\leqslant^P_{n^\alpha\text{-tt}}$-reductions for constant $\alpha < 1$. Later we also show a strong connection with the Small Span Theorem.

Recall that for a reducibility $\leqslant_r^P$, the *lower span* of a language A is defined as $\mathsf{P}_r(A) = \{B \mid B \leqslant_r^P A\}$, and the *upper span* of A as $\mathsf{P}_r^{-1}(A) = \{B \mid A \leqslant_r^P B\}$. The $\leqslant_r^P$-*degree* of A equals $\mathsf{P}_r(A) \cap \mathsf{P}_r^{-1}(A)$.

Theorem 7.2.1. *For any $\alpha < 1$,*

$$\mu_\mathsf{E}(\{A \in \mathsf{EXP} \mid \mu_\mathsf{EXP}(\mathsf{P}_{n^\alpha\text{-tt}}^{-1}(A)) \neq 0\}) = 0.$$

We first give an outline of the proof.

Fix a $\leqslant_{n^\alpha\text{-tt}}^P$-reduction M running in time n^c for some constant $c > 0$, and a language $A \in \mathsf{EXP}$. We would like to construct an EXP-martingale that succeeds on any language B for which $M^B = A$. Suppose we are given the initial segment w_i of χ_B corresponding to all strings of length less than m_i. See Figure 7.1. We can select an input x of length $n_i = m_i^{1/\epsilon}$ for some constant $\epsilon > 0$, and divide the available capital uniformly among the extensions w_{i+1}' of w_i corresponding to all strings of length less than m_{i+1} ($m_{i+1} \geqslant n_i^c$) for which $M^{w_{i+1}'}(x) = A(x)$. This way, our capital at the end of stage i is definitely not smaller than at the beginning, and in case only half or fewer of the extensions pass the consistency test on x, we actually double it or even better. In order to be able to bet on the languages $A \in \mathsf{EXP}$ for which this strategy fails on some language B such that $M^B = A$, we will perform the consistency check not for a single input x of length n_i, but for a certain collection $I_{M,i}$ of $n_i^\alpha + 1$ inputs x of length n_i: We distribute the available

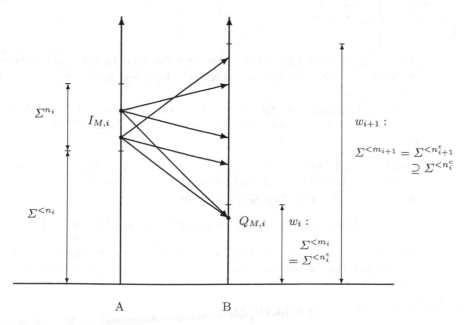

Fig. 7.1. Betting strategies at stage i

capital uniformly over all extensions w'_{i+1} for which $M^{w'_{i+1}}(x) = A(x)$ for every $x \in I_{M,i}$. If there is an input $x \in I_{M,i}$ for which only half or fewer of the extensions w'_{i+1} satisfy $M^{w'_{i+1}}(x) = A(x)$, we gain a factor of 2 or more in stage i while betting on B. We will try this strategy at every stage i, and we succeed on B if the latter situation occurs for infinitely many of them.

Now, suppose that for some B to which M reduces A, this situation only occurs for finitely many stages. So for almost all stages i, on any input $x \in I_{M,i}$ more than half of the extensions w'_{i+1} of w_i satisfy $M^{w'_{i+1}}(x) = A(x)$. We would like to construct an E-martingale that succeeds on any such $A \in \mathsf{EXP}$ by betting on these x's according to the majority vote of the extensions. We do not know the prefix w_i of χ_B we need for that, but we can guess the values of the bits in this prefix which M queries on inputs $x \in I_{M,i}$, i.e., divide our capital uniformly over all possible corresponding strategies. In order for this to work, we will make sure that the set $I_{M,i}$ consists of $n_i^\alpha + 1$ strings of length n_i on which M makes the *same* queries of length less than m_i. This implies we have to distribute our capital among no more than $2^{n_i^\alpha}$ strategies, and at least one of them will realize a relative gain of $2^{||I_{M,i}||} = 2^{n_i^\alpha+1} = 2 \cdot 2^{n_i^\alpha}$. So, if we do this at every stage with $\frac{2}{3}$ of the capital available at the beginning of that stage, and leave the other $\frac{1}{3}$ intact, we succeed on A: At almost all stages, we increase our capital with a factor of $\frac{2}{3} \cdot 2 = \frac{4}{3}$, and at the finitely many other stages, we do not lose all of it.

We define the stages as follows:

$$\begin{cases} m_0 = 1 \\ m_{i+1} = 2^{m_i} \\ n_i = m_i^{1/\epsilon}. \end{cases} \tag{7.1}$$

Note that, no matter for what constant c the reduction M runs in time n^c, the stages do not interfere at sufficiently high levels, i.e., $m_{i+1} \leqslant n_i^c$ for i sufficiently large.

Next, we show that for sufficiently large i, the sets $I_{M,i}$ exist for any $\leqslant_{n^\alpha\text{-tt}}^{\mathsf{P}}$-reduction M, and that we can construct them efficiently. Here we need the fact that $\alpha < 1$.

Lemma 7.2.1. *Let $\alpha < 1$, $\epsilon \in (0, 1 - \alpha)$, and m_i and n_i defined by (7.1). There is an integer i_0 such that for any $i \geqslant i_0$ and for any $\leqslant_{n^\alpha\text{-tt}}^{\mathsf{P}}$-reduction M, there is a set of strings $Q_{M,i}$ such that*

$$||\{x \in \{0,1\}^{n_i} \mid Q_M(x) \cap \{0,1\}^{<m_i} = Q_{M,i}\}|| \geqslant n_i^\alpha + 1,$$

where $Q_M(x)$ denotes the set of queries M makes on input x. Moreover, we can find the lexicographically first set $Q_{M,i}$ and the lexicographically first subset $I_{M,i}$ of

$$\{x \in \{0,1\}^{n_i} \mid Q_M(x) \cap \{0,1\}^{<m_i} = Q_{M,i}\}$$

with $||I_{M,i}|| = n_i^\alpha + 1$ in time 2^{2n_i}.

Proof (of Lemma 7.2.1). For sufficiently large i, the number of possible values of $Q_M(x) \cap \{0,1\}^{<m_i}$ for $x \in \{0,1\}^{n_i}$ is bounded by

$$\sum_{i=0}^{n_i^\alpha} \binom{2^{m_i}-1}{i} \leqslant (2^{m_i})^{n_i^\alpha} = 2^{n_i^{\alpha+\epsilon}} \leqslant \frac{2^{n_i}}{n_i^\alpha+1}, \tag{7.2}$$

from which the existence of $Q_{M,i}$ follows. A brute force search does the job.

We now formalize the above outline.

Proof (of Theorem 7.2.1). We use the notation from Lemma 7.2.1. Fix $A \in$ DTIME$[2^{n^k}]$. Let $\pi_{A,M}(w)$ be equal to 1 for $|w| < 2^{m_{i_0}}$, and be given by

$$\Pr_{\omega \sqsupseteq w}[(\forall x \in I_{M,i})\, M^\omega(x) = A(x)] \tag{7.3}$$

for $2^{m_{i_0}} \leqslant 2^{m_i} \leqslant |w| < 2^{m_{i+1}}$. We define the martingale $d_{A,M}$ as follows:

$$d_{A,M}(\lambda) = 1$$
$$d_{A,M}(wb) = \begin{cases} \frac{2 \cdot \pi_{A,M}(wb)}{\pi_{A,M}(wb)+\pi_{A,M}(w\bar{b})} \cdot d_{A,M}(w) & \text{if } \pi_{A,M}(wb) + \pi_{A,M}(w\bar{b}) \neq 0 \\ d_{A,M}(w) & \text{otherwise.} \end{cases}$$

This means that for any sufficiently large i (such that $i \geqslant i_0$ and stage $i+1$ does not interfere with stage i) and for any prefix w_i of length $2^{m_i}-1$, the martingale $d_{A,M}$ distributes $2^{2^{m_{i+1}}-2^{m_i}} \cdot d_{A,M}(w_i)$ uniformly over all extensions w'_{i+1} of w_i with $|w'_{i+1}| = 2^{m_{i+1}}-1$ for which $M^{w'_{i+1}}$ and A agree on the membership of every string in $I_{M,i}$.

The defining predicate of $\pi_{A,M}$ depends on $||I_{M,i}|| \cdot n_i^\alpha \in O((\log|w|)^{\frac{2\alpha}{\epsilon}})$ or fewer positions of ω not fixed by w. It follows that $\pi_{A,M}$ and $d_{A,M}$ can be computed in time $2^{(\log|w|)^{O(\frac{\alpha+k}{\epsilon})}}$.

We distinguish between two cases for the behavior of M and A: Either there are infinitely many stages i such that no matter what the prefix w_i is, there is always an input in $I_{M,i}$ on which only half or fewer of the extensions pass the consistency check between M and A; or else for almost all stages i, there is a prefix w_i such that for any input from $I_{M,i}$, a strict majority of the extensions of w_i make M and A agree on that input.

Case 1: $(\exists^\infty i)\,(\forall w \in \{0,1\}^{(2^{m_i})-1})\,(\exists x \in I_{M,i})\, \Pr_{\omega \sqsupseteq w}[M^\omega(x) = A(x)] \leqslant \frac{1}{2}$

Then for any $\omega = \chi_B$ such that M reduces A to B, and for any sufficiently large stage i for which the Case 1 condition holds,

$$d_{A,M}(w_{i+1}) \geqslant 2 d_{A,M}(w_i),$$

where w_j represents the prefix of ω of length $2^{m_j}-1$. This is because at least half of the extensions w'_{i+1} of w_i with $|w'_{i+1}| = 2^{m_{i+1}}-1$ fail some consistency test. It follows that $d_{A,M}(\omega) = \infty$, and that

$$\mu_{\mathsf{EXP}}(\{B \mid M \text{ reduces } A \text{ to } B\}) = 0. \tag{7.4}$$

Case 2: $(\forall^\infty i)\,(\exists w \in \{0,1\}^{(2^{m_i})-1})\,(\forall x \in I_{M,i})\,\Pr_{\omega \sqsupseteq w}[M^\omega(x) = A(x)] > \frac{1}{2}$
For any stage i and any $b \in \{0,1\}^{\|Q_{M,i}\|}$, let $\delta_{M,i,b}$ be the martingale with initial capital 1 that only bets on strings of $I_{M,i}$, and for such a string $x \in I_{M,i}$ bets all of its money according to the majority of $M^\omega(x)$ over all sequences $\omega \sqsupseteq v_i$, where v_i is the characteristic string of length $2^{m_i} - 1$ in which the bit corresponding to the j-th element of $Q_{M,i}$ equals the j-th bit of b, and all other bits are say 0. Ties are broken arbitrarily. The martingale

$$\delta_{M,i}(w) = \frac{1}{2^{\|Q_{M,i}\|}} \Sigma_b \delta_{M,i,b}(w)$$

has initial capital 1 and is computable in time $O(|w|^2)$. It has the property that

$$\delta_{M,i}(\chi_A|_{\{0,1\}^{<n_{i+1}}}) \geqslant \frac{2^{\|I_{M,i}\|}}{2^{\|Q_{M,i}\|}} \geqslant 2 = 2\delta_{M,i}(\chi_A|_{\{0,1\}^{<n_i}}),$$

provided i satisfies the Case 2 condition. Since almost all i's do, the following E-martingale δ_M succeeds on A: During stage i, it uses $\delta_{M,i}$ as a strategy on $\frac{2}{3}$ of the capital it has at the beginning of stage i, and does nothing with the other $\frac{1}{3}$.

Fix an enumeration M_j of all $\leqslant^P_{n^\alpha\text{-tt}}$-reductions such that we can compute $M_j(x)$ in time polynomial in $2^{|x|} + j$. Then the martingale system δ_{M_j} is E-uniform, so there is an E-martingale δ that succeeds on all languages A for which Case 2 applies for some $\leqslant^P_{n^\alpha\text{-tt}}$-reduction M. Consider any language $A \in \mathsf{EXP}$ not covered by δ. Since the martingale system d_{A,M_j} is EXP-uniform, equation (7.4) implies that the EXP-measure of $P^{-1}_{n^\alpha\text{-tt}}(A)$ is zero.   *(End of the proof of Theorem 7.2.1.)*

Luc Longpré noticed that Theorem 7.2.1 also holds for $\leqslant^P_{n^\alpha\text{-T}}$-reductions that make their queries in lexicographical order. It actually suffices that the queries are made in length non-decreasing order.

Theorem 7.2.2. *Let $\leqslant^P_r$ denote the reducibility by polynomial-time Turing machines that query no more than n^α strings on inputs of length n for some constant $\alpha < 1$, and make these queries in length non-decreasing order. Then*

$$\mu_\mathsf{E}(\{A \in \mathsf{EXP} \mid \mu_\mathsf{EXP}(P^{-1}_r(A)) \neq 0\}) = 0.$$

Proof. We can extend Lemma 7.2.1 as follows.

Lemma 7.2.2. *Let $\alpha < 1$, $\epsilon \in (0, 1-\alpha)$, and m_i and n_i defined by (7.1). There is an integer i_0 such that for any $i \geqslant i_0$, for any $\leqslant^P_r$-reduction M, and for any $b \in \{0,1\}^{n_i^\alpha}$, there is a set of strings $Q_{M,i,b}$ such that*

$$\|\{x \in \{0,1\}^{n_i} \mid Q^{<m_i}_{M,b}(x) = Q_{M,i,b}\}\| \geqslant n_i^\alpha + 1,$$

where $Q^{<m_i}_{M,b}(x)$ denotes the set of queries of length less than m_i which M makes on input x when the j-bit of b is given as the answer to the j-th query

of length less than m_i. Moreover, we can find the lexicographically first set
$Q_{M,i,b}$ *and the lexicographically first subset* $I_{M,i,b}$ *of*

$$\{x \in \{0,1\}^{n_i} \mid Q_{M,b}^{<m_i}(x) = Q_{M,i,b}\}$$

with $\|I_{M,i,b}\| = n_i^\alpha + 1$ *in time* 2^{2n_i}.

Note that $Q_{M,b}^{<m_i}(x)$ in Lemma 7.2.2 is well-defined, because the queries of length less than m_i which M^ω makes on input x only depend on the prefix of ω of length $2^{m_i} - 1$, since M^ω makes its queries in length non-decreasing order. More specifically, these queries only depend on the part of the prefix that specifies the answers to them, i.e., on b.

The betting strategy for $\mathsf{P}_r^{-1}(A)$ is the same as in Theorem 7.2.1, except that we use the set $I_{M,i,b}$ of Lemma 7.2.2 instead of the set $I_{M,i}$ of Lemma 7.2.1 in formula (7.3), where b is determined by the prefix of w of length $2^{m_i} - 1$.

The martingale $\delta_{M,i}$ is the average over several strategies. Now there is one strategy $\delta_{M,i,b}$ corresponding to every $b \in \{0,1\}^{n_i^\alpha}$, namely one with initial capital 1 that only bets on strings of $I_{M,i,b}$. On such a string $x \in I_{M,i,b}$, it bets all of its money according to the majority of $M^\omega(x)$ over all sequences $\omega \sqsupseteq v_{i,b}$, where $v_{i,b}$ is the characteristic string of length $2^{m_i} - 1$ in which the bit corresponding to the j-th query of M on input x equals the j-th bit of b, and all other bits are say 0.

The rest of the construction and the analysis are essentially the same as in the proof of Theorem 7.2.1.   *(End of the proof of Theorem 7.2.2.)*

Our results on the measure of complete languages follow directly from Theorem 7.2.1. By Theorem 7.2.2, they also hold for the more general reducibility introduced in Theorem 7.2.2.

Corollary 7.2.1. *For any $\alpha < 1$ and $C \in \mathsf{EXP}$, the $\leqslant_{n^\alpha\text{-tt}}^{\mathsf{P}}$-degree of C has* EXP*-measure zero. In particular, the classes of $\leqslant_{n^\alpha\text{-tt}}^{\mathsf{P}}$-complete languages for* NP*, the levels of the polynomial-time hierarchy,* PSPACE*, and* EXP *all have* EXP*-measure zero.*

Proof. Suppose not, then for any language A in the $\leqslant_{n^\alpha\text{-tt}}^{\mathsf{P}}$-degree of C, the EXP-measure of $\mathsf{P}_{n^\alpha\text{-tt}}^{-1}(A)$ is not zero, since it contains the $\leqslant_{n^\alpha\text{-tt}}^{\mathsf{P}}$-degree of C. But, by Theorem 7.2.1 this would imply that the E-measure of the $\leqslant_{n^\alpha\text{-tt}}^{\mathsf{P}}$-degree of C is zero.

For the class of $\leqslant_{n^\alpha\text{-tt}}^{\mathsf{P}}$-hard languages, we get:

Corollary 7.2.2. *For any $\alpha < 1$ and any complexity class $\mathcal{C}$ such that $\mu_\mathsf{E}(\mathcal{C} \cap \mathsf{EXP}) \neq 0$, the class of $\leqslant_{n^\alpha\text{-tt}}^{\mathsf{P}}$-hard languages for $\mathcal{C}$ has EXP-measure zero. In particular, the $\leqslant_{n^\alpha\text{-tt}}^{\mathsf{P}}$-hard languages for E and EXP have EXP-measure zero.*

Proof. By definition, for any language $A \in \mathcal{C}$, the $\leqslant^P_{n^\alpha\text{-tt}}$-hard languages for $\mathcal{C}$ are contained in $P^{-1}_{n^\alpha\text{-tt}}(A)$. If the class of $\leqslant^P_{n^\alpha\text{-tt}}$-hard languages for $\mathcal{C}$ does not have EXP-measure zero, Theorem 7.2.1 yields that $\mu_E(\mathcal{C} \cap \text{EXP}) = 0$.

The $\leqslant^P_{n^\alpha\text{-tt}}$-hard languages for NP, the levels of the polynomial-time hierarchy, and PSPACE also have EXP-measure zero, provided these classes themselves do not have E-measure zero.

   From Theorem 7.2.1, we can also deduce a Small Span Theorem. However, we have to settle for a more restrictive reducibility than $\leqslant^P_{n^\alpha\text{-tt}}$, because we need transitivity in the proof, and $\leqslant^P_{n^\alpha\text{-tt}}$ is in general not transitive for any constant $\alpha > 0$. It suffices to keep the number of queries subpolynomial, i.e., asymptotically smaller than n^ϵ for any $\epsilon > 0$. We write $A \leqslant^P_{n^{o(1)}\text{-tt}} B$ if there exists a subpolynomial function $f(n)$ such that $A \leqslant^P_{f(n)\text{-tt}} B$.

Theorem 7.2.3 (Small Span Theorem). *For any language A, at least one of the following holds:* $\mu_E(P_{n^{o(1)}\text{-tt}}(A) \cap \text{EXP}) = 0$ *or* $\mu_{\text{EXP}}(P^{-1}_{n^{o(1)}\text{-tt}}(A)) = 0$.

Proof. We distinguish between two cases:

- $P_{n^{o(1)}\text{-tt}}(A)$ contains a language B such that $\mu_{\text{EXP}}(P^{-1}_{n^{o(1)}\text{-tt}}(B)) = 0$. Then the transitivity of $\leqslant^P_{n^{o(1)}\text{-tt}}$ and the monotonicity of EXP-measure imply that $\mu_{\text{EXP}}(P^{-1}_{n^{o(1)}\text{-tt}}(A)) = 0$.
- $P_{n^{o(1)}\text{-tt}}(A) \cap \text{EXP}$ is included in $\{B \in \text{EXP} \mid \mu_{\text{EXP}}(P^{-1}_{n^\alpha\text{-tt}}(B)) \neq 0\}$ for any $\alpha > 0$. Then Theorem 7.2.1 says that $\mu_E(P_{n^{o(1)}\text{-tt}}(A) \cap \text{EXP}) = 0$.

For any language $A \in \text{EXP}$, Theorem 7.2.3 states that at least one of its lower span or upper span under $\leqslant^P_{n^{o(1)}\text{-tt}}$-reductions is small.

7.3 Complete Languages for **EXP** under Adaptive Reductions with n^c Queries

We now show how, in the case of EXP, we can extend the results of the previous section on the measure of complete languages from $\leqslant^P_{n^\alpha\text{-tt}}$-reductions for any $\alpha < 1$ to $\leqslant^P_{n^c\text{-T}}$-reductions for any constant c.

Theorem 7.3.1. *For any constant c, the class of $\leqslant^P_{n^c\text{-T}}$-complete languages for* EXP *has* EXP-*measure zero.*

The proof technique differs significantly. We exploit the diagonalization power of EXP against $\leqslant^P_{n^c\text{-T}}$-reductions to show that all $\leqslant^P_{n^c\text{-T}}$-complete languages for EXP share a structural property that allows the construction of an EXP-martingale succeeding on all of them. We first establish the structural property.

   Let $M_1, M_2, \ldots$ be an enumeration of $\leqslant^P_{n^c\text{-T}}$-reductions, where M_i runs in time n^i.

Lemma 7.3.1. *For any constant c, and for any $\leqslant^P_{n^c\text{-}T}$-complete language C for* EXP, *there is an index j such that*

$$(\forall n)\,(\forall x \in \{0,1\}^n)$$
$$M_j^C(\langle 0^j, x\rangle) = \text{minority}_{\omega \sqsupseteq \chi_C|_{\{0,1\}<n}}[M_j^\omega(\langle 0^j, x\rangle)]. \tag{7.5}$$

The right-hand side of (7.5) denotes the least probable value of $M_j^\omega(\langle 0^j, x\rangle)$ when ω is uniformly distributed over all extensions of the initial segment of χ_C corresponding to all strings of length up to n. Ties are broken in some fixed way, say always 0.

Proof (of Lemma 7.3.1). Let

$$D = \{\langle 0^i, x\rangle \mid \Pr_{\omega \sqsupseteq \chi_C|_{\{0,1\}<|x|}}[M_i^\omega(\langle 0^i, x\rangle) = 1] < \frac{1}{2}\}.$$

The above probability is a weighted sum of the accepting leaves of the reduction tree of M_i on input $\langle 0^i, x\rangle$. The weight of a leaf is only nonzero if on its path P all queries of length less than $|x|$ are answered consistent with C, and in that case its weight equals $2^{-q(P)}$, where $q(P)$ denotes the number of other queries made along P. Without loss of generality we are assuming here that on no path the reduction asks the same query more than once. So, we can decide D on instances $\langle 0^i, x\rangle$ of length n in time $2^{n^c}(n^c \cdot \text{time}_C(n) + n^i)$. Since $C \in$ EXP, this implies $D \in$ EXP, and since C is $\leqslant^P_{n^c\text{-}T}$-hard for EXP, that there is a $\leqslant^P_{n^c\text{-}T}$-reduction M_j reducing D to C. The index j satisfies (7.5) because for any $x \in \{0,1\}^n$,

$$M_j^C(\langle 0^j, x\rangle) = 1 \Leftrightarrow \langle 0^j, x\rangle \in D$$

$$\Leftrightarrow \Pr_{\omega \sqsupseteq \chi_C|_{\{0,1\}<n}}[M_j^\omega(\langle 0^j, x\rangle) = 1] < \frac{1}{2}$$

$$\Leftrightarrow \text{minority}_{\omega \sqsupseteq \chi_C|_{\{0,1\}<n}}[M_j^\omega(\langle 0^j, x\rangle)] = 1.$$

(End of the proof of Lemma 7.3.1.)

Lemma 7.3.1 provides a consistency test that eliminates at least half of the remaining possibilities. We now use it in a straightforward way to construct an EXP-martingale covering all $\leqslant^P_{n^c\text{-}T}$-complete languages for EXP.

Proof (of Theorem 7.3.1). For any index j, we construct a (uniform) EXP-martingale d_j that succeeds on any language C for which (7.5) holds. The martingale d_j has initial capital 1, and works in stages defined by

$$\begin{cases} n_1 = 1 \\ n_{i+1} = (n_i + j)^j. \end{cases}$$

The i-th stage starts when the martingale has to bet on the string 0^{n_i}. Let w_i denote the prefix seen up to that moment. During stage i, d_j distributes

$2^{2^{n_{i+1}}-2^{n_i}} \cdot d_j(w_i)$ uniformly over all extensions w'_{i+1} of w_i with $|w'_{i+1}| = 2^{n_{i+1}} - 1$ for which $M_j^{w'_{i+1}}(\langle 0^j, 0^{n_i} \rangle) = \text{minority}_{\omega \sqsupseteq w_i}[M_j^\omega(\langle 0^j, 0^{n_i} \rangle)]$.

Note that for any language C satisfying (7.5), d_j at least doubles its capital along C at every stage, so it succeeds on any such C. Therefore, by Lemma 7.3.1, the martingale system $(d_j)_j$ covers the class of $\leqslant_{n^c\text{-T}}^P$-complete languages for EXP.

Using the approach of Lemma 7.3.1, we can compute the minority and the probabilities underlying $d_j(w)$ in time $O(2^{(\log|w|+j)^c}(\log|w| + j)^j)$. So, the martingale system $(d_j)_j$ is EXP-uniform.

In an analogous way, we get the following theorem for E.

Theorem 7.3.2. *For any constant c, the class of $\leqslant_{cn\text{-T}}^P$-complete languages for* E *has* E*-measure zero.*

Ambos-Spies informed us recently that he and Lempp have a new proof of Theorems 7.3.1 and 7.3.2 [9].

7.4 Complete Languages for **EXP** under Nonadaptive Reductions

Theorem 7.3.1 cannot be improved using relativizable techniques, since it fails for unbounded growing exponent c in a world where BPP = EXP, and such a world exists [64]. This follows from the relativizable result of Allender and Strauss [5] that the class of languages that are not $\leqslant_T^P$-hard for BPP has E-measure zero. In this section, we will see what results we can get on the measure of the EXP-complete languages for polynomial-time reductions without an explicit bound an the number of queries, under the likely but nonrelativizing hypothesis MA $\neq$ EXP. We obtain:

Theorem 7.4.1. *The class of languages complete for* EXP *under $\leqslant_T^P$-reductions that make their queries in lexicographical order, has* E*-measure zero unless* EXP = MA. *In particular, the class of $\leqslant_{tt}^P$-complete languages for* EXP *(or* E*) has* E*-measure zero unless* EXP = MA.

The idea is the following. We will apply pseudo-random generators to approximate efficiently the probabilities underlying the martingales constructed in the previous section, and that way mimic their behavior by an easier-to-compute martingale. The pseudo-random generators whose existence is known to follow from the assumption MA $\neq$ EXP by Theorem 2.3.7, have superpolynomial security at infinitely many lengths. They will allow us to approximate the underlying probabilities well enough, but only at infinitely many lengths. Therefore, in order for the mimicking martingale to succeed, we will make sure we make a lot of money on these lengths. We will use the following lemma instead of Lemma 7.3.1 to do so.

Lemma 7.4.1. *Fix a pseudo-random generator computable in time 2^{an} for some constant $a > 1$, and with stretching $r(n)$. There is an oracle Turing machine T running in time 2^{2an} with the following property: For any language C complete for* EXP *under $\leqslant_T^P$-reductions that make their queries in lexicographic order, there is an index j of such a reduction M_j such that for any string x,*

$$
\begin{cases}
\Pr_{\omega \sqsupseteq \chi_{C|_{\{0,1\}^{<n}}}} [(\forall i \in I_n)\, M_j^\omega(\langle 0^j, x, 0^i \rangle) = \\
\qquad\qquad\qquad T^{C \cap \{0,1\}^{<n}}(\langle 0^j, x, 0^i \rangle)] \leqslant \frac{2}{n^3} \qquad\qquad (7.6) \\
(\forall i \in I_n)\, M_j^C(\langle 0^j, x, 0^i \rangle) = T^{C \cap \{0,1\}^{<n}}(\langle 0^j, x, 0^i \rangle),
\end{cases}
$$

where $n = |x|$ and $I_n = \{1, 2, \ldots, 3 \log n\}$, provided $r(n), S_G(n) \geqslant n^{j+1}$ and n is sufficiently large.

Lemma 7.4.1 also holds if we substitute 'length non-decreasing' for 'lexicographic'.

Proof (of Lemma 7.4.1). Consider an input $x \in \{0,1\}^n$, a prefix $w \in \{0,1\}^{2^n - 1}$, a string $b \in \{0,1\}^{3 \log n}$, and an index j such that M_j makes its queries in length non-decreasing order. Recall that M_j runs in time n^j. We can compute the probability

$$
\pi_j(x, w, b) = \Pr_{\omega \sqsupseteq w} [(\forall i \in I_n)\, M_j^\omega(\langle 0^j, x, 0^i \rangle) = b_i]
$$

as the fraction of strings $\beta \in \{0,1\}^{n^{j+1}}$ such that the predicate underlying π_j holds when the oracle queries of length less than n are answered according to w, and the k-th different query of length at least n is answered as β_k. The predicate depends on $o(n^{j+1})$ bits of the prefix w in total, because the queries of length less than n made by M are the same for any β. It follows from Theorem 2.2.7 that the test circuit has size n^{j+1} for sufficiently large n. Therefore, we can approximate $\pi_j(x, w, b)$ to within an additive term of $\frac{1}{n^4}$ using the pseudo-random generator G at length n, provided $r(n) \geqslant n^{j+1}$ and $S_G(n) \geqslant n^{j+1}$.

On input $\langle 0^j, x, 0^i \rangle$, the machine T^w will compute these approximations $\tilde\pi_j(x, w, b)$ to $\pi_j(x, w, b)$ for every $b \in \{0,1\}^{3 \log n}$, select the lexicographically first value $\tilde b$ for b that minimizes $\tilde\pi_j(x, w, b)$, and output the i-th bit of $\tilde b$. T can do this in time 2^{2an}.

Since there are n^3 possible settings for $b \in \{0,1\}^{3 \log n}$, there has to be a setting b^* such that $\pi_j(x, w, b^*) \leqslant \frac{1}{n^3}$. Therefore,

$$
\begin{aligned}
\pi_j(x, w, \tilde b) &\leqslant \tilde\pi_j(x, w, \tilde b) + \frac{1}{n^4} \\
&\leqslant \tilde\pi_j(x, w, b^*) + \frac{1}{n^4} \\
&\leqslant \tilde\pi_j(x, w, b^*) + \frac{2}{n^4}
\end{aligned}
$$

$$\leqslant \frac{1}{n^3} + \frac{2}{n^4}$$

$$\leqslant \frac{2}{n^3},$$

which establishes the first part of (7.6) for any language C.

Now fix a language C complete for EXP under $\leqslant^{\mathsf{P}}_{\mathsf{T}}$-reductions that make their queries in lexicographic order, and consider the language

$$D = \{\langle 0^j, x, 0^i \rangle \mid 1 \leqslant i \leqslant 3 \log |x| \text{ and } T^{C \cap \{0,1\}^{<|x|}}(\langle 0^j, x, 0^i \rangle) \text{ accepts}\}.$$

Since $C \in$ EXP, we can also decide D in EXP, and since C is hard for EXP under $\leqslant^{\mathsf{P}}_{\mathsf{T}}$-reductions that make their queries in lexicographic order, there is such a reduction M_j reducing D to C. This establishes the second part of (7.6). *(End of the proof of Lemma 7.4.1.)*

Lemma 7.4.1 gives a consistency test that eliminates a fraction at least $1 - \frac{2}{n^3}$ of the possibilities, and therefore multiplies the capital by a factor of $\frac{n^3}{2}$. For Lemma 7.3.1 these figures are $\frac{1}{2}$ and 2 respectively. We will now see how we can exploit the larger increase in capital to construct an E-martingale that succeeds on the complete languages for EXP under $\leqslant^{\mathsf{P}}_{\mathsf{T}}$-reductions that make their queries in lexicographical order, using the above pseudo-random generator once more.

Proof (of Theorem 7.4.1 for EXP*).* Fix a $\leqslant^{\mathsf{P}}_{\mathsf{T}}$-reduction M_j running in time n^j that makes its queries in lexicographical order. Let T be the oracle Turing machine given by Lemma 7.4.1 based on the pseudo-random generator G that follows from the hypothesis MA $\neq$ EXP by Theorem 2.3.7. Let

$$\pi_{j,m}(w) = \Pr_{\omega \sqsupseteq w}[(\forall i \in I_m) \, M_j^\omega(\langle 0^j, 0^m, 0^i \rangle) = T^{w \cap \{0,1\}^{<m}}(\langle 0^j, 0^m, 0^i \rangle)],$$

and consider

$$d_{j,m}(w) = \begin{cases} m^3 \cdot \pi_{j,m}(w) & \text{if } |w| \geqslant 2^m \\ 2 & \text{otherwise.} \end{cases}$$

The function $d_{j,m}(w)$ is computable in time $2^{O(\log^{j+1} |w|)}$, and the same is true of $d_j(w) = \sum_{m=1}^{\infty} \frac{1}{m^2} d_{j,m}(w)$. They are non-negative and satisfy the supermartingale inequality (2.4) for all strings w, except possibly for those of length $2^m - 1$. In case of a language C satisfying (7.6) for $x = 0^m$, the inequality also holds for $w \sqsubseteq \chi_C$ of length $2^m - 1$. Moreover, $d_{j,m}(\chi_C) = m^3$, and $d_j(\chi_C) = \infty$.

We now want to construct (super)martingales $\tilde{d}_{j,m}$ and $\tilde{d}_j$ that behave like $d_{j,m}$ and d_j along χ_C, and are computable uniformly in time $|w|^a$ for some constant a, i.e., independent of the running time of M_j. The key idea is to approximate efficiently the probability $\pi_{j,m}$ using the pseudo-random generator G as we did in the proof of Lemma 7.4.1. Following that approach, for some constant a_1, we can compute in time $|w|^{a_1}$ an approximation $\tilde{\pi}_{j,m}(w)$ of $\pi_{j,m}(w)$ to within $\epsilon_{j,m} = m^{-(j+4)}$, provided $r(m) \geqslant m^{j+1}$ and $S_G(m) \geqslant m^{j+4}$. By Theorem 2.3.7 (assuming MA $\neq$ EXP), infinitely many m satisfy the latter conditions; we call such m's good.

There are still two technical problems we have to solve in order to make sure that $\tilde{d}_{j,m}$ is a supermartingale: First, what to do along languages C for which (7.6) does not hold for $x = 0^m$, and what if m is not good? We will deal with that in a moment. Second, even for a good m along a language C satisfying (7.6) for $x = 0^m$, just replacing $\pi_{j,m}$ with $\tilde{\pi}_{j,m}$ in the definition of $d_{j,m}$ might not work. For example, if $\tilde{\pi}_{j,m}$ underestimates $\pi_{j,m}$ on input w, and overestimates it on input $w0$ and $w1$, condition (2.4) is violated. Note that such a situation can only occur in case the string corresponding to the position right after w is a query M_j^ω makes on some input of the form $\langle 0^j, 0^m, 0^i \rangle$ for some $i \in I_m$ and some $\omega \sqsupseteq w$. As the queries are made in lexicographical order, we can efficiently check the latter condition on w by running M_j^w on every input $\langle 0^j, 0^m, 0^i \rangle$ for $i \in I_m$, and there can be no more than $3m^j \log m$ prefixes w satisfying it along any sequence ω. Since the limit $\epsilon_{j,m}$ on the estimation error is such that $(3m^j \log m) \cdot \epsilon_{j,m}$ remains bounded, we can remedy this problem by accumulatively subtracting a term $2\epsilon_{j,m}$ from the approximation for $\pi_{j,m}$, and adding a constant to the resulting approximation for $d_{j,m}$. The former modification guarantees that condition (2.4) is met; the latter is needed after the former in order to keep the values non-negative. More precisely, we define

$$d_{j,m}^*(w) = \begin{cases} m^3 \tilde{\pi}_{j,m}(w) + 1 - 2q_{j,m}(w)m^3\epsilon_{j,m} & \text{if } |w| \geqslant 2^m \\ 4 & \text{otherwise,} \end{cases} \tag{7.7}$$

where $q_{j,m}(w)$ denotes the number of positions in w that correspond to a query M_j^w makes on an input of the form $\langle 0^j, 0^m, 0^i \rangle$ for some $i \in I_m$. Note that $0 \leqslant q_{j,m}(w) \leqslant q_{j,m}(\omega) \leqslant 3m^j \log m$ and that we can efficiently compute $q_{j,m}(w)$.

We solve the first problem by explicitly checking for each prefix w that the values $d_{j,m}^*$ proposes for the one bit extensions $w0$ and $w1$, satisfy the defining conditions of a supermartingale. If they do, we accept them; otherwise we enforce the conditions by not betting. So, we define the function $\tilde{d}_{j,m}$ as follows:

$$\tilde{d}_{j,m}(\lambda) = 4$$

$$\tilde{d}_{j,m}(wb) = \begin{cases} d_{j,m}^*(wb) & \text{if } d_{j,m}^*(w0) \geqslant 0 \text{ and } d_{j,m}^*(w1) \geqslant 0 \text{ and} \\ & d_{j,m}^*(w0) + d_{j,m}^*(w1) \leqslant 2\tilde{d}_{j,m}(w) \\ \tilde{d}_{j,m}(w) & \text{otherwise.} \end{cases} \tag{7.8}$$

It follows that $\tilde{d}_{j,m}$ is a supermartingale computable in time $|w|^{a_2}$ for some constant a_2 independent of M_j and m.

Claim 7.4.1. If m is good and sufficiently large, $\tilde{d}_{j,m}(w) = d_{j,m}^*(w)$ for any $w \sqsubseteq \chi_C$, where C is a language satisfying (7.6).

Proof. We show that $\tilde{d}_{j,m}(w) = d^*_{j,m}(w)$ for any $w \sqsubseteq \chi_C$ by induction on $|w|$. Clearly, the statement holds for $w = \lambda$. So, it suffices to argue for any string w that the conditions on the right-hand side of (7.8) are met, assuming that $\tilde{d}_{j,m}(w) = d^*_{j,m}(w)$.

If $|w| < 2^m - 1$, this is true because $d^*_{j,m}(v) = 4$ for $|v| < 2^m$. If $|w| \geqslant 2^m - 1$, the first two conditions on the right-hand side of (7.8) are satisfied, since for any string v of length $|v| \geqslant 2^m$,

$$d^*_{j,m}(v) \geqslant 1 - 2q_{j,m}(v)m^3\epsilon_{j,m} \geqslant 1 - 6\epsilon_{j,m}m^{j+3}\log m = 1 - \frac{6\log m}{m},$$

which is positive for sufficiently large m. In case $|w| = 2^m - 1$, the remaining condition is met because

$$
\begin{aligned}
d^*_{j,m}(w0) + d^*_{j,m}(w1) &\leqslant m^3(\tilde{\pi}_{j,m}(w0) + \tilde{\pi}_{j,m}(w1)) + 2 \\
&\leqslant m^3(\pi_{j,m}(w0) + \pi_{j,m}(w1) + 2\epsilon_{j,m}) + 2 \\
&= 2m^3(\pi_{j,m}(w) + \epsilon_{j,m}) + 2 \\
&\leqslant 2(2 + 1 + 1) \\
&= 2\tilde{d}_{j,m}(w).
\end{aligned}
$$

In case $|w| \geqslant 2^m$, the remaining condition certainly holds if $d^*_{j,m}(w0) = d^*_{j,m}(w1) = d^*_{j,m}(w)$. Otherwise, $q_{j,m}(w0) = q_{j,m}(w1) = q_{j,m}(w) + 1$, and we have that

$$
\begin{aligned}
& d^*_{j,m}(w0) + d^*_{j,m}(w1) \\
&= m^3(\tilde{\pi}_{j,m}(w0) + \tilde{\pi}_{j,m}(w1)) + 2 - 2(q_{j,m}(w0) + q_{j,m}(w1))m^3\epsilon_{j,m} \\
&\leqslant m^3(\pi_{j,m}(w0) + \pi_{j,m}(w1) + 2\epsilon_{j,m}) + 2 - 4(q_{j,m}(w) + 1)m^3\epsilon_{j,m} \\
&= 2m^3(\pi_{j,m}(w) - \epsilon_{j,m}) + 2 - 4q_{j,m}(w)m^3\epsilon_{j,m} \\
&\leqslant 2m^3\tilde{\pi}_{j,m}(w) + 2 - 4q_{j,m}(w)m^3\epsilon_{j,m} \\
&= 2d^*_{j,m}(w) \\
&= 2\tilde{d}_{j,m}(w).
\end{aligned}
$$

(End of the proof of Claim 7.4.1.)

So, for a good and sufficiently large m we get that

$$\tilde{d}_{j,m}(\chi_C) = d^*_{j,m}(\chi_C) \geqslant d_{j,m}(\chi_C) + 1 - (2q_{j,m}(\omega) + 1)m^3\epsilon_{j,m} \geqslant d_{j,m}(\chi_C)$$

for any language C satisfying (7.6). Since there are infinitely many good m's and $d_{j,m}(\chi_C) = m^3$, this implies that $\tilde{d}_j = \sum_{m=1}^{\infty} \frac{1}{m^2}\tilde{d}_{j,m}$ is a supermartingale that succeeds on any such language C. It is computable in time $|w|^a$ for some constant a independent of j.

Since for a standard enumeration M_i including all $\leqslant^P_T$-reductions that make their queries in lexicographical order and such that $M_i(x)$ is computable in time $(2^{|x|}+i)^{O(1)}$, the supermartingale system $\tilde{d}_i$ is E-uniform, Lemma 7.4.1 finishes the proof of the theorem.

7.5 Conclusion and Open Questions

We have shown that EXP and several other subclasses only have a few complete or hard languages under certain relatively weak reducibilities. On the other hand, most languages turn out to be hard for BPP under somewhat more powerful reductions. A very narrow gap between the power of the reductions remains, and bridging it would separate BPP from EXP and from certain other classes.

Here are a couple of problems for further research along these lines. The question of whether Theorem 7.2.1 holds for some constant $\alpha \geqslant 1$, remains open. A positive answer would be the best result provable by relativizable techniques, just as our results in Section 4 are optimal. By the same token, relativizable techniques cannot establish the Small Span Theorem for $\leqslant^P_{tt}$-reductions.

It seems unlikely that our approach allows one to establish Theorem 7.2.1 for $\alpha \geqslant 1$, because of Lemma 7.2.1. For some constant $\epsilon > 0$ and a given $\leqslant^P_{n^\alpha\text{-}tt}$-reduction M, this would require the construction of a set $I_{M,i}$ containing $n_i^\alpha + 1$ strings of length n_i and a set $Q_{M,i}$ of size n_i^α, such that all queries of length less than n_i^ϵ that M makes on inputs from $I_{M,i}$ are in $Q_{M,i}$. However, the following argument shows that for $\alpha \geqslant 1$, it is not even possible for $\|I_{M,i}\|$ to equal $\|Q_{M,i}\|$ when for every input $x \in \{0,1\}^{n_i}$ the queries are chosen from $\{0,1\}^{<n_i^\epsilon}$ in a Kolmogorov random way. The concatenation σ of all these queries is a Kolmogorov random string of length $2^{n_i} n_i^{\alpha+\epsilon}$. Given a listing of the elements of $Q_{M,i}$, we can describe the queries for elements of $I_{M,i}$ by pointers to that list. Assuming $\|I_{M,i}\| = \|Q_{M,i}\| = q$, this leads to a description of σ of length at most $qn_i^\epsilon + q(n_i + n_i^\alpha \log q) + (2^{n_i} - q)n_i^{\alpha+\epsilon} + O(\log q)$, which is asymptotically less than $|\sigma|$ as long as $\log q \leqslant cn_i^\epsilon$ for some constant $c < 1$. Since we have $\log q \in O(\log n_i)$, we get a contradiction to the Kolmogorov randomness of σ.

Ambos-Spies, Neis, and Terwijn [10] focused on E-measure, and they established the equivalent of Theorem 7.2.1 and the Small Span Theorem within E for $\leqslant^P_{k\text{-}tt}$-reductions for any constant k. A similar Kolmogorov argument as above indicates that our techniques are not powerful enough to extend these results to stronger reductions. Even the $\leqslant^P_{btt}$-case remains open.

8. The Frequency of Autoreducible Languages

This chapter asks the question how many languages in exponential time are autoreducible. We will study the problem within the framework of resource-bounded measure, as well as within the context of betting games, a notion which we will develop here and which provides an alternate to resource-bounded measure. Several approaches for separating BPP from EXP will come up. problem

8.1 Introduction

Lutz's theory of measure on complexity classes is now usually defined in terms of resource-bounded martingales. A martingale can be regarded as a gambling game played on unseen languages A. Let $s_1, s_2, s_3, \ldots$ be the standard lexicographic ordering of strings. The gambler G starts with capital $C_0 = \$1$ and places a bet $B_1 \in [0, C_0]$ on either "$s_1 \in A$" or "$s_1 \notin A$." Given a fixed particular language A, the bet's outcome depends only on whether $s_1 \in A$. If the bet wins, then the new capital C_1 equals $C_0 + B_1$, while if the bet loses, $C_1 = C_0 - B_1$. The gambler then places a bet $B_2 \in [0, C_1]$ on (or against) membership of the string s_2, then on s_3, and so forth. The gambler *succeeds* if G's capital C_i grows unboundedly. The class $\mathcal{C}$ of languages A on which G succeeds (and any subclass) is said to have *measure zero*. Lutz and others (see [90]) have developed a rich and extensive theory around this measure-zero notion, and have shown interesting connections to many problems in complexity theory.

We propose the generalization obtained by lifting the requirement that G must bet on strings in lexicographic order. That is, G may begin by choosing any string x_1 on which to place its first bet, and after the oracle tells the result, may choose any other string x_2 for its second bet, and so forth. Note that the sequences $x_1, x_2, x_3, \ldots$ (as well as $B_1, B_2, B_3, \ldots$) may be radically different for different oracle languages A – in complexity-theory parlance, G's queries are *adaptive*. The lone restriction is that G may not bet on the same string twice. We call G a *betting game*.

Our betting games remedy a possible lack in the martingale theory, one best explained in the context of languages that are "random" for classes $\mathcal{D}$ such as E or EXP. A language L is $\mathcal{D}$-*random* if L cannot be covered by

D. van Mehlkebeek: Randomness and Completeness in Computational Complexity, LNCS 1950, pp. 161–181, 2000.
© Springer-Verlag Berlin Heidelberg 2000

a $\mathcal{D}$-martingale. Based on one's intuition about random 0-1 sequences, the language $L' = \{flip(x) \mid x \in L\}$ should likewise be $\mathcal{D}$-random, where $flip(x)$ changes every 0 in x to a 1 and vice-versa. However, this closure property is not known for E-random or EXP-random languages, because of the way martingales are tied to the fixed lexicographic ordering of Σ^*. Betting games can adapt to easy permutations of Σ^* such as that induced by $flip$. Similarly, a class $\mathcal{C}$ that is *small* in the sense of being covered by a ($\mathcal{D}$-)betting game remains small if the languages $L \in \mathcal{C}$ are so permuted.

Our new angle on measure theory may be useful for attacking the problem of separating BPP from EXP. In Lutz's theory it is open whether the class of EXP-complete languages under polynomial-time Turing reductions has EXP-measure zero. If so, by results of Allender and Strauss [5], BPP $\neq$ EXP. Since there are oracles A such that BPP^A = EXP^A [64], this kind of absolute separation would be a major breakthrough. We show that the EXP-complete languages *can* be covered by an EXP-betting game – in fact, by an E-betting game. The one technical lack in our theory as a notion of measure is also interesting here: If the "finite unions" property holds for betting games (that is, $\mathcal{C}_1$ small and $\mathcal{C}_2$ small implies $\mathcal{C}_1 \cup \mathcal{C}_2$ small), then EXP $\neq$ BPP. Likewise, if Lutz's martingales do enjoy the permutation-invariance of betting games, then BPP $\neq$ EXP. Finally, we show that if an EXP-computable pseudo-random generator of security $2^{n^{\Omega(1)}}$ exists, then for every EXP-betting game G one can find an EXP-martingale that succeeds on all languages covered by G. Pseudo-random generators of higher security $2^{\Omega(n)}$ and computable in E likewise imply the equivalence of E-betting games and E-measure.

Measure theory and betting games help us to dig further into questions about pseudo-random generators and complexity-class separations. Our tool is the notion of an *autoreducible* language. Recall that a language L is $\leqslant_T^P$-*autoreducible* if there is a polynomial-time oracle Turing machine Q such that for all inputs x, Q^L correctly decides whether $x \in L$ without ever submitting x itself as a query to L. If Q is nonadaptive (i.e., computes a polynomial-time truth-table reduction), we say L is $\leqslant_{tt}^P$-*autoreducible*. We show that the class of $\leqslant_T^P$-autoreducible languages is covered by an E-betting game. Since every EXP-complete language is $\leqslant_T^P$-autoreducible by Theorem 5.4.1, this implies that the class of EXP-complete languages can be covered by an E-betting game. The subclass of $\leqslant_{tt}^P$-autoreducible languages provides the following tighter connection between measure statements and open problems about EXP.

- If the $\leqslant_{tt}^P$-autoreducible languages do not have E-measure zero, then EXP = MA.
- If the $\leqslant_{tt}^P$-autoreducible languages do not have E-measure one in EXP, then EXP $\neq$ BPP.

Since EXP $\neq$ MA is strongly believed, one would expect the class of $\leqslant_{tt}^P$-autoreducible languages to have E-measure zero. *Proving* this would yield a proof of EXP $\neq$ BPP.

The structure of this chapter is as follows. Section 8.2 introduces betting games, and shows that they are a generalization of martingales. Section 8.3 shows how to simulate a betting game by a martingale of perhaps-unavoidably higher time complexity. Section 8.4, however, demonstrates that strong pseudo-random generators (if there are any) allow one to compute the martingale in the same order of time. Section 8.5 presents our main results pertaining to autoreducible languages, including our motivating example of a concrete betting game. The concluding Section 8.6 summarizes open problems and gives prospects for future research.

8.2 Betting Games

To capture intuitions that have been expressed not only for Lutz measure but also in many earlier papers on random sequences, we formalize a betting game as an *infinite* process, rather than as a Turing machine that has *finite* computations on string inputs.

Definition 8.2.1. *A betting game G is an oracle Turing machine that maintains a "capital tape" and a "bet tape," in addition to its standard input, output, work and query tapes, and works in stages $i = 1, 2, 3 \ldots$ as follows: Beginning each stage i, the capital tape holds a nonnegative rational number C_{i-1}. The initial capital C_0 is some positive rational number. G computes a query string x_i to bet on, a bet amount B_i, $0 \leqslant B_i \leqslant C_{i-1}$, and a bet sign $b_i \in \{-1, +1\}$. The computation is legal so long as x_i does not belong to the set $\{x_1, \ldots, x_{i-1}\}$ of strings queried in earlier stages. G ends stage i by entering a special query state. For a given oracle language A, if $x_i \in A$ and $b_i = +1$, or if $x_i \notin A$ and $b_i = -1$, then the new capital is given by $C_i \doteq C_{i-1} + B_i$, else by $C_i \doteq C_{i-1} - B_i$. We charge M for the time required to write the numerator and denominator of the new capital C_i down. The query and bet tapes are blanked, and G proceeds to stage $i + 1$.*

Note that every oracle language A determines a unique infinite computation of G, which we denote by G^A. This includes a unique infinite sequence $x_1, x_2, \ldots$ of query strings, and a unique sequence $C_0, C_1, C_2, \ldots$ telling how the gambler fares against A.

Definition 8.2.2. *A betting game G runs in time $t(n)$ if for all oracles A, every query of length n made by G^A is made in the first $t(n)$ steps of the computation.*

Definition 8.2.3. *A betting game G succeeds on a language A, written $A \in S^\infty[G]$, if the sequence of values C_i in the computation G^A is unbounded. If $A \in S^\infty[G]$, then we also say G covers A.*

Our main motivating example where one may wish not to bet in lexicographic order, or according to any fixed ordering of strings, is deferred to Section 8.5.

There we will construct an E-betting game that succeeds on the class of $\leqslant^{\mathrm{P}}_{\mathrm{T}}$-autoreducible languages, which is not known to have Lutz measure zero in E or EXP.

We now want to argue that the more liberal requirement of being covered by a time $t(n)$ betting game, still defines a smallness concept for subclasses of DTIME$[t(n)]$ in the intuitive sense Lutz established for his measure-zero notion. The following result is a good beginning.

Theorem 8.2.1. *For every time $t(n)$ betting game G, we can construct a language that lies in* DTIME$[t(n)]$ *but is not covered by G.*

Proof. Let Q be a non-oracle Turing machine that runs as follows, on any input x. The machine Q simulates up to $t(|x|)$ steps of the single computation of G on empty input. Whenever G bets on and queries a string y, Q gives the answer that causes G to lose money, rejecting in case of a zero bet. If and when G queries x, Q does likewise. If $t(|x|)$ steps go by without x being queried, then Q rejects x.

The important point is that Q's answer to a query $y \neq x$ is the same as the answer when Q is run on input y. The condition that G cannot query a string x of length n after $t(n)$ steps have elapsed ensures that the decision made by Q when x is not queried does not affect anything else. Hence Q defines a language on which G never does better than its initial capital C_0, and so does not succeed.

In particular, the class E cannot be covered by an E-betting game, nor EXP by an EXP-betting game. Put another way, the "measure conservation axiom" [88] of Lutz's measure carries over to betting games.

To really satisfy the intuition of "small," however, it should hold that the union of two small classes is small. Our lack of meeting this "finite union axiom" will later be excused insofar as it has the nonrelativizing consequence BPP $\neq$ EXP. Theorem 8.2.1 is still good enough for the "measure-like" results we will obtain.

We note also that several robustness properties of Lutz's measure treated in Section 2.5.3 carry over to betting games. This is because we can apply the underlying transformations to the *capital function* c_G of G, which is defined as follows.

Definition 8.2.4. *Let G be a betting game, and $i \geqslant 0$ an integer.*

- *A play α of length i is a sequence of i-many oracle answers.*
- *$c_G(\alpha)$ denotes the capital C_i that G has at the end of the play α (before the next query).*

Note that α determines the first i-many stages of G (so $c_G(\alpha)$ is well-defined) together with the query and bet for the next stage. Note also that the function c_G is a martingale over plays α. The proof of Lemma 2.5.2 works for c_G. We obtain:

Lemma 8.2.1 (Slow-But-Sure Winnings Lemma for betting games).
Let G be a betting game that runs in time $t(n)$. Then we can construct a betting game G' running in time $(2^n t(n))^{O(1)}$ such that $c_{G'}(\lambda) = c_G(\lambda)$ and $S^\infty[G] \subseteq S^\infty[G']$, G' always makes the same queries in the same order as G, and:

$$(\forall \beta)\,(\forall \gamma)\, c_{G'}(\beta\gamma) > c_{G'}(\beta) - 2c_{G'}(\lambda) \tag{8.1a}$$

$$(\forall \alpha)\, c_{G'}(\alpha) < 2(|\alpha| + 1)c_G(\lambda). \tag{8.1b}$$

To begin comparing betting games and martingales, we note first that the latter can be considered a direct special case of betting games. Say a betting game G is *lex-limited* if for all oracles A, the sequence $x_1, x_2, x_3 \ldots$ of queries made by G^A is in lexicographic order. (It need not equal the lexicographic enumeration $s_1, s_2, s_3, \ldots$ of Σ^*.)

Theorem 8.2.2. *Let $\mathcal{T}(n)$ be a collection of time bounds that is closed under squaring and under multiplication by 2^n, such as $2^{O(n)}$ or $2^{n^{O(1)}}$. Then a class $\mathcal{C}$ has time $\mathcal{T}(n)$ measure zero iff $\mathcal{C}$ is covered by a time $\mathcal{T}(n)$ lex-limited betting game.*

Proof. From a martingale d to a betting game G, each stage i of G^A bets on s_i an amount B_i with sign $b_i \in \{-1, +1\}$ given by $b_i B_i = d(w1) - d(w)$, where w is the first $i - 1$ bits of the characteristic sequence of A. This takes $O(2^n)$ evaluations of d to run G up through queries of length n, hence the hypothesis on the time bounds $\mathcal{T}(n)$. In the other direction, when G is lex-limited, one can simulate G on a finite initial segment w of its oracle up to a stage where all queries have been answered by w and G will make no further queries in the domain of w. One can then define $d(w)$ to be the capital entering this stage. That this is a martingale and fulfills the success and run-time requirements is straightforward to check.

Hence in particular for measure on E and EXP, martingales are equivalent to betting games constrained to bet in lexicographic order. Now we will see how we can transform a *general* betting game into an equivalent martingale.

8.3 From Betting Games to Martingales

This section associates to every betting game G a martingale d_G such that $S^\infty[G] \subseteq S^\infty[d_G]$, and begins examining the complexity of d_G. Before defining d_G, however, we pause to discuss some subtleties of betting games and their computations.

Recall that $s_1, s_2, s_3, \ldots$ denotes the standard lexicographic ordering of Σ^*. For a language $A \subseteq \Sigma^*$ and a string $w \in \{0, 1\}^*$, we write $w \sqsubseteq A$ if for all i, $1 \leqslant i \leqslant |w|$, $s_i \in A$ iff the i-th bit of w is a 1. We will also regard w as a function with *domain* $\{s_1, \ldots, s_{|w|}\}$ and range $\{0, 1\}$, writing $w(s_i)$ for the i-th bit of w.

Given a finite initial segment w of an oracle language A, one can define the partial computation G^w of the betting game up to the stage i at which it first makes a query x_i that is not in the domain of w. Define $d(w)$ to be the capital C_{i-1} that G had entering this stage. It is tempting to think that d is a martingale and succeeds on all A for which G succeeds – but neither statement is true in general. The most important reason is that d may fail to be a martingale.

To see this, suppose x_i itself is the lexicographically least string not in the domain of w. That is, x_i is indexed by the bit b of wb, and $w1 \sqsubseteq A$ iff $x_i \in A$. It is possible that G^A makes a small (or even zero) bet on x_i, *and then goes back to make more bets in the domain of w, winning lots of money on them.* The definitions of both $d(w0)$ and $d(w1)$ will then reflect these added winnings, and both values will be greater than $d(w)$. For example, suppose G^A first puts a zero bet on $x_i = s_j$, then bets all of its money on $x_{i+1} = s_{j-1}$ not being in A, and then proceeds with $x_{i+2} = s_{j+1}$. If $w(s_{j-1}) = 0$, then $d(w0) = d(w1) = 2d(w)$.

Put another way, a finite initial segment w may carry much more "winnings potential" than the above definition of $d(w)$ reflects. To capture this potential, one needs to consider potential plays of the betting game outside the domain of w. Happily, one can bound the length of the considered plays via the running time function t of G. Let n be the maximum length of a string indexed by w, i.e., $n = \lfloor \log_2(|w|) \rfloor$. Then after $t(n)$ steps, G cannot query any more strings in the domain of w, so w's potential is exhausted. We will define $d_G(w)$ as an *average* value of those plays that can happen, given the query answers fixed by w. We use the following definitions and notation.

Definition 8.3.1. *For any $t(n)$-time-bounded betting game G and string $w \in \{0,1\}^*$, define:*

- *A play α is t-maximal if G completes the first $|\alpha|$ stages, but not the query and bet of the next stage, within t steps.*
- *A play α is G-consistent with w, written $\alpha \sim_G w$, if for all stages j such that the queried string x_j is in the domain of w, $\alpha_j = w(x_j)$. That is, α is a play that could possibly happen given the information in w. Also let $m(\alpha, w)$ stand for the number of such stages j whose query is answered by w.*
- *Finally, put $d_G(\lambda) = c_G(\lambda)$, and for nonempty w, with $n = \lfloor \log_2(|w|) \rfloor$ as above, let*

$$d_G(w) = \sum_{\alpha \ t(n)-maximal, \alpha \sim_G w} c_G(\alpha) \, 2^{m(\alpha,w)-|\alpha|} \ . \tag{8.2}$$

The weight $2^{m(\alpha,w)-|\alpha|}$ in (8.2) has the following meaning. Suppose we extend the simulation of G^w by flipping a coin for every query outside the domain of w, for exactly i stages. Then the number of coin flips in the resulting play α of length i is $i - m(\alpha, w)$, so $2^{m(\alpha,w)-i}$ is its probability. Thus $d_G(w)$ returns the suitably-weighted average of $t(n)$-step computations of G with w fixed.

One may verify that this is the same as averaging $d(wv)$ over all v of length $2^{t(n)}$ (or any fixed longer length), where d is the non-martingale defined at the beginning of this section.

Lemma 8.3.1. *The function $d_G(w)$ is a martingale.*

Proof. First we argue that

$$d_G(w) = \sum_{|\alpha'|=t(n),\alpha' \sim_G w} c_G(\alpha')\, 2^{m(\alpha',w)-t(n)}. \tag{8.3}$$

Observe that when $\alpha' = \alpha\beta$ and α is $t(n)$-maximal, $\alpha \sim_G w$ iff $\alpha' \sim_G w$. This is because none of the queries answered by β can be in the domain of w, else the definition of G running in time $t(n)$ would be violated. Likewise if $\alpha \sim_G w$ then $m(\alpha',w) = m(\alpha,w)$. Finally, since c_G is a martingale, $c_G(\alpha) = \sum_{|\beta|=t(n)-|\alpha|} c_G(\alpha\beta)\, 2^{|\alpha|-t(n)}$. These facts combine to show the equality of (8.2) and (8.3).

By the same argument, the right-hand side of (8.3) is unchanged on replacing "$t(n)$" by any $t' > t(n)$.

Now consider w such that $|w| + 1$ is not a power of 2. Then the "n" for $w0$ and $w1$ is the same as the "n" for $d_G(w)$. Let P_0 stand for the set of α of length $t(n)$ that are G-consistent with $w0$ but not with $w1$, P_1 for those that are G-consistent with $w1$ but not $w0$, and P for those that are consistent with both. Then the set $\{\alpha : |\alpha| = t(n),\ \alpha \sim_G w\}$ equals the disjoint union of P, P_0, and P_1. Furthermore, for $\alpha \in P_0$ we have $m(\alpha,w0) = m(\alpha,w) + 1$, and similarly for P_1, while for $\alpha \in P$ we have $m(\alpha,w0) = m(\alpha,w1) = m(\alpha,w)$. Hence,

$$
\begin{aligned}
d_G&(w0) + d_G(w1)\\
&= \sum_{\alpha \in P \cup P_0} c_G(\alpha)2^{m(\alpha,w0)-t(n)} + \sum_{\alpha \in P \cup P_1} c_G(\alpha)2^{m(\alpha,w1)-t(n)}\\
&= \sum_{\alpha \in P_0} c_G(\alpha)2^{m(\alpha,w0)-t(n)} + \sum_{\alpha \in P_1} c_G(\alpha)2^{m(\alpha,w1)-t(n)}\\
&\quad + 2\sum_{\alpha \in P} c_G(\alpha)2^{m(\alpha,w)-t(n)}\\
&= 2\sum_{\alpha \in P_0} c_G(\alpha)2^{m(\alpha,w)-t(n)} + 2\sum_{\alpha \in P_1} c_G(\alpha)2^{m(\alpha,w)-t(n)}\\
&\quad + 2\sum_{\alpha \in P} c_G(\alpha)2^{m(\alpha,w)-t(n)}\\
&= 2d_G(w).
\end{aligned}
$$

Finally, if $|w| + 1$ is a power of 2, then $d_G(w0)$ and $d_G(w1)$ use $t' \doteq t(n+1)$ for their length of α. However, by the first part of this proof, we can replace $t(n)$ by t' in the definition of $d_G(w)$ without changing its value, and then the second part goes through the same way for t'. Hence d_G is a martingale.

It is still the case, however, that d_G may not succeed on the languages on which the betting game G succeeds. To ensure this, we first use Lemma 8.2.1 to place betting games G into a suitable "normal form" satisfying the sure-winnings condition (8.1a).

Lemma 8.3.2. *If G is a betting game satisfying the sure-winnings condition (8.1a), then $S^\infty[G] \subseteq S^\infty[d_G]$.*

Proof. First, let $A \in S^\infty[G]$, and fix $k > 0$. Find a finite play β of G consistent with A such that $c_G(\beta) \geqslant k + 2c_G(\lambda)$; and a finite initial segment $w \sqsubseteq A$ long enough to answer every query made in β and long enough to make $t(n)$ in the definition (8.2) of $d_G(w)$ greater than $|\beta|$. Then every α of length $t(n)$ such that $\alpha \sim_G w$ has the form $\alpha = \beta\gamma$. The sure-winnings condition (8.1a) implies that the right-hand side of (8.2) defining $d_G(w)$ is an average over terms that all have size at least k. Hence $d_G(w) \geqslant k$. Letting k grow to infinity gives $A \in S^\infty[d_G]$.

Now we turn our attention to the complexity of d_G. If G is a time $t(n)$ betting game, it is clear that d_G can be computed deterministically in $O(t(n))$ *space*, because we need only cycle through all α of length $t(n)$, and all the items in (8.2) are computable in space $O(t(n))$. In particular, every E-betting game can be simulated by a martingale whose values are computable in deterministic space $2^{O(n)}$ (even counting the output against the space bound), and every EXP-betting game by a martingale similarly computed in space $2^{n^{O(1)}}$. However, we show in the next section that one can *estimate* $d_G(w)$ well without having to cycle through all the α, using a pseudo-random generator to "sample" only a very small fraction of the α's.

8.4 Sampling Results

First we determine the accuracy to which we need to estimate the values $d(w)$ of a hard-to-compute martingale. We state a stronger version of the result than we need in this section. In the next section, we will apply it to martingales whose "activity" is restricted to subsets J of $\{0,1\}^*$ in the following sense: For all strings $x \notin J$, and all w such that $s_{|w|+1} = x$, $d(w0) = d(w1) = d(w)$. Intuitively, a martingale d is inactive on a string x if there is no possible "past history" w that causes a nonzero bet to be made on x. For short we say that such a d is *inactive outside J*. Recall that $2^n \leqslant N < 2^{n+1}$.

Lemma 8.4.1. *Let d be a martingale that is inactive outside $J \subseteq \{0,1\}^*$, and let $(\epsilon(i))_i$ be a nonnegative sequence such that $\sum_{s_i \in J} \epsilon(i)$ converges to a number K. Suppose we can compute in time $t(n)$ a function $g(w)$ such that $|g(w) - d(w)| \leqslant \epsilon(N)$ for all w of length N. Then there is a martingale d' computable in time $(2^n t(n))^{O(1)}$ such that for all w, $|d'(w) - d(w)| \leqslant 4K + 2\epsilon(0)$.*

In this section, we will apply Lemma 8.4.1 with $J = \{0,1\}^*$ and $\epsilon(N) = 1/N^2 \approx 1/2^{2n}$. In Section 8.5.3 we will apply Lemma 8.4.1 in cases where J is finite.

Proof. First note that for any w (with $N = |w|$),

$$\left| g(w) - \frac{g(w0) + g(w1)}{2} \right|$$

$$\leqslant |g(w) - d(w)| + \left| \frac{d(w0) - g(w0)}{2} \right| + \left| \frac{d(w1) - g(w1)}{2} \right|$$

$$\leqslant \epsilon(N) + \epsilon(N+1). \tag{8.4}$$

In case $J = \{0,1\}^*$, we inductively define:

$$\begin{cases} d'(\lambda) = g(\lambda) + 2K + \epsilon(0) \\ d'(wb) = d'(w) + g(wb) - \frac{g(w0) + g(w1)}{2}. \end{cases}$$

Note that d' satisfies the average law (2.3), and that we can compute $d'(w)$ in time $O(2^n t(n))$.

By induction on $|w|$, we can show using the estimate provided by (8.4) that

$$g(w) + \epsilon(N) + 2 \sum_{i=N+1}^{\infty} \epsilon(i) \;\leqslant\; d'(w) \;\leqslant\; g(w) + 2 \sum_{i=0}^{N-1} \epsilon(i) + \epsilon(N) + 2K.$$

It follows that

$$d'(w) \geqslant g(w) + \epsilon(N)$$
$$= d(w) + (g(w) - d(w)) + \epsilon(N) \geqslant d(w),$$

and that

$$d'(w) = d(w) + (g(w) - d(w)) + (d'(w) - g(w))$$
$$\leqslant d(w) + \epsilon(N) + 2 \sum_{i=0}^{N-1} \epsilon(i) + \epsilon(N) + 2K$$
$$\leqslant d(w) + 4K + 2\epsilon(0).$$

This establishes the lemma in case $J = \{0,1\}^*$. The generalization to other subsets J of $\{0,1\}^*$ is straightforward.

(End of the proof of Lemma 8.4.1.)

Next, we will specify precisely which function f_G we will sample in order to estimate d_G, and how we will do it.

Let G be a $t(n)$-time-bounded betting game. Consider a prefix w, and let n denote the largest length of a string in the domain of w. With any string ρ of length $t(n)$, we can associate a unique "play of the game" G defined by using w to answer queries in the domain of w, and the successive bits of ρ

to answer queries outside it. We can stop this play after $t(n)$ steps – so that the stopped play is a $t(n)$-maximal α – and then define $f_G(w, \rho)$ to be the capital $c_G(\alpha)$. Note that we can compute $f_G(w, \rho)$ in linear time, i.e., in time $O(|w| + t(n))$. The proportion of strings ρ of length $t(n)$ that map to the same play α is exactly the weight $2^{m(\alpha,w)-|\alpha|}$ in (8.2) for $d_G(w)$. Letting E stand for mathematical expectation, this gives us:

$$d_G(w) = E_{|\rho|=t(n)}[f_G(w, \rho)].$$

We will now apply sampling using pseudo-random generators to obtain a good approximation $g(w)$ to this average. The following general result shows how pseudo-random generators can be used to approximate averages. It provides the accuracy and time bounds needed for applying Lemma 8.4.1 to get the desired martingale.

Theorem 8.4.1. *Let D be a pseudo-random generator computable in time $\delta(n)$ with seed length $s(n) = n$ and output length $r(n)$. Let $f : \{0,1\}^* \times \{0,1\}^* \to (-\infty, \infty)$ be a function that is computed in linear time on a Turing machine, and let $\ell, R, m : \mathbb{N} \to \mathbb{N}$ be time-constructible functions such that $\ell(N) \geqslant N$ and the following relations hold for any integer $N \geqslant 0$, $w \in \{0,1\}^N$, and $\rho \in \{0,1\}^{\ell(N)}$:*

$$|f(w, \rho)| \leqslant R(N)$$
$$r(m(N)) \geqslant \ell(N)$$
$$S_D(m(N)) \geqslant (\ell(N) + R(N))^6. \tag{8.5}$$

Then we can approximate

$$h(w) = E_{|\rho|=\ell(N)}[f(w, \rho)] \tag{8.6}$$

to within N^{-2} in time $O(2^{m(N)} \cdot (\ell(N) + R(N))^4 \cdot \delta(m(N)))$.

Proof. For any positive integer N, let $\mathcal{I}_N$ be a partition of the interval $[-R(N), R(N)]$ into subintervals of length $\frac{1}{2N^2}$. Note that $\|\mathcal{I}_N\| = 4N^2 R(N)$. Define for any $I \in \mathcal{I}_N$ and any string w of length N,

$$\pi(I, w) = \Pr_{|\rho|=\ell(N)}[f(w, \rho) \in I].$$

Using Theorem 2.2.7, the predicate underlying $\pi(I, w)$ can be computed by circuits of size $O(\ell(N) \log \ell(N))$. Since $S_D(m(N)) \in \omega(\ell(N) \log \ell(N))$, it follows that

$$\tilde{\pi}(I, w) = \Pr_{|\sigma|=m(N)}[f(w, D(\sigma)[1 \ldots \ell(N)]) \in I]$$

approximates $\pi(I, w)$ to within an additive error of $(S_D(m(N)))^{-1}$, and we can compute it in time $O(2^{m(N)} \cdot \ell(N) \cdot \delta(m(N)))$. We define the approximation $\tilde{h}(w)$ for $h(w)$ as

$$\tilde{h}(w) = \sum_{I \in \mathcal{I}_N} \tilde{\pi}(I, w) \min(I).$$

Since we can write $h(w)$ as

$$h(w) = \sum_{I \in \mathcal{I}_N} \pi(I, w) E_{|\rho| = \ell(N)}[f(w, \rho) \mid f(w, \rho) \in I],$$

we can bound the approximation error as follows:

$$|h(w) - \tilde{h}(w)|$$
$$\leqslant \sum_{I \in \mathcal{I}_N} \left(\pi(I, w) \cdot |E_{|\rho| = \ell(N)}[f(w, \rho) \mid f(w, \rho) \in I] - \min(I)| + \right.$$
$$\left. |\pi(I, w) - \tilde{\pi}(I, w)| \cdot \min(I) \right)$$
$$\leqslant \max_{I \in \mathcal{I}_N} (||I||) + ||\mathcal{I}_N|| \cdot (S_D(m(N)))^{-1} \cdot R(N)$$
$$\leqslant \frac{1}{2N^2} + 4N^2 \cdot R^2(N) \cdot (S_D(m(N)))^{-1} \leqslant \frac{1}{N^2}.$$

Computing $\tilde{h}(w)$ requires $||\mathcal{I}_N|| = 4N^2 R(N)$ evaluations of $\tilde{\pi}$, which results in the claimed upper bound for the time complexity of $\tilde{h}$.

(End of the proof of Theorem 8.4.1.)

Now, we would like to apply Theorem 8.4.1 to approximate $h = d_G$ given by (8.2) to within N^{-2}, by setting $f = f_G$ and $\ell(N) = t(n)$. However, for a general betting game G running in time $t(n)$, we can only guarantee an upper bound of $R(N) = 2^{t(n)} \cdot c_G(\lambda)$ on $|f(w, \rho)|$. Since S_D can be at most exponential, condition (8.5) would force $m(N)$ to be $\Omega(t(n))$. In that case, Theorem 8.4.1 can only yield an approximation computable in time $2^{O(t(n))}$, which is no faster than the straightforward exact computation of f mentioned at the end of Section 8.3. However, we can assume without loss of generality that G satisfies the slow-winnings condition (8.1b) of Lemma 8.2.1, in which case an upper bound of $R(N) \in O(N)$ holds. Then the term $\ell(N)$ in the right-hand side of (8.5) dominates, provided $t(n) \in 2^{\Omega(n)}$.

Taking everything together, we obtain the following result about transforming E- and EXP-betting games into equivalent E- respectively EXP-martingales.

Theorem 8.4.2. *If there is a pseudo-random generator computable in E with seed length n and security $2^{\Omega(n)}$, then for every E-betting game G, there exists an E-martingale d such that $S^\infty[G] \subseteq S^\infty[d]$. If there is a pseudo-random generator computable in EXP with seed length n and security $2^{n^{\Omega(1)}}$, then for every EXP-betting game G, there exists an EXP-martingale d such that $S^\infty[G] \subseteq S^\infty[d]$.*

Proof. By Lemma 8.2.1, we can assume that c_G satisfies both the sure-winnings condition (8.1a) as well as the slow-winnings condition (8.1b). Because of Lemma 8.3.2 and Lemma 8.4.1 (since the series $\sum_{i=1}^\infty \frac{1}{i^2}$ converges), it suffices to approximate the function $d_G(w)$ given by (8.2) to within N^{-2} in time $2^{O(n)}$ respectively $2^{n^{O(1)}}$, where $N = |w|$ and $n = \log N$.

Under the given hypothesis for E and using Corollary 2.3.1, we can meet the conditions for applying Theorem 8.4.1 to $h = d_G$ with $\ell(N) \in N^{O(1)}$, $R(N) \in O(N)$, and $m(N) \in O(\log N)$, and we obtain the approximation of d_G we need. The same holds in a similar manner for EXP, for which we have $\ell(N) \in 2^{(\log N)^{O(1)}}$, $R(N) \in O(N)$, and $m(N) \in (\log N)^{O(1)}$.

Finally, we note that the hypothesis in Theorem 8.4.2 holds if NP = P.

Corollary 8.4.1. *If* NP = P, *then for every* E-*betting game* G, *there exists an* E-*martingale* d *such that* $S^{\infty}[G] \subseteq S^{\infty}[d]$. *Similarly, if* NP $\subseteq$ DTIME$[2^{(\log n)^{O(1}}$ *then for every* EXP-*betting game* G, *there exists an* EXP-*martingale* d *such that* $S^{\infty}[G] \subseteq S^{\infty}[d]$.

Proof. By Corollary 2.2.1 and Theorem 2.3.8, the hypothesis NP = P implies that there exists a pseudo-random generator computable in E with seed length n, and output length and security $2^{\Omega(n)}$. Theorem 8.4.2 then yields the first result. The second result follows in a similar way.

8.5 Autoreducible Languages

An oracle Turing machine M is said to autoreduce a language A if it accepts A when given A as the oracle, and for all strings x, M^A on input x does not query x. That is, one can learn the membership of x by querying strings other than x itself. If M runs in polynomial time, we say that A is $\leqslant^P_T$-autoreducible. If M is also nonadaptive, then A is $\leqslant^P_{tt}$-autoreducible.

One can always code M so that for *all* oracles, it *never* queries its own input – then we call M an autoreduction. Hence we can define an effective enumeration $(M_i)_i$ of polynomial-time autoreductions, such that a language A is autoreducible iff there exists an i such that the language accepted by M_i^A equals A. The same goes for $\leqslant^P_{tt}$-autoreductions.

We will now demonstrate the importance of autoreducible languages for testing the power of resource-bounded measure.

8.5.1 Adaptively Autoreducible Languages

As stated in Section 8.1, if the $\leqslant^P_T$-autoreducible languages in EXP (or even the $\leqslant^P_T$-complete languages for EXP) are covered by an EXP-martingale, then EXP $\neq$ BPP, a nonrelativizing consequence. However, it is easy to cover them by an E-betting game. Indeed, the betting game uses its adaptive freedom only to "look ahead" at the membership of lexicographically greater strings, betting nothing on them.

Theorem 8.5.1. *There is an* E-*betting game G that succeeds on all $\leqslant_T^P$-autoreducible languages.*

Proof. Let $M_1, M_2, \ldots$ be an enumeration of $\leqslant_T^P$-autoreductions such that each M_i runs in time $n^i + i$ on inputs of length n. Our betting game G regards its capital as composed of infinitely many "shares" c_i, one for each M_i. Initially, $c_i = 1/2^i$. Letting $\langle \cdot, \cdot \rangle$ be a standard pairing function, inductively define $n_0 = 0$ and $n_{\langle i,j \rangle + 1} = (n_{\langle i,j \rangle})^i + i$.

During a stage $s = \langle i, j \rangle$, G simulates M_i on input $0^{n_{s-1}}$. Whenever M_i makes a query of length less than n_{s-1}, G looks up the answer from its table of past queries. Whenever M_i makes a query of length n_{s-1} or more, G places a bet of zero on that string and makes the same query. Then G bets all of the share c_i on $0^{n_{s-1}}$ according to the answer of the simulation of M_i. Finally, G "cleans up" by putting zero bets on all strings with length in $[n_{s-1}, n_s)$ that were not queries in the previous steps.

If M_i autoreduces A, then share c_i doubles in value at each stage $\langle i, j \rangle$, and makes the total capital grow to infinity. And G runs in time $2^{O(n)}$ – indeed, only the "cleanup" phase needs this much time.

Corollary 8.5.1. *Each of the following statements implies* BPP $\neq$ EXP.

1. *The class of $\leqslant_T^P$-autoreducible languages has* E-*measure zero.*
2. *The class of $\leqslant_T^P$-complete languages for* EXP *has* E-*measure zero.*
3. E-*betting games and* E-*martingales are equivalent.*
4. E-*betting games have the finite union property.*

The same holds if we replace E *by* EXP *in these statements.*

Proof. Let $\mathcal{C}$ stand for the class of languages that are not $\leqslant_T^P$-hard for BPP. Allender and Strauss [5] showed that $\mathcal{C}$ has E-measure zero, so trivially it is also covered by an E-betting game. Now let $\mathcal{D}$ stand for the class of $\leqslant_T^P$-complete languages for EXP. By Theorems 8.5.1 and 5.4.1, $\mathcal{D}$ is covered by an E-betting game.

If EXP = BPP, the union $\mathcal{C} \cup \mathcal{D}$ contains all of EXP, and:

- If $\mathcal{D}$ would have E-measure zero, so would $\mathcal{C} \cup \mathcal{D}$ and hence EXP, contradicting the measure conservation property of Lutz measure.
- If E-betting games would have the finite-union property, then $\mathcal{C} \cup \mathcal{D}$ and EXP would be covered by an E-betting game, contradicting Theorem 8.2.1.

Since statement 1 implies statement 2, and statement 3 implies statement 4, these observations suffice to establish the corollary for E. The proof for EXP is similar.

Since there is an oracle A giving $\mathsf{EXP}^A = \mathsf{BPP}^A$ [64], this shows that relativizable techniques cannot establish the equivalence of E-martingales and E-betting games, nor of EXP-martingales and EXP-betting games. They cannot refute it either, since there are oracles relative to which strong pseudo-random generators exist – all "random" oracles, in fact.

8.5.2 Nonadaptively Autoreducible Languages

It is tempting to think that the *non*-adaptively autoreducible languages should have E-measure zero, or at least EXP-measure zero, insofar as betting games are the adaptive cousins of martingales. However, it is not just adaptiveness but also the freedom to bet *out of the fixed lexicographic order* that adds power to betting games. If one carries out the proof of Theorem 8.5.1 to cover the class of $\leqslant_{tt}^P$-autoreducible languages, using an enumeration $(M_i)_i$ of $\leqslant_{tt}^P$-autoreductions, one obtains a *nonadaptive* E-betting game (defined formally below) that (independent of its oracle) bets on all strings in order given by a single permutation of Σ^*. The permutation itself is E-computable. It might seem that an E-martingale should be able to "untwist" the permutation and succeed on all these languages. However, our next results, which strengthen the above corollary, close the same "nonrelativizing" door on proving this with current techniques.

In order to formalize the strengthening of Corollary 8.5.1, we call a betting game G *nonadaptive* if the infinite sequence $x_1, x_2, x_3, \ldots$ of queries G^A makes is the same for all oracles A. If G runs in $2^{O(n)}$ time, and this sequence hits all strings in Σ^*, then the permutation π of the standard ordering $s_1, s_2, s_3, \ldots$ defined by $\pi(s_i) = x_i$ is both computable and invertible in $2^{O(n)}$ time. It is computable in this amount of time because in order to hit all strings, G must bet on all strings in $\{0, 1\}^n$ within the first $2^{O(n)}$ steps. Hence its i-th bet must be made in a number of steps that is singly-exponential in the length of s_i. And to compute $\pi^{-1}(x_i)$, G need only be run for $2^{O(|x_i|)}$ steps, since it cannot query x_i after this time. Since π and its inverse are both E-computable, π is a reasonable candidate to replace lexicographic ordering in the definition of E-martingales, and likewise for EXP-martingales. We say a class $\mathcal{C}$ has π-E-measure zero if $\mathcal{C}$ can be covered by an E-martingale that interprets its input as a characteristic string *in the order given by π*.

Theorem 8.5.2. *The class of $\leqslant_{tt}^P$-autoreducible languages can be covered by a nonadaptive E-betting game. Hence there is an E-computable and invertible permutation π of Σ^* such that this class has π-E-measure zero.*

Proof. With reference to the proof of Theorem 8.5.1, we can let $M_1, M_2, \ldots$ be an enumeration of $\leqslant_{tt}^P$-autoreductions such that each M_i runs in time $n^i + i$. The machine G in that proof automatically becomes nonadaptive, and since it queries all strings, it defines a permutation π of Σ^* as above with the required properties.

Corollary 8.5.2. *Each of the following statements implies* BPP $\neq$ EXP, *as do the statements obtained on replacing "E" by "EXP."*

1. *The class of $\leqslant_{tt}^P$-autoreducible languages has E-measure zero.*
2. *The class of $\leqslant_{tt}^P$-complete languages for* EXP *has E-measure zero.*
3. *Nonadaptive E-betting games and E-martingales are equivalent.*

4. *If two classes can be covered by nonadaptive E-betting games, then their union can be covered by an E-betting game.*
5. *For all classes C and all E-computable and invertible orderings π, if C has π-E-measure zero, then C has E-measure zero.*

Proof. It suffices to make the following two observations to argue that the proof of Corollary 8.5.1 carries over to the truth-table cases:

- The construction of Allender and Strauss [5] actually shows that the class of languages that are not $\leqslant_{tt}^P$-hard for BPP has E-measure zero.
- If EXP = BPP, Theorem 5.4.4 from Chapter 5 implies that all $\leqslant_{tt}^P$-complete languages for EXP are $\leqslant_{tt}^P$-autoreducible, because BPP $\subseteq \Sigma_2^P \subseteq \Delta_3^P \subseteq$ EXP.

Theorem 8.5.2 and the finite-unions property of Lutz's measures on E and EXP do the rest.

The last point of Corollary 8.5.2 formalizes that Lutz's definition of measure on E is invariant under all E-computable and invertible permutations. These permutations include *flip* from Section 8.1 and (crucially) π from Theorem 8.5.2. Hence this robustness assertion for Lutz's measure implies BPP $\neq$ EXP. Our "betting-game measure" (both adaptive and nonadaptive) does enjoy this permutation invariance, but asserting the finite-unions property for it also implies BPP $\neq$ EXP. The rest of this chapter explores conditions under which Lutz's martingales *can* cover classes of autoreducible languages, thus attempting to narrow the gap between martingales and betting games.

8.5.3 Covering Autoreducible Languages by Martingales

This puts the spotlight on the question: Under what hypotheses can we show that the $\leqslant_{tt}^P$-autoreducible languages have E-measure zero? Any such hypothesis must be strong enough to imply EXP $\neq$ BPP, but we hope to find hypotheses weaker than assuming the equivalence of (E- or EXP-) betting games and martingales, or assuming the finite-union property for betting games. Do we need strong pseudo-random generators to cover the $\leqslant_{tt}^P$-autoreducible languages? How close can we come to covering the $\leqslant_T^P$-autoreducible languages by an E-martingale?

Our final results show that the hypothesis MA $\neq$ EXP suffices. By Theorem 2.3.7, this assumption is only known to yield pseudo-random generators of super-polynomial security (at infinitely many lengths) rather than exponential security (at almost all lengths).

Theorem 8.5.3. *If MA $\neq$ EXP, then the class of $\leqslant_{tt}^P$-autoreducible languages has E-measure zero.*

We actually obtain a stronger conclusion.

Theorem 8.5.4. *If MA $\neq$ EXP, then the class of languages A autoreducible by polynomial-time oracle Turing machines that always make their queries in lexicographic order has E-measure zero.*

To better convey the essential sampling idea, we prove the weaker Theorem 8.5.3 before the stronger Theorem 8.5.4. The extra wrinkle in the latter theorem is to use the pseudo-random generator *twice*, to construct the set of "critical strings" to bet on as well as to compute the martingale.

Proof (of Theorem 8.5.3). Let $(M_i)_i$ enumerate the $\leqslant_{tt}^P$-autoreductions, with each M_i running in time n^i. Divide the initial capital into *shares* $s_{i,m}$ for $i, m \geqslant 1$, with each $s_{i,m}$ valued initially at $(1/m^2)(1/2^i)$. For each share $s_{i,m}$, we will describe a martingale that is active only on a finite number of strings x. The martingale will be active only if $i \leqslant m/(2\lceil \log_2 m \rceil)$ and $m \leqslant |x| \leqslant m^i$, and further only if x belongs to a set $J = J_{i,m}$ constructed below. Hence the martingale will be inactive outside J, and we will be able to apply Lemma 8.4.1. We will arrange that whenever M_i autoreduces A, there are infinitely many m such that share $s_{i,m}$ attains a value above 1 (in fact, close to m) along A. Hence the martingale defined by all the shares succeeds on A. We will also ensure that each active share's bets on strings of length n are computable in time 2^{an}, where the constant a is independent of i. This is enough to make the whole martingale E-computable and complete the proof.

To describe the betting strategy for $s_{i,m}$, first construct a set $I = I_{i,m}$ starting with $I = \{0^m\}$ and iterating as follows: Let y be the lexicographically least string of length m that does not appear among queries made by M_i on inputs $x \in I$. Then add y to I. Do this until I has $3\lceil \log_2 m \rceil$ strings in it. This is possible because the bound $3\lceil \log_2 m \rceil m^i$ on the number of queries M_i could possibly make on inputs in I is less than 2^m. Moreover, 2^m bounds the time needed to construct I. Thus we have arranged that

$$\text{for all } x, y \in I \text{ with } x < y, \ M_i(x) \text{ does not query } y. \tag{8.7}$$

Now let J stand for I together with all the queries M_i makes on inputs in I. Adapting ideas from Definition 8.3.1 to this context, let us define a finite Boolean function $\beta : J \to \{0, 1\}$ to be *consistent with M_i on I*, written $\beta \sim_I M_i$, if for all $x \in I$, M_i run on input x with oracle answers given by β agrees with the value $\beta(x)$. Given a characteristic prefix w, also write $\beta \sim w$ if $\beta(x)$ and $w(x)$ agree on all x in J and the domain of w. Since I and J depend only on i and m, we obtain a "probability density" function for each share $s_{i,m}$ via

$$\pi_{i,m}(w) = \Pr_{\beta \sim w} [\beta \sim_I M_i]. \tag{8.8}$$

The martingale $d_{i,m}$ standardly associated to this density (as in [88]) is definable inductively by $d_{i,m}(\lambda) = 1$ and

$$d_{i,m}(wb) = d_{i,m}(w)\frac{\pi_{i,m}(wb)}{\pi_{i,m}(w)} \tag{8.9}$$

for $b \in \{0, 1\}$. In case $\pi_{i,m} = 0$, we already have $d_{i,m}(w) = 0$, and so both $d_{i,m}(w1)$ and $d_{i,m}(w0)$ are set to 0.

Note that the values $\pi_{i,m}(wb)$ for $b = 0, 1$ can only differ from $\pi_{i,m}(w)$ if the string x indexed by b belongs to J; i.e., $d_{i,m}$ is inactive outside J.

Claim 8.5.1. If M_i autoreduces A, then for all sufficiently large m, if share $s_{i,m}$ could play the strategy $d_{i,m}$, then on A its value would rise to (at least) $m/2^i$. That is, $s_{i,m}$ would multiply its initial value by (at least) m^3.

Proof. First note that for any $w \sqsubseteq A$ long enough to contain J in its domain, $\pi_{i,m}(w) = 1$. We want to show that for any v short enough to have domain disjoint from I, $\pi_{i,m}(v) = 1/2^{||I||}$. To do this, consider any fixed 0-1 assignment β_0 to strings in $J \setminus I$ that agrees with v. This assignment determines the computation of M_i on the lexicographically first string $x \in I$, using β_0 to answer queries, and hence forces the value of $\beta(x)$ in order to maintain consistency on I. This in turn forces the value $\beta(x')$ on the next string x' in I, and so on. Hence only one out of $2^{||I||}$ possible completions of β_0 to β is consistent with M_i on I. Thus $\pi_{i,m}(v) = 1/2^{||I||}$. Since $d_{i,m}(w) = d_{i,m}(v) \cdot (\pi_{i,m}(w)/\pi_{i,m}(v))$ by (8.9), and $2^{||I||} = 2^{3\lceil \log_2 m \rceil} \geqslant m^3$, Claim 8.5.1 is proved.

The main obstacle now is that $\pi_{i,m}$ in (8.8), and hence $d_{i,m}(w)$, may not be computable in time 2^{an} with a independent of i. The number of assignments β to count is on the order of $2^{||J||} \approx 2^{m^i} \approx 2^{n^i}$. Here is where we use the E-computable pseudo-random generator D, with super-polynomial stretching and security, obtained via Theorem 2.3.7 from the hypothesis MA $\neq$ EXP. For all i and sufficiently large m, D stretches a seed s of length m into at least $3\lceil \log_2 m \rceil m^i$ bits, which are enough to define an assignment β_s to J (agreeing with any given w). We estimate $\pi_{i,m}(w)$ by

$$\hat{\pi}_{i,m}(w) = \Pr_{|s|=m}[\beta_s \sim_I M_i]. \tag{8.10}$$

Take $\epsilon = 1/m^{i+4}$. By Theorem 2.3.7 there are infinitely many "good" m such that $S_D(m) > m^{i+4}$.

Claim 8.5.2. For all large enough good m, *every* estimate $\hat{\pi}_{i,m}(w)$ satisfies $|\hat{\pi}_{i,m}(w) - \pi_{i,m}(w)| \leqslant \epsilon$.

Proof. Suppose not. First note that (8.8) and (8.10) do not depend on all of w, just on the up-to-$3\lceil \log_2 m \rceil m^i < m^{i+1}$ bits in w that index strings in J, and these can be hard-wired into circuits. The tests $[\beta \sim_I M_i]$ can also be done by circuits of size $o(m^{i+1})$, because a Turing machine computation of time r can be simulated by circuits of size $O(r \log r)$ (see Theorem 2.2.7). Hence we get circuits of size less than $S_D(m)$ achieving a discrepancy greater than $1/S_D(m)$, a contradiction. This proves Claim 8.5.2.

Finally, observe that the proof of Claim 8.5.1 gives us not only $d_{i,m}(w) \geqslant \pi_{i,m}(w) \cdot m^3$, but also $d_{i,m}(w) = \Theta(\pi_{i,m}(w) \cdot m^3)$, when $w \sqsubseteq A$. For $w \sqsubseteq A$ and good m, we thus obtain estimates $g(w)$ for $d_{i,m}(w)$ within error bounds $\epsilon' = \Theta(\epsilon) = \Theta(1/m^{i+1})$. Now applying Lemma 8.4.1 for this $g(w)$ and $J = J_{i,m}$ yields a martingale $d'_{i,m}(w)$ computable in time 2^{an}, where the constant a is independent of i. This $d'_{i,m}(w)$ is the martingale computed by the actions of share $s_{i,m}$. Since $K = \sum_{s_i \in J} \epsilon' = ||J|| \epsilon' \leqslant (1/m) \cdot 3\lceil \log_2 m \rceil = o(1)$, we actually obtain $|d'_{i,m}(w) - d_{i,m}(w)| = o(1)$, which is stronger than what we needed to conclude that share $s_{i,m}$ returns enough profit.

(End of the proof of Theorem 8.5.3.)

To prove Theorem 8.5.4, we need to construct sets $I = I_{i,m}$ with properties similar to (8.7), in the case where M_i is no longer a $\leqslant_{tt}^P$-autoreduction, but makes its queries in lexicographic order. To carry out the construction of I, we use the pseudo-random generator D a second time, and actually need only that M_i on input 0^m makes all queries of length $< m$ before making any query of length $\geqslant m$. To play the modified strategy for share $s_{i,m}$, however, appears to require that all queries observe lexicographic order.

Proof (of Theorem 8.5.4). Recall that the hypothesis $\mathsf{EXP} \neq \mathsf{MA}$ yields a pseudo-random generator D computable in time $2^{O(m)}$ and stretching m bits to $r(m)$ bits such that for all i, all sufficiently large m give $r(m) > m^i$, and infinitely many m give hardness $S_D(m) > m^i$. Let $(M_i)_i$ be a standard enumeration of $\leqslant_T^P$-autoreductions that are constrained to make their queries in lexicographic order, with each M_i running in time $O(n^i)$. We need to define strategies for "shares" $s_{i,m}$ such that whenever M_i autoreduces A, there are infinitely many m such that share $s_{i,m}$ grows its initial capital from $1/m^2 2^i$ to $1/2^i$ or more. The strategy for $s_{i,m}$ must still be computable in time 2^{am} where a is independent of i.

To compute the strategy for $s_{i,m}$, we note first that $s_{i,m}$ can be left inactive on strings of length $< m$. The overall running time allowance $2^{O(m)}$ permits us to suppose that by the time $s_{i,m}$ becomes active and needs to be considered, the initial segment w_0 of A (where A is the language on which the share happens to be playing) that indexes strings of length up to $m - 1$ is known. Hence we may regard w_0 as fixed. For any $\alpha \in \{0,1\}^{m^i}$ let $M_i^\alpha(x)$ stand for the computation in which w_0 is used to answer any queries of length $< m$ and α is used to answer all other queries. Because of the order in which M_i makes its queries, those queries y answered by w_0 are the same for all α, so that those answers can be coded by a string u_0 of length at most m^i. Now for any string y of length equal to m, define

$$P(x, y) = \Pr_\alpha[M_i^\alpha(x) \text{ queries } y].$$

Note that given u_0 and α, the test "$M_i^\alpha(x)$ queries y" can be computed by circuits of size $O(m^{i+1})$. Hence by using the pseudo-random generator D at length m, we can compute uniformly in E an approximation $P_D(x, y)$ for $P(x, y)$ such that for infinitely many m, said to be "good" m, *all* pairs x, y give $|P_D(x, y) - P(x, y)| \leqslant \epsilon_m$, where we choose $\epsilon_m = 1/m^4$.

Here is the algorithm for constructing $I = I_{i,m}$. Start with $I = \varnothing$, and while $||I|| < 3\log_2 m$, do the following: Take the lexicographically least string $y \in \Sigma^m \setminus I$ such that for all $x \in I$, $P_D(x, y) \leqslant \epsilon_m$. The search for such a y will succeed within $||I|| \cdot m^{i+4}$ trials, since for any particular x, there are fewer than m^{i+4} strings y overall that will fail the test. (This is so even if m is not good, because it only involves P_D, and because P_D involves simulating $M_i^{D(\sigma)}$ over all seeds σ.) There is enough room to find such a y provided $||I||m^{i+4} \leqslant 2^m$, which holds for all sufficiently large m. The whole construction of I can be completed within time 2^{2am}. It follows that for any sufficiently large good m and $x, y \in I$ with $x < y$, $\Pr_\alpha[M_i^\alpha(x) \text{ queries } y] < 2\epsilon_m = 2/m^4$.

At this point we would like to define J to be "I together with the set of strings queried by M_i on inputs in I" as before, but unlike the previous case where We acknowledge the dependence of the strings queried by M_i on the oracle A by defining

$$J_A \doteq I \cup \{y \mid (\exists x \in I)\, M_i^A(x) \text{ queries } y\}.$$

Let $r = m^i \cdot \lceil 3 \log m \rceil$. Then $||J_A|| \leqslant r$; that is, J_A has the same size as J in the previous proof. This latter definition will be OK *because* M_i makes its queries in lexicographic order. Hence the share $s_{i,m}$, having already computed I without any reference to A, can determine the strings in J_A on which it should be active on the fly, in lexicographic order. Thus we can well-define a mapping β from $\{0,1\}^r$ to $\{0,1\}$ so that for any $k \leqslant r$, $\beta(k) = 1$ means that the query string y that happens to be kth in order in the on-the-fly construction of J_A is answered "yes" by the oracle. Then we may write J_β for J_A, and then write $\beta(y) = 1$ in place of $\beta(k) = 1$. Most important, given any $x \in I$, every such β well-defines a computation $M_i^\beta(x)$. This entitles us to carry over the two "consistency" definitions from the proof of Theorem 8.5.3:

- $\beta \sim w$ if $\beta(y) = w(y)$ for all $y \in J_\beta$;
- $\beta \sim_I M_i$ if for all $x \in I$, $M_i^\beta(x)$ equals (i.e., "agrees with") $\beta(x)$.

Finally, we may apply the latter notion to initial subsets of I, and define for $1 \leqslant \ell \leqslant 3 \log m$ the predicate $R_\ell(\beta)$ as

$$(\beta \sim_{x_1,\ldots,x_\ell} M_i) \wedge (\forall j, k : 1 \leqslant j \leqslant k \leqslant \ell)\, M_i^\beta(x_j) \text{ does not query } x_k.$$

Claim 8.5.3. For all ℓ, $\Pr_\beta[R_\ell(\beta)] \leqslant 1/2^\ell$.

Proof. For the base case $\ell = 1$, $\Pr_\beta[R_1(\beta)] = 1/2$, because $M_i(x)$ does not query x_1, M_i being an autoreduction, and because whether $\beta \sim_{x_1} M_i$ depends only on the bit of β corresponding to x_1. Working by induction, suppose $\Pr_\beta[R_{\ell-1}(\beta)] \leqslant 1/2^{\ell-1}$. If $R_{\ell-1}(\beta)$ holds, then taking β' to be β with the bit corresponding to x_ℓ flipped, $R_{\ell-1}(\beta')$ also holds. However, at most one of $R_\ell(\beta)$ and $R_\ell(\beta')$ holds, again because $M_i(x_\ell)$ does not query x_ℓ. Hence $\Pr_\beta[R_\ell(\beta)] \leqslant (1/2)\Pr_\beta[R_{\ell-1}(\beta)]$, and this proves Claim 8.5.3. (It is possible that neither $R_\ell(\beta)$ nor $R_\ell(\beta')$ holds, as happens when $M_i^\beta(x_j)$ queries x_ℓ for some j, but this does not hurt the claim.)

Now we can rejoin the proof of Theorem 8.5.3 at (8.8), defining the probability density function $\pi_{i,m}(w) = \Pr_{\beta \sim w}[\beta \sim_I M_i]$. We get a martingale $d_{i,m}$ from $\pi_{i,m}$ as before, and this represents an "ideal" strategy for share $s_{i,m}$ to play. The statement corresponding to Claim 8.5.1 is:

Claim 8.5.4. If M_i autoreduces A and m is good and sufficiently large, then the ideal strategy for share $s_{i,m}$ multiplies its value by at least $m^3/2$ along A.

Proof. Note that we constructed $I = \{x_1, \ldots, x_{3\log m}\}$ above so that for all $j < k$, $\Pr_\alpha[M_i^\alpha(x_j)$ queries $x_k] \leqslant 2/m^4$. It follows that

$$\Pr[(\exists j, k : 1 \leqslant j \leqslant k \leqslant 3\log m)\ M_i(x_j) \text{ queries } x_k]$$
$$\leqslant \binom{\lceil 3\log m\rceil}{2} \cdot \frac{2}{m^4} \leqslant \frac{1}{m^3},$$

provided $m \geqslant \lceil 3\log m\rceil^2$. Hence, using Claim 8.5.3 with $\ell = 3\log m$, we get:

$$\Pr_\beta[\beta \sim_I M_i] \leqslant \frac{1}{2^{3\log m}} + \frac{1}{m^3} = \frac{2}{m^3}.$$

Since the β defined by A satisfies $\beta \sim_I M_i$, it follows by the same reasoning as in Claim 8.5.1 that $d_{i,m}$ profits by at least a fraction of $m^3/2$ along A. This proves Claim 8.5.4.

Finally, we (re-)use the pseudo-random generator D as before to expand a seed s of length m into a string β_s of (at least) $r = 3\lceil\log_2 m\rceil m^i$ bits. Given any w, β_s well-defines a β and a set J_β of size at most r as constructed above, by using w to answer queries in the domain of w and β_s for everything else. We again obtain the estimate $\hat\pi_{i,m}(w) = \Pr_{|s|=m}[\beta_s \sim_I M_i]$ from (8.10), with the same time complexity as before. Now we repeat Claim 8.5.2 in this new context:

Claim 8.5.5. For all large enough good m, every estimate $\hat\pi_{i,m}(w)$ satisfies $|\hat\pi_{i,m}(w) - \pi_{i,m}(w)| \leqslant \epsilon$.

Proof. If not, then for some fixed w the estimate fails. The final key point is that because M_i always makes its queries in lexicographic order, the queries in the domain of w that need to be covered are the same for every β_s. Hence the corresponding bits of w can be hard-wired by circuitry of size at most r. The test $[\beta_s \sim_I M_i]$ can thus still be carried out by circuits of size less than m^{i+1}, and we reach the same contradiction of the hardness value S_D.

Finally, we want to apply Lemma 8.4.1 to replace $d_{i,m}(w)$ by a martingale $d'_{i,m}(w)$ that yields virtually the same degree of success and is computable in time $2^{O(n)}$. Unlike the truth-table case we cannot apply Lemma 8.4.1 verbatim because we no longer have a single small set J that d' is active on. However, along any language A, the values $d'_{i,m}(w)$ and $d'_{i,m}(wb)$ ($b = 0$ or 1) can differ only for cases where b indexes a string in the small set J corresponding to A, and one may check that the argument and bounds of Lemma 8.4.1 go through unscathed in this case. This finishes the proof of Theorem 8.5.4.

8.6 Conclusion and Open Questions

The initial impetus for this chapter was a simple question about measure: Is the pseudo-randomness of a characteristic sequence invariant under simple permutations such as that induced by *flip*? The question for *flip* is tantalizingly still open. However, in Section 8.5.2 we showed that establishing a "yes" answer for any permutation that intuitively *should* preserve the same complexity-theoretic degree of pseudo-randomness, or even for a single specific such permutation as that in the simple proof of the nonadaptive version of Theorem 8.5.1, would have the nonrelativizing consequence that $\mathsf{EXP} \neq \mathsf{BPP}$.

Our "betting games" in themselves are a natural extension of Lutz's measures for deterministic time classes. They preserve Lutz's original idea of "betting" as a means of "predicting" membership in a language, without being tied to a fixed order of which instances one tries to predict, or to a fixed order of how one goes about gathering information on the language. We have shown some senses in which betting games are robust and well-behaved. We also contend that some current defects in the theory of betting games, notably the lack of a finite-unions theorem pending the status of pseudo-random generators, trade off with lacks in the resource-bounded measure theory, such as being tied to the lexicographic ordering of strings.

The main open problems in this chapter are interesting in connection with the BPP versus EXP problem problem. Among the many measure statements in the last section that imply $\mathsf{BPP} \neq \mathsf{EXP}$, the most constrained and easiest to attack seems to be item 4 in Corollary 8.5.2. Indeed, in the specific relevant case starting with the assumption $\mathsf{BPP} = \mathsf{EXP}$, one is given a nonadaptive E-betting game G and an E-martingale d, and to obtain the desired contradiction that proves $\mathsf{BPP} \neq \mathsf{EXP}$, one need only construct an EXP-betting game G' that covers $S^\infty[G] \cup S^\infty[d]$. What we *can* obtain is a "randomized" betting game G'' that flips one coin at successive intervals of input lengths to decide whether to simulate G or d on that interval. (The intervals come from the proof of Theorem 8.5.2.) Any hypothesis that can derandomize this G'' implies $\mathsf{BPP} \neq \mathsf{EXP}$.

Stepping back from trying to prove $\mathsf{BPP} \neq \mathsf{EXP}$ outright or trying to prove that these measure statements are equivalent to $\mathsf{BPP} \neq \mathsf{EXP}$, we also have the problem of narrowing the gap between $\mathsf{BPP} \neq \mathsf{EXP}$ and the sufficient condition $\mathsf{EXP} \neq \mathsf{MA}$ used in our results. Moreover, does $\mathsf{EXP} \neq \mathsf{MA}$ suffice to make the $\leqslant_T^P$-autoreducible languages have E-measure zero? Does that suffice to simulate every betting game by a martingale of equivalent complexity? We also inquire whether there exist oracles relative to which $\mathsf{EXP} = \mathsf{MA}$ but strong pseudo-random generators still exist. Our work seems to open opportunities to tighten the connections among pseudo-random generators, the structure of classes within EXP, and resource-bounded measure.

References

1. L. Adleman. Two theorems on random polynomial time. In *Proceedings of the 19th IEEE Symposium on Foundations of Computer Science*, pages 75–83. IEEE, 1978.
2. L. Adleman and M. Huang. Recognizing primes in random polynomial time. In *Proceedings of the 19th ACM Symposium on the Theory of Computing*, pages 462–469. ACM, 1987.
3. R. Aleliunas, R. Karp, R. Lipton, L. Lovász, and C. Rackoff. Random walks, universal traversal sequences, and the complexity of maze problems. In *Proceedings of the 20th IEEE Symposium on Foundations of Computer Science*, pages 218–223. IEEE, 1979.
4. E. Allender, K. Reinhardt, and S. Zhou. Isolation, matching, and counting: Uniform and nonuniform upper bounds. *Journal of Computer and System Sciences*, 59:164–181, 1999.
5. E. Allender and M. Strauss. Measure on small complexity classes, with applications for BPP. In *Proceedings of the 35th IEEE Symposium on Foundations of Computer Science*, pages 807–818. IEEE, 1994.
6. N. Alon, O. Goldreich, J. Håstad, and R. Peralta. Simple constructions of almost k-wise independent random variables. *Journal of Random Structures and Algorithms*, 3(3):289–304, 1992.
7. N. Alon, J. Spencer, and P. Erdős. *The Probabilistic Method*. John Wiley and Sons, 1992.
8. K. Ambos-Spies. P-Mitotic sets. In E. Börger, G. Hasenjäger, and D. Roding, editors, *Logic and Machines*, volume 177 of *Lecture Notes in Computer Science*, pages 1–23. Springer-Verlag, 1984.
9. K. Ambos-Spies, S. Lempp, and G. Mainhardt. Randomness vs. completeness: On the diagonalization strength of resource-bounded random sets. In *Proceedings of the 23rd International Symposium on the Mathematical Foundations of Computer Science*, volume 1450 of *Lecture Notes in Computer Science*. Springer-Verlag, 1998.
10. K. Ambos-Spies, H.-C. Neis, and S. Terwijn. Genericity and measure for exponential time. *Theoretical Computer Science*, 168(1):3–19, 1996.
11. D. Angluin. Queries and concept learning. *Machine Learning*, 2(4):319–342, 1988.
12. R. Armoni, A. Ta-Shma, A. Wigderson, and S. Zhou. $SL \subseteq L^{\frac{4}{3}}$. In *Proceedings of the 29th ACM Symposium on the Theory of Computing*, pages 230–239. ACM, 1997.
13. S. Arora, C. Lund, R. Motwani, M. Sudan, and M. Szegedy. Proof verification and the hardness of approximation problems. *Journal of the ACM*, 45(3):501–555, 1998.
14. V. Arvind and J. Köbler. On pseudorandomness and resource-bounded measure. In *Proceedings 17th Conference on the Foundations of Software Tech-*

nology and Theoretical Computer Science, volume 1346 of *Lecture Notes in Computer Science*, pages 235–249. Springer-Verlag, 1997.

15. V. Arvind, J. Köbler, and M. Mundhenk. On bounded truth-table, conjunctive, and randomized reductions to sparse sets. In *Proceedings of the 12th Conference on Foundations of Software Technology and Theoretical Computer Science*, volume 652 of *Lecture Notes in Computer Science*, pages 140–151. Springer-Verlag, 1992.

16. L. Babai. Trading group theory for randomness. In *Proceedings of the 17th ACM Symposium on the Theory of Computing*, pages 421–429. ACM, 1985.

17. L. Babai, L. Fortnow, and C. Lund. Non-deterministic exponential time has two-prover interactive protocols. *Computational Complexity*, 1:3–40, 1991.

18. L. Babai, L. Fortnow, N. Nisan, and A. Wigderson. BPP has subexponential time simulations unless EXPTIME has publishable proofs. *Computational Complexity*, 3:307–318, 1993.

19. L. Babai, W. Kantor, and E. Luks. Computational complexity and the classification of finite simple groups. In *Proceedings of the 24th IEEE Symposium on Foundations of Computer Science*, pages 162–171. IEEE, 1983.

20. L. Babai and E. Luks. Canonical labeling of graphs. In *Proceedings of the 15th ACM Symposium on the Theory of Computing*, pages 171–183. ACM, 1983.

21. L. Babai and S. Moran. Arthur-Merlin games: a randomized proof system, and a hierarchy of complexity classes. *Journal of Computer and System Sciences*, 36:254–276, 1988.

22. L. Babai, N. Nisan, and M. Szegedy. Multiparty protocols, pseudorandom generators for logspace, and time-space trade-offs. *Journal of Computer and System Sciences*, 45:204–232, 1992.

23. R. Beigel and J. Feigenbaum. On being incoherent without being very hard. *Computational Complexity*, 2(1):1–17, 1992.

24. C. Bennett and J. Gill. Relative to a random oracle, $P^A \neq NP^A \neq co - NP^A$ with probability one. *SIAM Journal on Computing*, 10:96–113, 1981.

25. L. Berman and J. Hartmanis. On isomorphism and density of NP and other complete sets. *SIAM Journal on Computing*, 6(2):305–322, 1977.

26. M. Blum and S. Micali. How to generate cryptographically strong sequences of pseudo-random bits. *SIAM Journal on Computing*, 13:850–864, 1984.

27. R. Boppana, J. Håstad, and S. Zachos. Does co-NP have short interactive proofs? *Information Processing Letters*, 25:127–132, 1987.

28. A. Borodin. On relating time and space to size and depth. *SIAM Journal on Computing*, 6:733–744, 1977.

29. A. Borodin, J. von zur Gathen, and J. Hopcroft. Fast parallel matrix and GCD computations. *Information and Control*, 52:241–256, 1982.

30. N. Bshouty, R. Cleve, R. Gavaldà, S. Kannan, and C. Tamon. Oracles and queries that are sufficient for exact learning. *Journal of Computer and System Sciences*, 52(3):421–433, 1996.

31. H. Buhrman, S. Fenner, and L. Fortnow. Results on resource-bounded measure. In *Proceedings of the 24th International Colloquium On Automata, Languages and Programming*, volume 1256 of *Lecture Notes in Computer Science*, pages 188–194. Springer-Verlag, 1997.

32. H. Buhrman, L. Fortnow, and T. Thierauf. Nonrelativizing separations. In *Proceedings of the 13th IEEE Conference on Computational Complexity*, pages 8–12. IEEE, 1998.

33. H. Buhrman, L. Fortnow, and L. Torenvliet. Using autoreducibility to separate complexity classes. In *Proceedings of the 36th IEEE Symposium on Foundations of Computer Science*, pages 520–528. IEEE, 1995.

34. H. Buhrman, L. Fortnow, D. van Melkebeek, and L. Torenvliet. Separating complexity classes using autoreducibility. *SIAM Journal on Computing*, 29(5):1497–1520, 2000.

35. H. Buhrman and E. Mayordomo. An excursion to the Kolmogorov random strings. *Journal of Computer and System Sciences*, 54(3):393–399, 1997.

36. H. Buhrman and D. van Melkebeek. Hard sets are hard to find. In *Proceedings of the 13th IEEE Conference on Computational Complexity*, pages 170–180. IEEE, 1998.

37. H. Buhrman and D. van Melkebeek. Hard sets are hard to find. *Journal of Computer and System Sciences*, 59(2):327–345, 1999.

38. H. Buhrman, D. van Melkebeek, K. Regan, D. Sivakumar, and M. Strauss. A generalization of resource-bounded measure, with an application. In *Proceedings of the 15th Symposium on Theoretical Aspects of Computer Science*, volume 1373 of *Lecture Notes in Computer Science*, pages 161–171. Springer-Verlag, 1998.

39. H. Buhrman, D. van Melkebeek, K. Regan, D. Sivakumar, and M. Strauss. A generalization of resource-bounded measure, with application to the BPP vs. EXP problem. *SIAM Journal on Computing*, 30(2):576–601, 2000.

40. J. Cai, A. Naik, and D. Sivakumar. Bounded truth-table reductions of P. Technical Report TR-95-42, Department of Computer Science, State University of New York at Buffalo, September 1995.

41. J. Cai, A. Naik, and D. Sivakumar. On the existence of hard sparse sets under weak reductions. In *Proceedings of the 13th Symposium on Theoretical Aspects of Computer Science*, volume 1046 of *Lecture Notes in Computer Science*, pages 307–318. Springer-Verlag, 1996.

42. J. Cai and D. Sivakumar. Sparse hard sets for P: Resolution of a conjecture of Hartmanis. *Journal of Computer and System Sciences*, 58(2):280–296, 1999.

43. J. Cai and D. Sivakumar. Resolution of Hartmanis' conjecture for NL-hard sparse sets. *Theoretical Computer Science*, 240(2):257–269, 2000.

44. A. Chandra, D. Kozen, and L. Stockmeyer. Alternation. *Journal of the ACM*, 28:114–133, 1981.

45. B. Chor and O. Goldreich. On the power of two-point based sampling. *Journal of Complexity*, 5:96–106, 1989.

46. A. Clementi, J. Rolim, and L. Trevisan. Recent advances towards proving P = BPP. *Bulletin of the European Association for Theoretical Computer Science*, 64:96–103, February 1998.

47. S. Cook. The complexity of theorem-proving procedures. In *Proceedings of the 3rd ACM Symposium on the Theory of Computing*, pages 151–158. ACM, 1971.

48. S. Cook. Short propositional formulas represent nondeterministic computations. *Information Processing Letters*, 26:269–270, 1988.

49. S. Cook and P. McKenzie. Problems complete for deterministic logarithmic space. *Journal of Algorithms*, 8:385–394, 1987.

50. W. Eberly. Very fast parallel polynomial arithmetic. *SIAM Journal on Computing*, 18(5):955–976, 1989.

51. J. Feigenbaum and L. Fortnow. On the random-self-reducibility of complete sets. *SIAM Journal on Computing*, 22:994–1005, 1993.

52. S. Fenner, L. Fortnow, and S. Kurtz. Gap-definable counting classes. *Journal of Computer and System Sciences*, 48(1):116–148, 1994.

53. L. Fortnow. The role of relativization in complexity theory. *Bulletin of the European Association for Theoretical Computer Science*, 52:229–244, 1994.

54. L. Fortnow. Counting complexity. In L. Hemaspaandra and A. Selman, editors, *Complexity Theory Retrospective II*, pages 81–107. Springer-Verlag, 1997.

55. J. Friedman. A note on matrix rigidity. Technical Report TR-308-91, Department of Computer Science, Princeton University, 1990.

56. O. Goldreich and L. Levin. A hard-core predicate for all one-way functions. In *Proceedings of the 21st ACM Symposium on the Theory of Computing*, pages 25–32. ACM, 1989.

57. O. Goldreich, S. Micali, and A. Wigderson. Proofs that yield nothing but their validity or all languages in NP have zero-knowledge proof systems. *Journal of the ACM*, 38:691–729, 1991.

58. S. Goldwasser and S. Micali. Probabilistic encryption. *Journal of Computer and System Sciences*, 28:270–299, 1984.

59. S. Goldwasser and M. Sipser. Private coins versus public coins in interactive proof systems. In S. Micali, editor, *Randomness and Computation*, volume 5 of *Advances in Computing Research*, pages 73–90. JAI Press, Greenwich, 1989.

60. J. Hartmanis. On log-tape isomorphisms of complete sets. *Theoretical Computer Science*, 7(3):273–286, 1978.

61. J. Hartmanis, P. Lewis, and R. Stearns. Hierarchies of memory limited computations. In *The 6th Annual Symposium on Switching Circuit Theory and Logical Design*, pages 179–190. IEEE, 1965.

62. J. Hartmanis and R. Stearns. On the computational complexity of algorithms. *Transactions of the American Mathematical Society*, 117:285–306, 1965.

63. J. Håstad, R. Impagliazzo, L. Levin, and M. Luby. A pseudorandom generator from any one-way function. *SIAM Journal on Computing*, 28(4):1364–1396, 1999.

64. H. Heller. On relativized exponential and probabilistic complexity classes. *Information and Compuation*, 71:231–243, 1986.

65. S. Homer and L. Longpré. On reductions of NP sets to sparse sets. *Journal of Computer and System Sciences*, 48(2):324–336, 1994.

66. J. Hong. On some deterministic space complexity problems. In *Proceedings of the 12th ACM Symposium on the Theory of Computing*, pages 310–317. ACM, 1980.

67. N. Immerman. Nondeterministic space is closed under complementation. *SIAM Journal on Computing*, 17(5):935–938, 1988.

68. R. Impagliazzo. Hard-core distributions for somewhat hard problems. In *Proceedings of the 36th IEEE Symposium on Foundations of Computer Science*, pages 538–545. IEEE, 1995.

69. R. Impagliazzo and A. Wigderson. P=BPP unless E has sub-exponential circuits: Derandomizing the XOR lemma. In *Proceedings of the 29th ACM Symposium on the Theory of Computing*, pages 220–229. ACM, 1997.

70. R. Impagliazzo and A. Wigderson. Randomness vs. time: De-randomization under a uniform assumption. In *Proceedings of the 39th IEEE Symposium on Foundations of Computer Science*, pages 734–743. IEEE, 1998.

71. D. Juedes and J. Lutz. The complexity and distribution of hard problems. *SIAM Journal on Computing*, 24(2):279–295, 1995.

72. R. Kannan. Circuit-size lower bounds and non-reducibility to sparse sets. *Information and Control*, 55:40–56, 1982.

73. H. Karloff. A Las Vegas RNC algorithm for maximum matching. *Combinatorica*, 6:387–391, 1986.

74. R. Karp and R. Lipton. Turing machines that take advice. *L'Enseignement Mathématique*, 28(2):191–209, 1982. A preliminary version appeared in STOC 1980.

75. A. Klivans and D. van Melkebeek. Graph nonisomorphism has subexponential size proofs unless the polynomial hierarchy collapses. In *Proceedings of the 31st ACM Symposium on the Theory of Computing*, pages 659–667. ACM, 1999.

76. R. Ladner. Mitotic recursively enumerable sets. *Journal of Symbolic Logic*, 38(2):199–211, 1973.

77. R. Ladner. The circuit value problem is log-space complete for P. *SIGACT News*, 6(2):18–20, 1975.

78. R. Ladner. On the structure of polynomial time reducibility. *Journal of the ACM*, 22:155–171, 1975.

79. R. Ladner and N. Lynch. Relativization of questions about logspace computability. *Mathematical Systems Theory*, 10(1):19–32, 1976.

80. C. Lautemann. BPP and the polynomial hierarchy. *Information Processing Letters*, 17:215–217, 1983.

81. H. Lewis and C. Papadimitriou. Symmetric space-bounded computation. *Theoretical Computer Science*, 19(2):161–187, 1982.

82. J. H. van Lint. *Introduction to Coding Theory*. Springer-Verlag, 1991.

83. N. Littlestone. Learning when irrelevant attributes abound: A new linear-threshold algorithm. *Machine Learning*, 2:285–318, 1988.

84. L. Longpré. Personal communication, 1997.

85. L. Lovász. On determinants, matchings and random algorithms. In L. Budach, editor, *Fundamentals of Computing Theory*. Akademia-Verlag, Berlin, 1979.

86. C. Lund, L. Fortnow, H. Karloff, and N. Nisan. Algebraic methods for interactive proof systems. *Journal of the ACM*, 39:859–868, 1992.

87. J. Lutz. Category and measure in complexity classes. *SIAM Journal on Computing*, 19(6):1100–1131, 1990.

88. J. Lutz. Almost everywhere high nonuniform complexity. *Journal of Computer and System Sciences*, 44:220–258, 1992.

89. J. Lutz. A small span theorem for P/poly-Turing reductions. In *Proceedings of the 10th IEEE Structure in Complexity Theory Conference*, pages 324–330. IEEE, 1995.

90. J. Lutz. The quantitative structure of exponential time. In L. Hemaspaandra and A. Selman, editors, *Complexity Theory Retrospective II*, pages 225–260. Springer-Verlag, 1997.

91. F. MacWilliams and N. Sloane. *The Theory of Error-Correcting Codes*. North-Holland, 1981.

92. S. Mahaney. Sparse complete sets for NP: Solution of a conjecture of Berman and Hartmanis. *Journal of Computer and System Sciences*, 25(2):130–143, 1982.

93. W. McColl. Complexity hierarchies for boolean functions. *Acta Informatica*, 11:71–77, 1978.

94. D. van Melkebeek. Reducing P to a sparse set using a constant number of queries collapses P to L. In *Proceedings of the 11th IEEE Conference on Computational Complexity*, pages 88–96. IEEE, 1996.

95. D. van Melkebeek. Deterministic and randomized bounded truth-table reductions of P, NL, and L to sparse sets. *Journal of Computer and System Sciences*, 57(2):213–232, 1998.

96. D. van Melkebeek. The zero-one law holds for BPP. *Theoretical Computer Science*, 244(1–2):283–288, 2000.

97. A. Meyer and L. Stockmeyer. The equivalence problem for regular expressions with squaring requires exponential space. In *Proceedings of the 13th IEEE Symposium on Foundations of Computer Science*, pages 125–129. IEEE, 1972.

98. P. Bro Miltersen. Relativizable pseudorandom generators and extractors. Comment to ECCC Technical Report TR98-055, 1998.

99. K. Mulmuley. A fast parallel algorithm to compute the rank of a matrix over an arbitrary field. *Combinatorica*, 7(1):101–104, 1987.

100. J. Naor and M. Naor. Small-bias probability spaces: Efficient constructions and applications. *SIAM Journal on Computing*, 22(4):838–856, 1993.
101. N. Nisan. Pseudorandom generators for space-bounded computation. *Combinatorica*, 12:449–461, 1992.
102. N. Nisan. On read-once vs. multiple access to randomness in logspace. *Theoretical Computer Science*, 107:135–144, 1993.
103. N. Nisan and A. Ta-Shma. Symmetric *logspace* is closed under complement. *Chicago Journal of Theoretical Computer Science*, 1995.
104. N. Nisan and A. Wigderson. Hardness vs. randomness. *Journal of Computer and System Sciences*, 49:149–167, 1994.
105. M. Ogihara. Sparse hard sets for P yield space-efficient algorithms. *Chicago Journal of Theoretical Computer Science*, 1996.
106. M. Ogiwara and A. Lozano. On sparse hard sets for counting classes. *Theoretical Computer Science*, 112(2):255–275, 1993.
107. M. Ogiwara and O. Watanabe. On polynomial-time bounded truth-table reducibility of NP sets to sparse sets. *SIAM Journal on Computing*, 20(3):471–483, 1991.
108. M. Paterson and I. Wegener. Nearly optimal hierarchies for network and formula size. *Acta Informatica*, 23:217–221, 1986.
109. N. Pippenger. On simultaneous resource bounds. In *Proceedings of the 20th IEEE Symposium on Foundations of Computer Science*, pages 307–311. IEEE, 1979.
110. L. Pitt and M. Warmuth. Prediction preserving reducibility. *Journal of Computer and System Sciences*, 41(3):430–467, 1990.
111. P. Pudlák and Z. Vavřín. Computation of rigidity of order n^2/r for one simple matrix. *Comment. Math. Univ. Carolinae*, 32:213–218, 1991.
112. M. Rabin. A probabilistic algorithm for testing primality. *Journal of Number Theory*, 12, 1980.
113. D. Ranjan and P. Rohatgi. On randomized reductions to sparse sets. In *Proceedings of the 7th IEEE Structure in Complexity Theory Conference*, pages 239–242. IEEE, 1992.
114. A. Razborov. On rigid matrices. Manuscript in Russian.
115. A. Razborov and S. Rudich. Natural proofs. *Journal of Computer and System Sciences*, 55(1):24–35, 1997.
116. K. Regan, D. Sivakumar, and J. Cai. Pseudorandom generators, measure theory, and natural proofs. In *Proceedings of the 36th IEEE Symposium on Foundations of Computer Science*, pages 26–35. IEEE, 1995.
117. J. Robson. *N* by *N* checkers is Exptime complete. *SIAM Journal on Computing*, 13:252–267, 1984.
118. S. Rudich. Super-bits, demi-bits, and $\tilde{NP}$/qpoly-natural proofs. In *Proceedings of the 1st International Symposium on Randomization and Approximation Techniques in Computer Science*, volume 1269 of *Lecture Notes in Computer Science*, pages 85–93. Springer-Verlag, 1997.
119. M. Saks and S. Zhou. $BP_HSPACE(s) \subseteq DSPACE(s^{3/2})$. *Journal of Computer and System Sciences*, 58(2):376–403, 1999.
120. W. Savitch. Relationships between nondeterministic and deterministic tape complexities. *Journal of Computer and System Sciences*, 4:177–192, 1970.
121. W. Savitch. Maze recognizing automata and nondeterministic tape complexity. *Journal of Computer and System Sciences*, 7:389–403, 1973.
122. M. Schaefer. Graph Ramsey theory and the polynomial hierarchy. In *Proceedings of the 31st ACM Symposium on the Theory of Computing*, pages 592–601. ACM, 1999.

123. C. Schnorr. The network complexity and the Turing machine complexity of finite functions. *Acta Informatica*, 7:95–107, 1976.

124. A. Shamir. IP = PSPACE. *Journal of the ACM*, 39:869–877, 1992.

125. M. Sipser. A complexity theoretic approach to randomness. In *Proceedings of the 15th ACM Symposium on the Theory of Computing*, pages 330–335. ACM, 1983.

126. R. Solovay and V. Strassen. A fast Monte-Carlo test for primality. *SIAM Journal on Computing*, 6:84–85, 1977. See also erratum 7:118, 1978.

127. P. Spira. On time-hardware complexity tradeoffs for Boolean functions. In *Proceedings of the 4th Hawaii Symposium on System Sciences*, pages 525–527. Western Periodicals Company, North Hollywood, 1971.

128. L. Stockmeyer. The polynomial-time hierarchy. *Theoretical Computer Science*, 3:1–22, 1976.

129. M. Sudan, L. Trevisan, and S. Vadhan. Pseudorandom generators without the XOR lemma. Technical Report TR-98-074, Electronic Colloquium on Computational Complexity, 1999. Revision 1.

130. R. Szelepcsényi. The method of forced enumeration for nondeterministic automata. *Acta Informatica*, 26:279–284, 1988.

131. S. Toda. PP is as hard as the polynomial-time hierarchy. *SIAM Journal on Computing*, 20(5):865–877, 1991.

132. S. Toda and M. Ogiwara. Counting classes are at least as hard as the polynomial-time hierarchy. *SIAM Journal on Computing*, 21(2):316–328, 1992.

133. B. Trakhtenbrot. On autoreducibility. *Dokl. Akad. Nauk SSSR*, 192:1224–1227, 1970. In Russian. English translation in [134].

134. B. Trakhtenbrot. On autoreducibility. *Soviet Mathematics–Doklady*, 11:814–817, 1970.

135. L. Trevisan. Construction of extractors using pseudo-random generators. In *Proceedings of the 31st ACM Symposium on the Theory of Computing*, pages 141–148. ACM, 1999.

136. L. Valiant. Graph-theoretic arguments in low-level complexity. In *Proceedings of the 6th Symposium on Mathematical Foundations of Computer Science*, volume 53 of *Lecture Notes in Computer Science*, pages 162–176. Springer-Verlag, 1977.

137. L. Valiant and V. Vazirani. NP is as easy as detecting unique solutions. *Theoretical Computer Science*, 47:85–93, 1986.

138. A. Yao. Theory and applications of trapdoor functions. In *Proceedings of the 23rd IEEE Symposium on Foundations of Computer Science*, pages 80–91. IEEE, 1982.

139. A. Yao. Coherent functions and program checkers. In *Proceedings of the 22nd ACM Symposium on the Theory of Computing*, pages 84–94. ACM, 1990.

140. S. Žàk. A Turing machine time hierarchy. *Theoretical Computer Science*, 26:327–333, 1983.

Notation Index

Subject Index